The Control of Childbirth

The Control of Childbirth

Women Versus Medicine Through the Ages

PHYLLIS L. BRODSKY

Foreword by Mary Ann Shah

McFarland & Company, Inc., Publishers

Jefferson, North Carolina, and London

5/09

LIBRARY OF CONGRESS CATALOGUING-IN-PUBLICATION DATA

Brodsky, Phyllis L., 1936–
    The control of childbirth : women versus medicine through the
ages / Phyllis L. Brodsky ; foreword by Mary Ann Shah.
      p.   cm.
    Includes bibliographical references and index.

    ISBN 978-0-7864-3362-9
    softcover : 50# alkaline paper ∞

    1. Childbirth—History.   2. Obstetrics—History.   I. Title.
RG51.B76   2008
618.4—dc22
                                            2008005564

British Library cataloguing data are available

Cover photographs ©2007 Shutterstock

Manufactured in the United States of America

McFarland & Company, Inc., Publishers
  Box 611, Jefferson, North Carolina 28640
   www.mcfarlandpub.com

To
Drs. Edna Quinn and Thomas Erskine,
who have inspired and encouraged me
throughout this effort.

Acknowledgments

FOREMOST, I AM GRATEFUL TO MY HUSBAND, Allen Brodsky, an author and editor in his own right, who has supported and encouraged me from the beginning and has always believed in me. He patiently critiqued and edited each chapter as it was completed and each time I revised it and was always there when I needed him. Thank you sweetheart for all you have given me.

My dear friend and colleague, Dr. Edna Quinn, Professor Emeritus, Salisbury University in Maryland, Certified Nurse Midwife, and author of Chapter 10 of this book, inspired and encouraged me from the beginning, with love and never-ending enthusiasm. Edna's husband, Dr. Thomas Erskine, also Professor Emeritus, Salisbury University, has encouraged me throughout. Tom and Edna helped in the planning and organizing of the Second International Conference on "Global Outlook on Gender Issues" organized by Salisbury University and Srinakharinwirot University in Bangkok, Thailand, January 7 to 9, 1999. Tom and Dr. Amporn Srisermbhok, Dean, Faculty of Humanities at Srinakharinwirot, planned and organized this conference with over 200 participants from 18 countries, with over 85 interdisciplinary papers presented. Edna, who was planning the section on Women's Health Care Issues, suggested I give a paper on the history of childbirth in America. This opportunity, in part, inspired me to begin writing this book. I am indebted to them both.

Susan Beverly edited my entire manuscript and was so very helpful, supportive, and encouraging. Thank you, Susan. Sherry Gamble, another dear friend, artist and former nurse, also offered great help. Thank you, Sherry, for your love, efforts, and encouragement.

The First Saturday Writers' Club members, in Berlin, Maryland, have been an inspiration to me for the past eight years, since I began the book and first joined the club. During meetings, each member reads something he or she has written and then receives comments and feedback from the others. In this very positive way, we all benefit from each other. I have learned so much from this group. Elizabeth Patera, the facilitator of the club, former English teacher and writer of children's books and teaching materials, has been so very helpful and enthusiastic in sharing her wisdom and experiences. Other members of the club, Betty Cianci, Fran Carlson, Sue Coleburn, Dr. J. H. Williams, Jean Fullerton, Jo Hanagan, Dale Cathell, Nelson Lynch, Tom Range, and Susan Beverly, to name but a few, offered wonderful advice and gentle constructive suggestions. Nelson Lynch, a great writer of satirical fantasy, once told me to "quit rewriting and get on with the book." This was an excellent piece of advice. I am indebted to all the members of this group.

Frances Levy, a friend and freelance writer, offered me suggestions for an appropriate title as I struggled to find the best fit. She also sent me Andre Bernard's book, *Now All We Need Is a Title*. After reading excerpts from famous authors, I realized I wasn't alone in this search. I am grateful to Lisa Lilley for her support and encouragement in writing this book and giving me permission to interview her in relating her childbirth experiences.

I wish to thank Pollinger Limited, publishers of Grantly Dick-Read's book, *Childbirth Without Fear*, who gave me permission to extract excerpts and quotes from that book. Ruth Needham of Pollinger has been very helpful in obtaining this permission. Thank you Ruth.

I extend my gratitude to JeriLyn Holston-Andrews, head librarian of the Ocean Pines branch of the Worcester County Library, in Maryland, who obtained most of the numerous reference books I requested for my research. The librarians at the National Library of Medicine were also helpful to me during the unending hours I spent there.

My son Stephen Neff and wife Teresa, daughter Beth-Ellen Berry and husband John, daughter Lisa Kowalewski and husband Rick, stepdaughter Karen Passero and husband Vito, stepson Jay Brodsky and wife Laura, and my wonderful grandchildren Rebecca, Sarah, and MaryBeth Berry, Lorena Kowalewski, David and Michael Samuel Neff, and Carmella Passero all have rallied behind me and believed in me for all these years. Thank you, my loving family.

Contents

Foreword

by Mary Ann Shah

I AM IN AGREEMENT WITH PHYLLIS BRODSKY's premises regarding the changing culture of childbirth over the last century, how we have succumbed to each popular trend along the way, and where we stand today. Her book will enhance informed decision-making by helping to demystify the choices contemporary women must make about birth, health care, and whom they choose as their providers of care.

It is my passionate belief that women are being disempowered by contemporary technologies that ensure "childbirth without pain" and now "childbirth without labor." I offer three analogous situations to bolster my argument.

Would Mount Everest climbers feel the same sense of exhilaration upon reaching the summit if helicopters were available to lift them from peak to peak when the going gets rough? Similarly, would anyone bother to participate in marathons if volunteers lined up along the way to pull exhausted runners to the finish lines in "American Flyer" red wagons? Or, to take the analogy just one step further, would a serious composer consider "giving birth" to a flawless composition that had been computer generated? I contend that the mountaineer, the marathoner, and the musician all experience a tremendous sense of self-fulfillment when they are able to laboriously—and sometimes even painfully—overcome the challenges of nature with their own innate talents.

Conversely, a new birth culture seems to be emerging in which more and more women are now demanding painless labors—or no labors at all—even before they experience their first contraction. In my opinion, this compromises the very wonder and awe that belongs to a woman alone when she valiantly attempts to bring her baby into this world through her own efforts, notwithstanding the compassionate support and vigilant monitoring she will require from a midwife or physician into whose hands she entrusts her care. And, to be sure, obstetric intervention may be

1

unavoidable even in the best of circumstances, because of some disharmony between the natural forces of labor: the "powers" (uterine muscle strength), the "passenger" (fetal size and position), the "passageway" (pelvic space and contours), and the "psyche" (maternal mental and emotional status). Thus, birth attendants must always be prepared to intervene with all the "miracles" that modern medicine has to offer whenever the physiologic process of passage goes awry; at the same time, they must also serve as public adversaries against indiscriminate practices and blissful ignorance.

We cannot afford to forget the "Twilight Sleep" era of almost a half-century ago when the joy of birth all but disappeared thanks to technologic "advances" that rendered women out of control of the birth experience. Injections of labor "cocktails" (combinations of the drugs scopolamine, Phenegran, and Demerol), inductions of labor with potent uterine stimulants (oxytoxins), forceps deliveries, episiotomies, and general anesthetics prevailed, expediting the escape of babies from the wombs of their unawake and unaware mothers. Those of us who bore witness to such practices can attest to the deleterious effects they had on childbearing families. Human dignity was lost as frightened women labored without the support of loved ones, were shaved of pubic hair, had their lower bowels cleansed by intrusive enemas, were fed intravenously and denied even sips of water, vomited from the effects of narcotics, had to be catheterized to relieve their bladders of urinary retention, became agitated and uncooperative as they uncharacteristically screamed and cursed, were confined to labor beds where they frequently had to be physically restrained until birth was imminent, and then were rushed on stretchers to sterile delivery rooms where they were strapped to narrow tables with their legs suspended in metal stirrups.

To compound these atrocities, worried expectant fathers and grandparents were exiled to waiting rooms; babies were born sluggish, frequently requiring resuscitation; and early parent/child bonding was compromised as newborns were whisked off to nurseries where they remained isolated, except for scheduled feeding times when they were wheeled to their mothers' bedsides to be fed bottles of formula. The "drug 'em up/drag 'em out" abuses probably persisted because women were duped into thinking that labor and delivery could be fast, easy, and without sensation. Most were unaware of the high price that such "sedation" had cost them since their conscious memories of the horrific events that ensued were obliterated by pharmacologically induced amnesia.

Thankfully, rationality gradually prevailed and twilight sleep disappeared off the birth option radar screen. But then, cesarean section rates began to skyrocket as liability issues prompted many physicians to practice defensively by surgically removing one out of every three to four babies via abdominal incisions, rather than risking bad outcomes from long or difficult labors. This trend seemed to level off in recent years; but now, new phenomena appear to be gaining increased popularity. In fact, it is estimated that more than seventy percent of pregnant women are currently seeking epidurals for labor pain relief while the availability of cesarean section as a consumer choice is picking up steam within the obstetric community. It is particularly worrisome that fewer and fewer women are seeking childbirth preparation as they surrender control to the lures of modern technology.

I certainly do not equate epidurals ("consciousness without sensation") with twilight sleep ("sensation without consciousness"), nor do I think that chemical analgesia, anesthesia, and surgery are inappropriate obstetric interventions when used with cautionary discretion. However, I am concerned that we could very well be on a slippery slope. Admittedly, medical research has not, to date, demonstrated that epidurals for labor pain relief cause any significant adverse effects in mothers or babies; however, one cannot ignore the longer labors, the increased likelihood of instrumental deliveries (vacuum extractors, forceps, cesareans), and the array of other perplexing outcomes (e.g., maternal fever, neonatal jaundice) that have been linked to their usage. Moreover, the maternal risks associated with cesarean section (e.g., infection, blood clots, hemorrhage) are well documented. Above all, science has yet to prove that optimal integrity of the mother/baby couple and the family unit is not best preserved by the least technologically manipulated labors.

Is there no lesson to be learned from diethylstilbesterol (DES), a drug administered to millions of pregnant women from the 1940s through the 1970s to prevent miscarriage and premature delivery until it was linked to cancer in DES-exposed daughters? And, what about the public uproars that ensued during the last three decades over belated warnings about the potential toxicity of thalidomide (fetal abnormalities), nicotine (pulmonary and cardiovascular compromise), and Fen-Phen diet pills (valvular heart disease)? Now, we are embroiled in a new exposé over hormone replacement therapy for post-menopausal women. Has the lure of remaining youthful backfired and actually predisposed many women to breast cancer, heart attacks, strokes, and blood clots?

In conclusion, I submit the following: more evidence about the relative safety (or possible non-safety) of "elective" medical technologies must be scientifically gathered; compassionate emotional support and non-pharmacologic comfort measures should always be the first lines of defense to enhance optimal physiologic functioning; midwives and physicians must be prepared to supplement "high-touch/low-tech care" with "high-tech interventions" whenever the well-being of mother and/or baby warrants their use; expectant couples must be helped to explore their goals for birth more fully by being offered full disclosure and informed consent regarding the potential maternal/infant, benefits/risks associated with all birthing options; women must be educated about how powerful they and their bodies really are, that with the proper education and labor support, most can deliver their babies with little or no intervention, and that birth is both a natural and sacred event and an empowering life experience. Ultimately, a woman's birth choices must be respected and supported as long as her own safety and well-being and that of her unborn child are not being compromised because of a lack of education or choice.

Mary Ann Shah, CNM, MS, FACNM
Immediate Past President of the American College of Nurse-Midwives
Editor Emeritus of the *Journal of Midwifery & Women's Health*

Preface

THE CONTROL OF CHILDBIRTH: *Women Versus Medicine Through the Ages* is a history of childbirth practices that takes the reader on a journey through time and reveals what childbirth was like from ancient, medieval, and modern times, up to the present. This history is important in helping the reader understand how the earliest customs evolved into later practices, leading to the options now available for the safest birth outcomes.

My interest in this issue began when I was a young nursing student and observed the ways in which childbirth was managed at that time, in the late 1950s, and developed further in succeeding years as an obstetric nurse and nursing educator. From my own experiences as well as from an extensive review of journal and book literature, I have described both the positive and negative changes through the ages and their consequences, brought about by the evolution of scientific knowledge and the societal and political changes that influenced childbirth practices.

This book focuses mainly on Western history. In the beginning, when women attended women, childbirth was considered a natural event, one phase of a woman's life cycle, until men entered the birth chamber. Men's attitudes toward women played a major role in how women healers, midwives, and women in general were viewed and thus treated. The book reveals what women lost when they traded in their midwives and their female network for male practitioners and surrendered the familiar ambience of their own homes for hospitals. It demonstrates how and why the management of normal childbirth became improperly medicalized in cases in which normal childbirth should have been allowed to proceed naturally. There is now scientific evidence that such obstetric interventions are not indicated in normal labor and they do not do what they were intended to do (such as prevent untoward outcomes). These interventions might even prolong labor and birth, incurring other attendant risks. In this account of the experiences of childbirth throughout the ages, there is an important message for historians, for those in the health professions and for all women, particularly those of childbearing age.

This subject has always been dear to my heart, having witnessed childbirth practices and attitudes of health professionals in the field for decades as an obstetric nurse and nursing and childbirth educator. This book handles the history of childbirth differently from other books written on the subject in that it focuses on how women become excluded from the process, why the power shifted, how and why women's control of their own experience in childbirth was lost, and how women can regain that control.

Phyllis L. Brodsky • Berlin, Maryland

Introduction

YOU HAVE GATHERED BY NOW that this book is about childbirth. My first encounter with this special event was when I was in my first year of nursing school in 1955; my sister, Marcia, was in labor at my parents' home. As Marcia's labor progressed, she just walked around the house to ease her discomfort. She moaned and complained at times, but didn't seem to be in any great distress until she was soon ready to give birth. Her husband, who was also with us, then called the doctor who said he didn't think she was ready to come to the hospital yet. Well, she was. I remember her holding onto the bed post, grunting and crying that the baby was coming. At that point, my mother, sister, and her husband got into the car and "flew" to the hospital. About fifteen minutes later, my mother called me to tell me, "It's a boy!" (It generally took about twenty minutes or so to get to the hospital from our home.) I didn't learn until later in my senior year as a student nurse what it was like to labor in hospitals. My sister was fortunate that she got to the hospital just in time, better yet that she labored at home, and of course best of all to have had a healthy baby.

My desire to specialize in obstetric nursing was crystallized in 1957 during my labor and delivery rotation as a senior nursing student. Those were the days of "twilight sleep," which was the heavy use of narcotics and scopolamine (a drug that produces amnesia, but also intensifies the sedative effects of narcotics). I wanted to witness the joy of childbirth, but instead I witnessed women being literally "knocked out" while their babies were "dragged out" by the obstetricians. I wanted to be an "OB" nurse, but it didn't take me long to be disillusioned and to question the ways in which labor and birth were managed.

In the early and middle years of the twentieth century, women had no idea that childbirth could be conducted differently than it was at the time. They were afraid to deal with any pain, willingly submitting their bodies to their physicians without questioning. One particular obstetrician, who was one of the busiest, wealthiest, and most beloved by his patients, answered all his patients' fantasies. His "standing orders" were to administer Demerol 100 mg and scopolamine 1/150th of a grain every two hours. It was perhaps unfortunate that the mothers took no part in their own birth experiences and remembered nothing; but it was worse yet that their babies were born blue, floppy, and sedated. I remember how difficult it was to stimulate these sleepy babies. This protocol was pretty much the norm during those times.

During delivery, women were placed flat on their backs with their legs strapped into stirrups (this was known as the "lithotomy" position). Because women were so sedated, they didn't have the urge or the strength to push on their own, nor was it possible to bear down while flat on their backs with their legs suspended above them. Forceps were then needed on practically all deliveries. But first a long cut (the episiotomy) was made from the woman's vagina toward her rectum to make room for inserting the forceps to pull the baby out. Instead of women birthing their babies; their babies were "delivered" from them.

There was one incident that had a profound effect on me. A woman was wheeled into the labor and delivery unit creating quite a disturbance because she was already "pushing," ready to give birth. There was no time to shave her pubic hair, give her an enema, administer medication, or to perform any other interventions. As soon as she was put on a stretcher headed for the delivery room, her baby just came out naturally and quickly, screaming, squirming, and pink all over. The doctors and nurses were quite disturbed because there was no time for "preparation" and her baby was born "out of sepsis." But I hadn't seen a baby arrive into the world in this beautiful condition before and knew then that this natural birth was the way it should be. This baby was not blue, sleepy, or floppy as most of the other newborns were that I had witnessed coming into the world. Instead, this baby was pink and crying (as newborns are supposed to do to aerate their lungs). I told myself that this was how I wanted to have my baby when my time came.

When I became pregnant in 1958, I read Grantly Dick-Read's book, *Childbirth Without Fear*, as suggested by my former OB nursing instructor. I informed my obstetrician that I didn't want medication if I could do without it. He was different from the others and accommodated me. During the course of my labor, I had only one very small dose of Demerol. During delivery, however, with my legs up in stirrups and on my back, I wasn't able to effectively "push" Stephen out. No one, in the 1950s, ever conceptualized that squatting was a better alternative. At that point, my doctor told me he would have to use forceps. I suddenly became fearful and then it hurt. So before the forceps were applied, my doctor suggested a small dose of nitrous oxide gas (a short-acting anesthesia used at that time during the actual birth), to which I agreed.

The important issue is that I made some decisions and my obstetrician went along with me, which most women of that era didn't have the opportunity to do. During my next two labors, which were short, I didn't have any medication, except for nitrous oxide during the actual births, for the same reason as in my first birth.

Even today, I find that women in childbirth are expected to conform to accepted practices even though such practices may not be in their best interests. For example, when I was teaching childbirth classes in 1999, a couple attending my class was expecting their second child. During the woman's first birth, which took place in a different state, she had a completely natural birth, attended by a midwife. Unable to find a midwife who took private cases where she currently lived, she selected a female obstetrician. This couple discussed their upcoming "birth plan" with me. I was quite surprised when their doctor later called me, sounding quite perturbed, and questioned me about this patient's "birth plan." Perhaps the couple's needs clashed with the doctor's need for control. Control and power are major themes in revealing the evolution of childbirth practices throughout the ages.

Through my many years of practicing and teaching obstetric nursing, I have observed so many wonderful births, but at times I was also dismayed about the ways they were managed, and I even witnessed some abuses. For example, I've seen women being examined too frequently for the benefit of practice by interns and residents, episiotomies performed even when women have specifically stated they didn't want to be cut, and amniotic membranes ruptured prematurely. I recall one incident in which pain relief was withheld from a teenage girl who was in hard, painful labor for over twenty-four hours. I urged her doctor, in vain, to order an epidural. We've come a long way from the practices of the early and middle twentieth century, but today childbirth is still not quite accepted as a natural phenomenon. In fact I feel there is a regression of sorts happening, as technological interventions in normal births continue to escalate and cesarean births continue to climb.

Through the ages, childbirth moved from a natural state, to interference, through epidemics of puerperal fever, and then to the sterile environment of hospitals. My hope is that, in relating the history of childbirth practices through the ages and where we stand today, I can help women regain the power to birth their babies in ways that work best for them, while accessing the expertise of their caregivers and technological advancements when and if it becomes necessary.

CHAPTER 1

Childbirth in Primitive and Ancient Times

When the prehistoric woman went into labor, she prepared a bed with piles of leaves and soft grass in the heart of a thicket in the forest, hidden from wild beasts. First she walked around her secluded area, stopping now and then to rub her belly. She labored alone silently as her pains increased in intensity and frequency. She didn't moan or cry out, an invitation to wild beasts. When she felt the urge to bear down, she squatted down, grunting quietly. Shortly her baby was born. She tied the cord with a strong weed or piece of sturdy grass and severed it with her teeth or a sharp stone. She then nursed her baby to keep him quiet as the afterbirth was expelled. She bathed him in a nearby stream, then wrapped him in her garment, packed him on her back and walked off to find her mate.[1]

THIS IS PERHAPS WHAT IT WAS LIKE to give birth in the earliest of times, before recorded history. Nobody was there to tell the woman when or how to push in a certain position, or any other way to manage her labor and birth. She was in total control and she was physiologically capable and prepared to bear children with only nature as her assistant.

Primitive women were constantly moving, running, and climbing to survive. Their bodies were well developed and muscular, making them physically fit for the task of childbirth. Constant motion allowed the fetus to be literally "shaken into that position in which it best adapts itself into the maternal parts" so birth becomes easy.[2] Primitive women also had small babies, so they rarely had obstructed labors. Women did what they needed to do to minimize the pains of childbirth. They walked, moved about, and changed positions to cope with their discomforts. They drank

11

if they were thirsty, ate if they were hungry, and rested if they were tired. They squatted when they felt the urge to bear down. No one had to tell them when to do so; there were no rules. These upright positions naturally allow the gravitational forces to help the unborn baby descend through his mother's pelvis and align himself in the best position for birth.

Depending on the culture or degree of social development, parturient women (during labor and birth) may or may not have been assisted by others. In many primitive societies, most women were not. Then there came a time when she began to seek the support and comfort from others. Men had attended their wives during birth from time to time in some early societies, mainly if needed for their strength.

There is a legend about the early settlers on the Island of Borneo, known as the Dayoks. A man named Kelile, a Dayok, was hunting in the forest and happened upon the big monkeys. He observed a female monkey that was crying out as she crouched down while giving birth. Her mate stayed close by her side throughout her birth. Kelile's mate was pregnant at the time. When the birth pains came to her, Kelile did as the male monkey had done; he stayed close to his mate and comforted her.[3]

In a later stage of social development, men were excluded from the birth ritual and women began to take their places. Roles, in general, were divided between the sexes, such that men were the hunters and defenders and women were the gatherers. As gatherers, women learned the earth's rich bounty for food and medicine. Women's base was the home, so they naturally held the caring role (for the children, the sick, and in childbirth). Women were the original physicians, healers, and midwives.

By observing many births, women gained much knowledge and skill in their roles as birth attendants. In the gathering of plants and herbs, women learned which ones had medicinal properties to soothe the pangs of labor and perhaps speed up a prolonged labor. Women were empiricists, having learned from nature, observing and practicing their art through the ages. Their wisdom and skills were shared between them and then passed on to the next generation.

The experienced woman of the family took charge and became the expert in childbirth. She was the forerunner of the midwife. Icelandic folklore describes the childbirth attendant as a woman sitting between the knees of the laboring woman, chanting, massaging, kneading the laboring woman's belly, and waving leaden amulets.

Long ago, birth was a mysterious event, because there were no explanations of how, why, or when pregnancy ended. Some primitive and ancient societies believed that the baby chose the time to be born, when he or she was ready. If the mother labored too long, attempts were made to coax the baby out with the promise of food or other offerings and if that didn't work, the unborn baby was threatened with punishment, such as having a horse charging toward the mother and turning away at the last moment.[4] This technique was supposed to frighten the baby out of the womb, but imagine the reaction of the poor mother-to-be. Superstition, taboos, and rituals played a large role in childbirth. The purposes of the rituals were mainly to ensure a speedy and safe birth and to keep evil spirits in check. Also, to prevent evil spirits from entering the home, all windows and doors were kept tightly closed. When labor and birth were very difficult or if the baby was deformed, evil spirits were to blame. Prayers, magic, sacrifices, and amulets were employed to entice the baby to make a safe and speedy entry.

Over time women became more skilled. But when births became too difficult, they would reluctantly call upon the shaman (medicine man) or priest, who would employ various techniques and rituals to lure the baby out.[5] When all else failed, men would extract the baby with crude tools.

Depending upon the culture, women varied in their interpretation and expression of pain, as is true in this day and age. Among the Navajo Indians, birth was a social event. Sensations of labor were not interpreted as painful. Rituals included sprinkling pollen on the laboring woman's abdomen and stroking her abdomen in a circular motion to stimulate her labor and promote comfort. Soothing conversation and music also provided diversion from the discomfort. In contrast, the Cuna Indian women of Panama had much anxiety and fear of childbirth. Prior to their labor, they went to the medicine man for freshly brewed medicinal tea. But when in actual labor, they hid from him and only allowed women to attend them. Midwives would keep the medicine man informed of the birthing woman's progress.[6]

The history of childbirth embodies the history of women and how they were viewed through the ages. In the beginning women were highly valued; they were regarded as the supreme race among the sexes. They were the goddesses, the queens, and the designated healers. The goddesses represented the heavens, the earth, nature, fertility, birth, and death. It was mainly women who originally discovered the earth's bounty and its healing properties.

The oldest deities were represented as women. The goddesses reigned throughout much of the known world and were known as Inanna in Sumer, Ishtar in Mesopotamia, Sekhmet in Egypt, and Artemis and Eileithyia in Greece, and Freyja in Scandinavia. This "gynolatric" period probably extended from the Stone Age (about 10,000 to 6,000 years ago) into the Bronze Age (about 1200 B.C.). This was also known as the "mythological" age, when the world was magical and the great Goddess was "mistress of stars and heaven, the beauty of nature, generating womb, nurturing power of earth and fertility, fulfiller of all needs, but also the power of death and the horror of decay and annihilation."[7] When the deities were in the image of women, women were valued, but when male gods replaced the goddesses, women became devalued and then subordinated. Women's monopoly of the healing arts was later stolen from them.

The ways in which man views his universe changes along with cultural and societal evolutions. Jeanne Achterberg, in her book *Woman as Healer*, describes the changing concepts of evolving cultures through the ages and the effects of such change on man's belief systems. "The cosmology of culture is the belief system that describes the nature of the universe, including creation of myths.... A culture's cosmology determines who assumes positions of leadership and honor."[8] Anthropological discoveries from pre-classical and ancient pasts have provided clues about women in positions of leadership and as the healers in these early times. Female figurines from the Stone Age, surrounded by animal and creature motifs, have been unearthed from European and Asian continents. These motifs represent "woman's connection to life, regeneration, wisdom, and the mysteries of her inner being."[9]

Excavations have unearthed evidence of a civilization, the Sumerians, who existed around 5000 to 4000 B.C. or earlier, located between the Euphrates and Tigris rivers, which flowed into the Persian Gulf. This city-state was known as Sumer. The Sumerians lived in earthen huts and erected tower-like temples. They also used a type of writing, scratched on clay.[10]

Unearthed relics from these excavations provided evidence that women held the role of healers. Prescriptions for pain relief, surgical tools, charms, and amulets were discovered in the gravesite of Queen Shubad of Ur, who reigned about 3500 B.C. A clay pot, assumed to be used for distilling plants into medicines, was found in another gravesite from about 5500 B.C. There is further evidence that women participated in sacred activities and served as priestess-physicians. Hundreds of plants used for healing were found in the Sumerian pharmacopoeia.[11]

Other archeological discoveries in Denmark revealed similar evidence of worship of female deity and women healers during the Bronze Age. Unearthed bodies of women, in remarkable states of preservation, were buried with herbal remedies, such as yarrow, chamomile, and ferns. Objects found buried with women were associated with the healing rituals of the shaman. Throughout the world women have served (and in some primitive cultures still serve) as shamans and sages (wise women). Shamans were "technicians of the sacred" and were among the most honored ranks of healers.[12]

In the pre-classical cultures of the Near and Middle East, healing was exclusively a woman's prerogative until the third millennium, B.C. In Sumer, Assyria, Egypt, and Greece, women were believed to be ordained by the goddesses to practice healing. Drawings found on the walls of ancient temples represent women as priestesses and physicians.[13] The first recorded woman physician was Peseshet, an Egyptian woman, who was an overseer of women physicians, about 2500 B.C.[14] Egyptian queens, Mentukelop in 2300 B.C. and Cleopatra in 100 B.C., were notable physicians. Because there weren't enough priestesses to attend all of the confinements, midwifery was "sub-contracted" to women who were trusted to practice within the cultural and religious requisites.[15]

The mysteries of childbirth in ancient times have been revealed through excavated relics and the written word. Some of the oldest known written records were the Egyptian papyri, the oldest of which was discovered by George Embers in 1872. The Embers papyrus, written about 1550 B.C., contained records on methods to diagnose pregnancy, speed up labor, relieve labor pain, and treat women's diseases. Similar records were found in other discovered papyri. Relics from ancient civilizations show women attending women in childbirth. A bas-relief in the ancient temple in Luxor depicts a queen from the Eighteenth Dynasty sitting on a birthing chair and surrounded by four women attending her.[16]

Passages in the Bible, other historical literature, and artifacts suggest how childbirth was conducted in ancient times. No one knows for sure. Depending on the cultural and societal norms of the times and places, most likely women attended in childbirth and birthing women found solace in their arms. Like today, women were fearful of pain and of dying in childbirth. But midwives were resourceful, working with natural ways, allowing a woman's own physiology and body movements to help ease her physical discomforts. Religious rituals also played a role in helping the parturient woman relax and ease both physical and emotional discomforts.

In her book *The Red Tent*, Anita Diamant described Leah's first birth; although fiction seemed to symbolize the ways of childbirth in ancient times. The description is summarized as follows: When Inna, the head midwife, arrived, "she made her [Leah] lie on her side and rubbed her back and thighs with a mint-scented oil. Inna smiled into Leah's face and said, 'the baby is nearly at the door.' Whenever a contraction came, Inna had words for Leah only. She praised her, reassured her, and told her 'good, good, good, my girl.'"[17] Leah's sisters and slaves also gave her constant physical and emotional support. Through the ages, women found many ways to comfort women in childbirth.

As cultures and societies continued to evolve, women's place of honor in some societies began to change. Intellectual functioning replaced the magical thinking that was prevalent in the Mythological Age, ushering in the "androlatric" period at the onset of the Iron Age, probably about 1200 B.C.[18] Migrations and Indo-European invasions led to cultural exchanges between the Egyptian, Greek, Roman, and Hebrew civilizations.[19] A new cosmology was beginning. The sexes were seen as separate and man began to view himself as the dominant of the two. By about 1000 B.C., worship of male deities had replaced worship of female goddesses, although worship of the Earth Mother did reemerge episodically.

During times of upheaval, such as natural disasters, famine, sickness, and wars, large cultural and social changes usually occur. Such was the case around 500 B.C. when cataclysmic geological events in Scandinavia caused rising waters and colder temperatures, forcing people to migrate to higher terrains. About the same time, marauding tribes invaded the land and the image of woman changed. The darker gods of war were replacing the earth goddesses.[20] As women began to lose their place of honor, their value as healers began to dwindle. However, women continued to practice healing in their families, especially the peasant populations. Woman's role as healer was being challenged, but midwifery remained her realm throughout ancient, medieval, and early modern history.

Man's interest in medicine and surgery coincided with the practice of embalming, which goes as far back as 2300 B.C. Men gained knowledge of anatomy and surgery through embalming, leading the way to the establishment of medical schools in ancient Greece and Egypt. Women were restricted from entering these centers of learning. In time, "male medicine began to stand for knowledge and discovery," while women's medicine was believed to be associated with superstition.[21]

Ancient Greek civilization was advanced and had highly skilled physicians, surgeons, and midwives. Greek medicine evolved in connection with the schools of philosophy and logic. The priests were the first male medical practitioners. Then lay assistants to the priests took over the role of healing so the priests could concentrate more on their religious duties. The sick were housed in great temples, such as the Temple of Asklepios and were attended to by lay assistants.[22]

The road was paved for the establishment of the Greek schools of medicine, the most famous of which began in Cos about 400 B.C. Ancient physicians did not attend to women during childbirth, which was beneath their dignity.[23] This task belonged only to women. The most famous of the Greek physicians was a man named Hippocrates, who was born about 460 B.C. on the island of Cos. Learning medicine from his physician father, Hippocrates became famous for his predictions, cures, and teaching.[24] He believed that health was governed by four humors—blood, phlegm, choler, and black choler. Balance of these four humors represented health, whereas imbalance represented sickness.

Hippocrates moved to Athens after his father's death. While there, he continued to study and he raised the craft of medicine from superstition, linked with the priesthood, to a science based on clinical observation. He believed that theory alone was not enough to bring about a cure; it must be based on observation and facts, "experience and reason together."[25]

Hippocrates, who became known as the "Father of Medicine," had little time for obstetrics because midwives were plentiful. He did, however, teach some aspects of pregnancy and childbirth. For example, he hypothesized that the fetus controlled the mechanism of labor and was responsible for his own birth by breaking his mother's bag of waters. Hippocrates also believed that the mother's pelvic bones separated to accommodate the head of the fetus passing through, regardless of the size of the baby's head.[26] Hippocrates advocated that the woman should sit or kneel upon a stool while giving birth.[27]

He taught that head presentations were favorable and feet presentations were unfavorable. When birth didn't follow its natural course, he recommended podalic version, which was practiced among physicians and surgeons of his day.[28] Podalic version was a technique by which the physician would reach his hand up into the woman's uterus, grasp the baby's feet, and then turn the baby and deliver him feet first. This practice might have saved some babies from inevitable death and possibly more mothers from death if the baby was impacted.

If the fetus was indeed truly impacted and couldn't be extracted by podalic version, then delivery was effected by using iron hooks to deliver the dead baby piece-meal.[29] Midwives only called upon the physician or surgeon in desperation to save the mother's life.

Hippocrates died in 375 B.C., but his teachings lived on. His theories were kept alive by students and graduates of the School of Cos and followed Alexander the Great through Syria, Palestine, Egypt, and India.[30]

Other physicians who taught and wrote about obstetrics and gynecology mainly dealt with the abnormal. Men didn't become involved with childbirth except in life-threatening situations. Midwives were plentiful, experienced, skilled, and highly respected. Because men assisted only in the most difficult cases, they were ignorant about the natural processes and conduct of *normal* labor and birth. Hippocrates wrote, "Do not refuse to believe women on matters concerning parturition" and Aetuis wrote, "It is needless to give a treatise on midwifery, because from long experience, not only do midwives, but also other women know this subject perfectly."[31]

Although some men began competing with women healers, there were several women—Lais, Artemisia, and Agnodice, to name a few—who wrote medical books and made significant contributions to medicine, gynecology, and obstetrics. By the fourth century B.C., Greek women were forbidden to practice medicine. However, then, as in other eras, female patients were reluctant to be examined by male practitioners. Agnodice disguised herself as a man and attended medical school. She had a successful practice until her fraud was discovered and she went on trial. Her women patients protested so strongly that Agnodice was acquitted and the law prohibiting women physicians was revoked. In the second century A.D., a woman named Cleopatra (not the queen) wrote a treatise on gynecology that was used extensively up to the sixth century by physicians and by midwives up until the sixteenth century.[32]

Pythias, Aristotle's wife, worked alongside her husband and studied the function of body tissues and process of reproduction. It is believed that some medical men who became famous borrowed their works from women healers and midwives. Such was the case with Moschian of the sixth century A.D., who, like others, was believed to have plagiarized Cleopatra's works, without acknowledging her.[33] Moschian was later credited as the first male author to describe natural labor.[34]

The first physicians were Greek, Egyptian, and Roman. The great Roman physician, Cornelius Celsus (first century A.D.), lived during the reign of Augustus. Celsus compiled his *De Medicina*, from the works of many other authors and included some details of anatomy and gynecology. He accepted Hippocrates' theory that the unborn child played an active role in his birth. He recommended various remedies for diseases of the womb, but his writings on obstetrics only dealt with the abnormal births. If the fetus was dead, Celsus described the procedure to extract it as Hippocrates had described.[35] Celsus left natural births to the midwives. He also held women healers and midwives in high regard.

Women physicians and midwives were also highly respected in Rome. Many healers were from aristocratic families during the early centuries following the birth of Christ. For example, Mark Antony's wife, Octavia, wrote a book on the prescriptions she used in her healing practice. Some of these remedies included lard, wine, cardamom seeds, spikenards, and cinnamon for pain relief. She also combined lard, rose leaves, cypress, and wintergreen to form a salve to rub on the abdomen to ease the pains of childbirth.[36]

A famous ancient male physician, Soranus of Ephesus, studied and practiced in Rome during the time of Trojan and Hadrean, about A.D. 98 to A.D. 138. Soranus was a prolific writer. His works on medicine also included aspects of midwifery.[37] Soranus was considered to have been the first specialist in obstetrics. He described the management of normal labor and, like Hippocrates before him, advocated that women sit upon the birth stool during birth. He also described and practiced the technique of podalic version for difficult births, as did Hippocrates. Moreover, his writings also included the structure of the uterus, its appendages and the anatomic position of the fetus in the uterus.[38]

Soranus taught the midwives how to perform vaginal examinations in order to determine how labor was progressing. If labor was slow, Soranus taught the midwives how to induce or stimulate labor by emptying the woman's urinary bladder, giving her an enema of oil, water and honey, and pouring egg whites into her vagina to soften the cervix.[39] He also wrote what he believed to be the qualifications of a good midwife; that "she should have a good memory, be ambitious and stick to her job, be of good moral conduct that she may be trusted; she must show good sense and be of strong constitution."[40] Soranus referred to the midwife as the medicae or sagae (wise woman). He was a strong advocate for midwives, whom he obviously trusted and respected.

Galen was born in Asia Minor in A.D. 130, studied in Alexandria, and later practiced in Rome. He was a prolific writer and left a library of some 400 works. Although he did not write a formal treatise on midwifery, his theories about it were scattered throughout his works. Like his predecessors, he advocated podalic version and extraction by mutilation if necessary. Galen's views were highly accepted. His views remained unchallenged until the seventeenth century.[41] Some of his writings were believed to be plagiarized from contributions of women healers.

Physicians were writing about midwifery, but not practicing the art unless called to difficult births. Midwifery was a vocation bestowed only upon women, who had their own techniques to make their work easier. The birth stool was an important symbol of childbirth from ancient times and thereafter. It was alluded to in the Bible: "When ye do the office of midwife to the Hebrew women and see them upon the stools...."[42] The Hebrew word *ovnayim* means two stones or a stone trough with its lid. It was believed that in ancient times women gave birth while sitting on the corner of this trough or on the round opening of the trough.[43]

It is instinctive for women to crouch down when the pangs of labor are the most intense and the baby is ready to enter the world. A stool aids this natural physiologic position to give birth, and also allows room for the midwife to be able to help guide the baby out of the mother's womb. If a stool was not on hand at the time of birth, the lap of the husband or of one of the women attending the birth would suffice. This person was able to assist the mother-to-be by applying pressure on her belly.

The birth stool or chair took on different forms and shapes through the ages. One early, simplistic stool was shaped in the form of the letter Y. One of the women in attendance or the husband would sit on the rounded knob of the stool (behind the parturient woman) and support her. Moschian, a physician of the sixth century A.D., described a chair that looked like a barber's chair with a crescent-shaped opening in the seat.[44] The birth stool served a practical purpose and was used for centuries.

Following the birth of Christ, the cosmology began to change again. By the second century, the city of Rome was overcrowded and plagued by filth, disease, contaminated drinking water, and clogged sewers. There was no such thing as sanitation. The dead were buried with the garbage in public refuse pits.[45] In times of upheaval, man experiences powerlessness and fear; when threatened he needs to attribute his failings to another force or group of people. Women healers, among other groups, became scapegoats and so began to lose their esteem in the healing arts. However, they continued to take care of sick family members and the sick among the peasant populations in their communities. Midwives were still highly regarded.

By the time the Roman Empire fell during the fourth century, one all-powerful god had replaced the Roman gods and goddesses. Women's healing practices became interpreted as paganism, since women used herbs, charms, and incantations in their healing. These practices were contrary to the techniques of the temple priests, and therefore, the sagae (healers, wise women) were seen as a threat to Christian doctrine. Because there were no known causes of natural disasters, disease, death or other calamities, these occurrences were believed to be due to demons, which women healers had the power to call up at will.[46] Since birth control was limited to mainly the use of certain herbs and was therefore unreliable, abortions were common. The herbs used to induce abortions were deadly in the wrong doses and highly poisonous. Women healers thus became seen as poisoners.

During the Christian era, healing became associated with spirituality and religious charity. There were some women of nobility who were sanctioned to practice healing within the bounds of Christian doctrine. Some of these wealthy women of high social status laid the groundwork for the establishment of charitable organizations to care for the sick, indigent, and dying. Three famous Roman matrons, Marcella, Fabiola, and Paula, devoted their lives to healing. Fabiola, who converted to Christianity after the death of her second husband, used her fortune to care for the sick and poor and founded the first Christian hospital in her own palace in A.D. 390.[47] She practiced surgery as well as nursing.

The art of healing and midwifery was not accomplished by way of reading books or by working in a laboratory. Nature was the laboratory and education came from their elders, from observation and continuous practice. In all probability, women in biblical times had little difficulty during childbirth, as it was written in the book of Exodus, "for they are lively, and are delivered ere the midwives come unto them."[48] If birth did become difficult, midwives knew what to do for the most part.

In her book, *Reading Birth and Death*, Jo Murphy-Lawless described women as being the "central agent" in determining the management of their own births, before management and technology ushered in the realm of men.[49] Richard and Dorothy Wertz referred to traditional childbirth as a "social birth" because there usually were several women in attendance who pampered, nurtured, and bustled about throughout the labor, birth and afterward.[50] The care and nurturing of the mother during labor, birth, and the weeks that followed became known as the *lying-in* period. Women took care of the new mother, other children in the family, prepared the meals and performed the other household chores.

The ways of childbirth from the beginnings of time were women's domain. The practice of midwifery remained only in the hands of women for thousands of years. During the Middle Ages, when all the scientific knowledge was lost in a sea of ignorance, darkness, superstition, and religious fanaticism, midwives were caught up in the misogynistic exploits of the Christian leaders of that era.

CHAPTER 2

The Middle Ages: An Era of Despair and Persecution

When the head midwife arrived, she gave Kristin something to help
her sleep, and then added cushions and straw to the bed prepared on
the floor. She got Kristin bedded down and covered her with rugs and
then "placed small stone pots with herbs in them against the fire."
The lady midwives came, one after another, and said, "She should
walk about the room as long as she could bear." The women divided
themselves into two groups, so that one group slept while the other
group watched and attended. The head midwife encouraged Kristen
to scream "when you feel the pain sore—take no heed of the sleepers.
We are here for naught but to help you, poor child." [1]

THIS PASSAGE WAS TAKEN from the fictional novel, *Kristin Lavransdot-*
ter II, The Mistress of Husaby, by Sigrid Undset, written in 1921.
Childbirth during the Middle Ages was basically unchanged from previous eras. Because there is scant recorded history about how childbirth
was conducted during the early middle ages, information has been
extracted from the few works written by women healers, from relics and
artifacts, from myth, and from what men have written about women
healers. Early fictional literature also suggests how it might have been.
There was little change from previous eras. Women were still the major
players; they provided the same comfort measures, used rituals and magic,
and basically let nature take its course.

While attending birth, midwives still carried their own birthing chair
and an array of potions and herbal remedies. Some of these remedies eased
the discomfort of labor or helped speed it along. Potions consisted of
strange and exotic concoctions, such as doves' dung, ants' eggs, virgin's

hair, and other bizarre remedies.[2] Healing and midwifery were composed of a mixture of Pagan and Christian rituals.

The Middle Ages began with the fall of the Roman Empire in the year A.D. 476 and lasted until the fall of Constantinople in 1453. It was a time of strife, famine, disease, stagnation, and despair that lasted for a thousand years. In these dark ages, knowledge and achievements of ancient times were lost. Belief in the devil and the religious interpretation of evil as cause of disease and disaster replaced any rational thought. This era was marked by men's suppression and subordination of women. The thousand years that composed the Middle Ages were wretched times for all mankind, and women suffered the most.

After the fall of pagan Rome, the social and economic structure of the Roman Empire was in ruins. The church became authoritative and gradually developed into an ecclesiastical monarchy with a central organization of deacons, priests, and bishops. The Pope had become the most powerful figure in Western Europe by the early middle ages. The priests hid ancient manuscripts and persecuted authors of current works.[3] The scientific knowledge and achievements of the ancient Hebrews, Greeks, and Romans were soon lost in a sea of ignorance and religious fervor. For three centuries no literature or science was produced. Trade and travel were prohibited. Only cruelty, stupidity, stagnation and strife prevailed and all things that seemed to make life desirable were perishing.[4]

The ancient libraries were destroyed by barbarian invasions and the ancient Greek and Roman philosophies were suppressed by the anti–Hellenic and anti–Roman policies of Christianity. However, many of the ancient texts were retrieved by the Arab conquerors. After Islam was established in A.D. 632, Arab tribes conquered much of the civilized world. Arab and Jewish scholars translated and preserved many of the Greek and Roman texts, founded new libraries and universities, established an efficient hospital system and introduced pharmacy and chemistry into medical practice. There were also several notable Arab and Jewish physicians who wrote original works.[5]

The civilization of Western Europe during the middle ages was shattered and without rational, political or social structure. It was a world that had become miserable. Also, there were no means of sanitation and disease was rampant. The bubonic plague that ravished Europe during the sixth century ushered in the period of centuries known as the Dark Ages. The plague spread across Europe by the Goths, Huns, and other marauding and migrating tribes and it devastated civilization.[6] Smallpox and other deadly diseases probably contributed to the death toll. As disease and war raged, cities and towns crumbled.

The insecurity and chaos of these dark ages led men to seek leaders among more powerful men, who called themselves lord, count or duke. The powerful ruled large areas of the countryside and the common man became a vassal (tenant) of a piece of the land. The feudal system, as described by Wells, "was anything but systematic"; instead it was confusing and roughly organized.[7] The majority of the people were serfs and the lords were aristocrats. Each lord created his own laws. Thus, private law usurped public law. The feudal system was a highly dysfunctional society and the peasants' lives were nightmarish. They lived in common with their relatives, forming a single household, in which they intermarried and interbred—"a mass of human beings getting up and going to bed together, eating bread off one platter and meat out of one pot."[8] Peasants living in overcrowded conditions were poorly nourished and in poor health. Peasant women were pregnant for most of their lives.

Men ruled society, but women had dominion over the home and were caregivers, healers, and midwives. It was the wise woman who was consulted by the ill and troubled. Just as in ancient times, women healers and midwives shared their knowledge of herbs, cures, and methods with each other, and they passed it on to the next generation. However, if a healer's cure failed, she could be labeled a witch.

Medical treatment was non-existent for the peasants, but the rich hired Arab or Jewish physicians. Moses Maimonides (1135–1204) was the most famous Jewish physician and medical writer of the medieval period. He was critical of Galen's teachings. "Emperors and kings and popes and the richest barons had sundry doctors of Salerno, or Moorish and Jewish physicians, but the whole world consulted the 'Saga' or 'wise woman.'"[9] Wise women were the only practitioners for the common people and from whom the wretched serfs and their abused wives could seek relief from illness.

Women's healing practices included pagan rituals and methods used for centuries prior to the advent of Christianity. Since the Christian leaders' beliefs conflicted with paganism, women healers were seen as spiritually deficient and considered open to temptation by the devil. Moreover, the Church was against healing in general because it believed that sickness was God's punishment for their sins.[10] Therefore, women healers were not looked upon favorably. However, they continued to practice among the peasant population since no one else would.

There were a few women healers who stood out among others and were respected for their wisdom. One such woman was Trotula of Salerno, who was said to be well educated and a distinguished medical teacher at the medical facility of Salerno, Italy. Salerno, established about A.D. 1000, became one of the most important medical centers and universities in Europe, and was open to female students (a rarity in those times). Faculty included Greek, Jewish, Arab, Latin, and even women scholars. Women physicians were also on the faculty, the most famous of whom were Trotula and Adella. Trotula headed the department of obstetrics and gynecology and wrote her treatise on these disciplines. She was a particularly skilled diagnostician, emphasizing the importance of examining the pulse and the urine. Some women who joined religious orders to take on the vocation of nursing, were respected as caregivers.

There was a need for nurses during the Crusades, at which time medical orders were established within the church. It was mostly women from wealthy families who joined these orders or became nuns. However, nuns were not allowed to own property, so the Church took over any property left to these women, which added to the wealth of the church. Among the peasant population, healing was still the realm of women.

Midwives continued in their vocation unimpeded except for the fact that the Church oversaw midwifery as it did everything else. If the midwives ran into difficulty while assisting at childbirth, they were expected to call in the priest for guidance, not a physician. It wasn't always practical or safe to bring a dying newborn to the church, so the midwives were taught how to perform the baptism.[11] According to the Church, the most important function of the midwife was to baptize the baby before its birth if it seemed likely that it would die. To accomplish this, the midwife used a pump-like instrument to squirt water into the woman's vagina and uterus.[12]

Disease, violence, and corruption continued to be a way of life. The Crusades, taking place during the eleventh to the twelfth centuries, contributed to the rampant spread of disease. Because disease and affliction were attributed to sin or possession by the devil, people went to the Church for cure. But the Church had little to offer. Women healers continued to be the real practitioners. Although some of their remedies were magical, many of them were effective. However, some were outright dangerous. Wise women and midwives ran the risk of either failing to cure or of poisoning their patients. It did take audacity and wisdom to determine the correct dosages. Some believed that the wise women were sorceresses.

By the eleventh century, the Church began to relax its stance on healing after the founding of the medical school in Salerno and other emerging universities in Europe. The Church continued, however, to maintain control of medical study by requiring the curriculum to include the study of theology. Medical schools also managed to include the ancient "classics" of medical theory, postulated by Hippocrates and Galen, which had been retrieved by Arabic and Jewish scholars, in their curriculum. These schools didn't teach actual healing methods. This knowledge was obtained from women healers. The priests still maintained a hold on medical practice by requiring physicians to first call in a priest to advise them before administering any treatment. In addition, physicians were forbidden to treat any patient who refused confession.[13]

Society slowly began to change during the High Middle Ages (1000 to 1300). When competition among tradesmen increased, the tools, agriculture, economy, and nutrition improved. These changes were spurred when barbarian tribes from the East and North stopped invading, staked claims, and settled in Europe. This period was characterized by greater mobility, when common men began to seek out separate hamlets and live apart.[14]

A class of merchants, bankers, and craftsmen emerged and university education began to revive. In the thirteenth century, in England and other European countries, men in the same crafts and professions banded together to form guilds. Because they used the same tools and techniques, physicians and apothecaries joined forces and barbers joined with surgeons, an alliance that became known as "barber-surgeons." These guilds provided the individual man with a sense of esteem and status. When the guilds were organized, standards were set and examinations had to be passed by members of the various guilds.[15]

The physicians and apothecaries' guild achieved a much higher status than did the barber-surgeons' guild. This latter group sought ways to improve their status through the years. If a midwife was attending a very difficult birth, in desperation she might call in a barber-surgeon. Barber-surgeons lacked any knowledge of the structure of the human body, but they used instruments sanctioned by law, which midwives were forbidden to use. These crude instruments served only to mutilate and extract the dead baby by dismemberment. Blunt and sharp hooks and knives were used to compress or crush the baby's skull, a procedure referred to as "embryotomy." Another instrument called a fillet was used to extract the baby in pieces.

If the unborn baby was alive before the arrival of the barber-surgeon, he or she surely died soon after. What about the mother? If she did survive any of these procedures, one can't even imagine the excruciating pain and injury she had to sustain. The barber-surgeons were skilled in mutilation, but knew nothing about the human body or mechanisms of childbirth. It was only on rare and critical occasions that the barber-surgeons were summoned and then only to possibly save the mother's life. The life of the unborn child was hopeless at this point.

Health did not improve significantly for the peasant population who lived within the walled, crowded cities where poor diet, lack of sanitation, filth and disease continued to prevail. Many women developed rickets from deficiency of vitamin D and calcium and were left with deformed pelvic bones through which a baby could not pass during childbirth. So in situations such as these, it was often necessary to call upon the feared barber-surgeon. Women who still lived in rural areas of the countryside had access to more milk and vitamin D through work outdoors in the sun. They were healthier, in general, and for the most part had easier births.

During the late Middle Ages (about the years between 1000 to 1500), the Christian Church of Rome became more powerful, sought to impose its doctrine on the whole world, and dominate western European society. By the thirteenth century, the Church had become so dogmatic, that instead of wanting to see the "Kingdom of God established in the hearts of men," they sought power to dominate mankind.[16] A morbid anxiety arose within the Church that men would lose faith and begin to doubt its teachings. So the Christian Church consolidated its teachings in the Counsels of Trent and became totally intolerant of any other religious beliefs or ideologies. Those people who did express ideologies or novel thoughts that contradicted Christian doctrine were accused of heresy. Heresy was a crime because those who held opinions counter to the teachings of the Church demonstrated an intellectual arrogance in opposition to divine law.[17]

The Church's hope for world dominion led to the papal Inquisition, a powerful instrument of suppression. In their mad search for heretics, poor and insignificant women were major targets in a world of suppression and the major victims of the misogynous Church leaders.

Women were devalued in a world ruled by men. Their chief value was only to breed and rear children and to serve their husbands. The contempt for women intensified into a cataclysmic state of misogyny that led to the mass murder of thousands upon thousands of women, most of whom were women healers and midwives, accused of witchcraft and heresy. The Middle Ages have been described as "ten whole centuries of a languor no previous age has known and that so oppressed mankind."[18]

In the centuries following the birth of Christ, Christianity only gradually penetrated downward from the upper to the lower social classes. Initial attempts by the early Church to convert whole nations to Christianity, meant conversion of the rulers only. But the masses, particularly the lower classes of people and those living in less inhabited areas of the countryside, continued to believe in their own gods and continued to practice their ancient religions.[19] Those who embraced these ancient beliefs and rituals by late medieval times were believed to be practicing witchcraft. Such organized religions had been around for centuries, but were diabolic in the eyes of the now strong Christian Church. The "rituals took place at night rather than day, were in the hands of women rather than men."[20] So the ancient pagan (or peasant) religion became known as the "witch cult" and those who embraced this religion were called "witches."

A common practice of the witch cult was the witches' Sabbath, an assembly of members who gathered to worship their gods. During these gatherings, various rites were practiced, such as feasts and dancing, indicating that this was a joyous religion. The most practiced ceremonies seemed to be for the purpose of securing fertility of the land, and often securing human and animal fertility as well. The witches generally traveled to their meetings by foot or horseback. Because of a common practice of anointing their bodies with mind-altering herbal salves that induced a feeling of flying, superstition promoted the belief that the witches traveled in the air on brooms.[21]

Ancient beliefs and customs were gradually incorporated into some Christian rites through the centuries, such as May Day, Halloween, Yule, and Easter. The witches had their own benign male gods, whom they worshiped and described in the form of a male deer or a man with horns, hooves for feet, and frequently a large erected penis symbolizing potency and fertility. It was the Christian judges who labeled these gods the Devil, or Satan, Lucifer, etc.[22] Of course, anyone who worshiped the Devil was accused of heresy.

When a society is threatened by a group of people whose beliefs and conduct differ from those of the larger and stronger group, such conduct is disturbing, constitutes a mystery, and is therefore a threat to the larger society. The witches were such a threat to the powerful Christian Church and its doctrines. The ancient cult was deviant, in the eyes of the Church. Although witchcraft existed for centuries, it became the foundation of an organized movement that sought to protect society from danger.[23] The sorceress who healed, the midwife who attended births, the individual who thought for herself or himself, the fornicator who lusted too much, and the Jew who rejected the divinity of Jesus were all viewed as deviant, and were categorized as heretics. When rulers are fearful of losing power, they intensify their domination. Furthermore, during bad times, such as disasters, famine, or epidemics, the powerful seek a scapegoat and then seek to cure society by killing the scapegoat.[24] The ultimate scapegoats were women healers, midwives, Jews, and any others who didn't follow the doctrines of the Christian Church.

What was the basis of the Church's misogyny? The witch cult was "heretical, erotic, and largely in the hands of women; it was evil and terrifying." "Witches were alleged to use the devil's power to murder, maim, make sterile, ruin crops, and so forth."[25] Women healers and midwives were empiricists, relying on experiment and their own observations. The church was anti-empiricist and so accused women of using magical powers to heal or harm. Furthermore, women represented sexuality and so were accused of sexual crimes against men. Sexual pleasure came from the devil and so it was, therefore, condemned. The peasant society that practiced its ancient rituals was also highly organized. The witches were a triple threat to the church; they were women, they belonged to a pagan cult, and they were empirical healers.[26] Women paid dearly for these transgressions.

From another viewpoint, there were three major forces that contributed to the Church's misogyny. The first was the masculinity of God. There was a time when women goddesses were revered, but when God became viewed in the image of man, the image of women changed. Second was her original sin, which was used as an excuse to subjugate women. For this women suffered a double punishment—to bear children in pain and to be subservient to men. Lastly, so it was believed, they worshiped the devil.[27] All these explanations may offer some insight into the minds of powerful and ignorant men, but there truly is no ethic behind the horrors and mass murder of women that occurred during this time in history.

Women were feared and hated. Those believed to be witches were hunted everywhere by the inquisitors. In the year 1215, Pope Innocent III convened the Fourth Lateran Council of more than 1500 dignitaries from all over Europe, who came to Rome to address the issue.[28] By 1234, the Papal Inquisition was established and Pope Innocent IV issued the infamous Bull (that authorized the imprisonment, torture and execution of heretics). There followed four agonizing centuries for accused witches, most of whom were women. Midwives were prime targets. They were an identifiable group. A passage in the *Malleus Maleficarum* (the manual written to identify witches and dictate their punishments) stated, "Midwives surpass all other witches in their crimes."[29]

There were other forces that contributed to the unrest and misogyny during these medieval times. With the emergence of trade, specialized crafts, and better agriculture between 1000 and 1300, Europe's population doubled and soon exceeded its food supply. The most serious famines occurred between 1315 and 1317, due to heavy rainfall and cold temperatures. The One Hundred Years War between France and England that began in 1346 led to financial devastation. Overcrowding, filth, and poor nutrition were some probable factors that led to the black plague pandemic that occurred between 1347 to 1350, and spread across Europe by land and sea, from Italy to France, Spain, England, Germany, and Scandinavia. The plague, known as the Black Death, killed between thirty and forty percent of Europe's population. Of course, the peasant population suffered the most. Medieval people speculated as to the causes. Some said it was some unknown contagion due to "bad air," but most blamed supernatural beings, such as angels, demons, or witches.[30]

In the meantime, physicians began to gain esteem and played a role in the persecution of women. These men, who began competing with women healers in the marketplace, were later recruited to serve as witnesses at the witch trials. By the thirteenth century, university-trained physicians had already become established as secular professionals. On the other hand, women were forbidden to practice without a license, yet were not admitted into universities or allowed to sit for licensing exams.

Among the peasant population, women healers continued to practice their art in a society that was still basically rural. Healing was a relatively new role for men since it was a practice that traditionally belonged to women. Physicians charged high fees, which the peasants weren't able to pay. University physicians, who didn't even want to serve the poor population, nevertheless scorned women healers, whom they believed were inherently ignorant.

A fourteenth-century English physician, John of Mirfield, chided women healers as "worthless and presumptuous women (who) usurp this profession to themselves and abuse it; who, possessing neither natural ability nor professional knowledge, make the greatest possible mistakes (thanks to their stupidity) and very often kill their patients."[31] These men conveniently disregarded women's long history of empirical practice, yet medical treatment was not based on either scientific or empirical knowledge, but on irrational theory and bizarre logic.

Medical theory was based on astrology, alchemy and on the writings of Galen, who was a dogmatic rationalist without the inquiring genius of Hippocrates. Physicians treated their patients with leeches and incantations.[32] There was much hypocrisy in the reasoning that men were intellectually superior. But, because these men had attended the universities they gained power.

The new medical profession, supported by the ruling classes, repudiated the skills of the non-professionals. Men believed that women's vast knowledge of plants and healing remedies came from the devil since women did not receive a medical education. The Church declared, "If a woman dare to cure without having studied she is a witch and must die."[33] However, licensing laws, which sanctioned only university-trained physicians to practice, were difficult to enforce because few doctors actually attended the universities. However, these laws were selectively used against the uneducated women healers. The fathers of science, such as

Francis Bacon, St. Thomas Aquinas, and others, kindled the outrage of women healers as practitioners of magic.[34] The Church's abhorrence of women healers equaled their abhorrence of magic. This exclusion of women from their healing roles became a theme for centuries.

Although women's healing role was challenged and usurped by men, women still held the reigns on midwifery. Women midwives continued to practice without competition from men because it was beneath the dignity of male physicians to care for women during birth or to treat women's ailments. Furthermore, men were not permitted in the birth chamber. It was against modesty and decency to permit men anywhere near. Through the ages, women managed childbirth well and were the experts. But midwives were a vulnerable group. Midwifery was a fairly risky vocation. The mother was at risk of dying in childbirth due to complications, and efforts to save the baby often failed.

If a deformed or stillborn baby were delivered, the midwife could be blamed and accused of witchcraft. A midwife could also be accused of witchcraft if her patient died in childbirth, or even if she displeased the parturient woman. Using herbs to relieve the pain of childbirth was considered a sin because pain during childbirth was punishment for Eve's original sin. Midwives were accused of performing abortions, poisoning, casting evil spells against their patients, and other heinous crimes during the witch hunts.

To the church, empiricism and sexuality both represented surrender to the senses. Even when the healer's magic and medicinal treatments were successful, they were seen as interfering with God's will. Some medical men in Europe played a role in the witch hunts by identifying the witches and by supporting the prosecutors. Such was the case of Jacobu Felicie, who was brought to trial in 1322, accused by the faculty of medicine at the University of Paris of healing internal wounds and abscesses. She was charged for illegal practice and that "as woman—she dare to cure at all."[35]

Not only were women healers a threat to physicians, but they were also a threat to the doctrines of the Church. Their methods were an affront to the authority of the Church because their magic was an appeal to a power other than the Christian god.[36] Women were also accused if they learned their art in the traditional ways. They could be blamed for anything that went awry or for any conceivable reason. Blame provided the blamer with a sense of control in times of chaos and disaster, which certainly described these late Middle Ages.

Men believed that women were placed on this earth only to preserve the species and to serve men. If women strayed from this role, they were labeled as evil and as devil worshipers. Women accused of witchcraft were hunted everywhere in an era of madness that began in the fourteenth century. It was insidious at first, escalated during the fifteenth century, peaked during the sixteenth century and did not cease until the seventeenth century.

The earliest known trials for witchcraft occurred in Ireland in 1324 and in France, when in 1440, a follower of Joan of Arc was burned following her account of her god who appeared to her in human form.[37] The fifteenth century marked open war against "the last remains of heathenism in the famous Bull of Innocent VIII" when, in 1484, he spoke of the "outbreak of Witchcraft."[38] In this proclamation, the Pope gave power to the inquisitors, who represented the church, to imprison and punish anyone straying from the catholic faith.[39] The Reverends Jacob Sprenger and Heinrich Kramer composed their infamous work, the *Malleus Maleficarum* (*The Hammer of Witches*), in the time between their adventure in Rome and their mission decreed by the Pope in 1484.[40]

The *Malleus*, circulated in 1486, was the most authoritative catechism of demonology, and had gone through fourteen editions by 1520.[41] Sprenger gathered notes from the stories of the accused sorceresses regarding their powers, to be used against them during their inquisitions. To Sprenger, sorcery was the same as heresy, so every sorcerer was a heretic as was every free thinker a sorcerer. "For the chiefest heresy of all, Witchcraft or sorcery, special Directoria (manuals) were compiled in the so-called *Malleus* (hammer) for the detection and punishment of Witches and Sorceresses."[42] This manual remained the guide of the tribunals of the Inquisition and Sprenger became the authority on questions of demonology.

Sprenger and Kramer explained why women were more susceptible to witchcraft than were men. They "have slippery tongues, ... since they are feebler both in mind and body, it is not surprising that they should come more under the spell of witchcraft."[43] Women were accused of copulating with the devil, of rendering men impotent, and were even accused for having sexual pleasure. Kramer and Sprenger reasoned that it is mostly women who are witches because "all witchcraft comes from carnal lust, which is in women insatiable."[44] The charges of witchcraft covered a multitude of sins, such as political subversion, blasphemy, lewdness, and of "every misogynist fantasy harbored by the monks and priests who officiated over the witch-hunts."[45] Midwives were also accused of offering herbs to ease the pain of childbirth, for contraceptive aid, and to bring on abortions. There seemed to be no end to the bizarre reasoning to the accusations of practicing witchcraft.

Criteria for the existence of witchcraft were established in the *Malleus*. Physicians were called upon to be expert witnesses at the witch trials to determine whether a person's disease was caused by natural phenomena or by witchcraft. After all, physicians, so it was believed, were the expert diagnosticians. Physicians were competing with women healers in the marketplace so this was their opportunity to eliminate them. One method of diagnosis was to determine whether or not someone's illness was due to a poisonous infection manifested by ill humors in the blood or stomach or was a result of witchcraft. If the illness wasn't due to poisonous infection, then it was due to witchcraft. Another method of diagnosis was the pouring of molten lead into a bowl of water. If the lead condensed into an image, then the illness was, of course, due to witchcraft.[46]

The three principal methods used to identify a witch were confessions, witch's marks, and ordeal by water. Confessions were sought under torture since the witch herself was the only witness, and of course, if she confessed she was guilty. Witch's marks could be any skin lesion, such a birthmark, mole, scar, or other mark found on her body. These marks, which were believed to be the brand of the devil, were evidence that she was a witch. If no marks were found, it was believed that the marks were there, but invisible. How does one detect invisible marks? Stick her with pins all over her body. If she did not have pain or bleeding at the site of the pin prick, then these were the sites of the invisible marks and so she was guilty of witchcraft.[47] If she did bleed or feel pain, she was innocent. Lucky her; however, at this point she could no longer endure more pain and so she confessed anyway.

This method of diagnosis was also profitable, because there followed a new profession of pin prickers. And guess who some of these men might be? You guessed it; physicians were recruited to join the group of common prickers. The third method of case finding, ordeal by water, probably saved her from burning at the stake. She would be tied hands to (opposite) feet and then thrown into deep water. If she floated she was guilty, but if she drowned, she was innocent. If she was lucky, then maybe her torturers would rescue her in time. The aim of the witch trials was to "proclaim the existence, prevalence, and the dangerousness of witches and the power and mercy of the inquisitors and judges."[48] It seems that the Church succeeded in this endeavor. Moreover, the accusers were rewarded monetarily.

There were conflicting accounts in regard to the methods of inquiry used during the trials. Actual accounts of the individual witches were taken from legal records of the trials and from the records of the inquisitors. One needs to keep in mind that these accounts might be meaningless because the inquisitors used leading questions to elicit confessions. Torture was not used in some countries. The means of execution varied among the different countries. In England, the condemned witches were executed by hanging and then burned. In Scotland, they were strangled at the stake prior to burning, but they were burned alive in France, Spain, and Germany.[49]

The witch trials peaked in the second half of the sixteenth century, but continued into the seventeenth century. Thousands upon thousands of women were accused of witchcraft, tortured, and executed during the height of the witch craze that spanned three centuries in Western Europe. The total number of women killed in Europe is difficult to estimate since the inquisitors and civil authorities kept poor records. Some historians have estimated that the number of women killed in the holocaust was in the millions. The witch craze ended at the dawn of the age of enlightenment. It came to an end when the powerful Church of Rome lost its stranglehold on the governments across Europe, which were becoming more secular.

The Middle Ages came to an end in political and social upheaval when the outrages of these times troubled the consciences of some men who sought to return to the fundamentals of Christianity.[50] The Church of Rome had been touting itself throughout the Middle Ages to be the only true religion. As those centuries came to an end, persons of influence began to break away from the all-powerful Church and wanted to form more liberal governments and branches of the Christian religion. The new branches rejected some of the dogma and wanted to focus on the basic teachings of Christ.

The awakening of intellectual energy and desire for free thought was stimulated by the introduction of paper from the East and the appearance of printed books. The art of printing was discovered in Germany in the early fifteenth century, and improved upon by Johannes Gutenberg in 1455. It was introduced into England in 1470, fostering the acquisition of knowledge. Philosophical discussion, in addition to theological study, was beginning to reemerge in the universities. Arabic medical texts were rediscovered and translated into Latin. Medicine emerged as a profession by the end of the Middle Ages. Medical schools were already flourishing in Salerno, Bologna, Paris, and Oxford. The Medical School of Salerno even had a department of obstetrics and gynecology and admitted female students.[51]

The Renaissance and the madness of the witch craze occurred concurrently. But times were changing as rational thought resurfaced and the flames of science and the arts were rekindled. In addition to seeking social justice and reformation within the church, men once again sought free intellectual discussion. Women continued to struggle to hold onto their healing professions.

CHAPTER 3

The Sixteenth Century: A Renaissance

When her bag of waters broke, she was helped to the stool, "leaning backward, in manner upright." Her midwife sat before her to "diligently observe and wait." The midwife "anointed [her hands] with oyle of almonds or oyle of those white lilies, rule and direct everything as shall seeme best. Also [she] must instruct and comfort [the woman], not only refreshing her with good meate and drinke, but also with sweet words, giving her hope of a good speedie deliverance." [1]

THIS QUOTE WAS IN RICHARD JONAS'S BOOK, *The Byrth of Mankynde* (the first book written for midwives), translated from Latin into English in 1540. As pointed out by Harvey Graham in his book, *Eternal Eve,* the passage basically describes the ways midwives attended women in childbirth for centuries—birthing women sat upright on a stool; the midwife comforted them with food, drink, soothing words and chants, and lubricated their hands to stretch the birth canal and help ease the infant out. Of course, there were other activities and rituals that will be described in further detail later in the chapter.

At the dawn of the sixteenth century, there was an awakening in the arts and sciences. Medicine began to emerge as a profession as more physicians, who began receiving university educations, gained status. They also gained further status by becoming members of the College of Physicians, which was established in London in 1518 by a charter from King Henry VIII.[2] Although there was an awakening in the sciences, the new medical profession was far from scientific or even empirical in practice. Physicians' methods of treating sicknesses and disease were crude and ineffective. Although experiments and quantitative methods were beginning to be applied to physiology, medical remedies were based on theoretical propositions, based on Galen's teachings, instead of empirical wisdom. Medical thought was explained by the classical assumptions regarding the state of body fluids (humors), which were bile, blood, and phlegm, as had been taught by Hippocrates in ancient times.[3] Bleeding and purging were the remedies used to treat diseases and Galen's theories still continued to dominate medical education. There was no concept of sepsis, so there were no measures taken to prevent infection or the spread of disease. Also, there was no such thing as anesthesia for pain relief during surgical procedures, except for the use of certain herbal extracts, such as opium poppy, henbane, and mandrake root. Heavy alcohol intoxication also provided some relief.

The intellectual awakenings and scientific discoveries of the Renaissance led to a better understanding of anatomy, although for years the church forbade dissections. It wasn't until the late 1400s that Pope Sixtus permitted students to dissect human bodies, as long as church authorities gave their permission.[4] Education in the great medical centers of the sixteenth century, such as Paris, Montpellier, Bologna, and Padua, was mainly didactic and theoretical. Students occasionally observed clandestine dissections made by a barber. Anatomical study began at the University of Bologna, School of Law, for legal purposes, necessitating postmortem examinations.[5] Those interested in the study of anatomy, such as scientists and artists, bought bodies stolen at night from gravesites.

Andreas Versalius, the first modern anatomist, who was born in Brussels in 1514 and studied medicine in Paris, became frustrated with only didactic learning. He traveled to Italy in 1536 to continue his studies. There he dissected human bodies in his laboratory and gave lectures on anatomy at the University of Padua. (Scholars could travel as desired because language, spoken and taught in Latin, was not a barrier.) Famous artists of the era, such as Michelangelo, Benevenuto, Cellini, Raphael, Dürer, and da Vinci, also contributed greatly to the growing knowledge of the structure of the human body. Leonardo's drawings include his famous 1492 study of human proportions called *Vitruvian Man*. His 1513 drawing of a female—although partly incorrect—was a detailed attempt to illustrate the body's circulatory and other systems. Versalius wrote the first scientific textbook on anatomy, *De Humani Corporis Fabrica* (*On the Structure of the Human Body*), published in 1543. Versalius confirmed some, but disproved most of Galen's anatomical descriptions, which were based on animal dissections.[6] Bodies for study were still difficult to obtain.

The Company of Barber-Surgeons, granted a Royal Charter by King

Henry VIII in 1540, was allowed to dissect the bodies of just four executed criminals each year.[7] However, there were few available "official" corpses for centuries, and what few there were decomposed quickly in warm weather due to lack of embalming. Grave robbing was one solution and was widespread until the early 1800s.

Let us not forget that while sixteenth century physicians were striving to advance in knowledge and status, women healers and midwives were still being persecuted as witches in this century. The emerging medical elite continued to compete with the traditional women healers and disparaged them as ignorant, uneducated, and therefore not qualified to treat patients. However, the so-called educated men gained status and recognition in belonging to a gentlemanly occupation. Men approached healing from a mechanistic perspective, different from women's caring and sensitive approach.

Francis Bacon advanced the concept that woman was linked to nature; except that she was not revered in the same sense as she was in ancient times. Instead she was viewed as an inferior being. Bacon, who had attended the witch trials, later "transposed trial language into the new science to extract her secrets."[8] Most men of science truly believed that women were inferior and even believed that their brains were smaller than men's. However, there were exceptions to this mindset. Agrippa von Nettesheim praised the wise woman whose divination and predictions were superior to those of the philosophers and astrologers. There had been notable women who provided the impetus for medical advancement. For example, the Christian mystic, Hildegard of Bingen (1100–1179) had remarkable medical insight and wrote two medical manuscripts covering disease, physiology, and plant, animal and mineral medicines. In her *Physica*, she wrote on the concept of virginity and directions for the hygiene of pregnancy.

Although medicine was emerging as a male-dominated profession, in competition with women healers, childbirth remained in the hands of women. Midwives continued to let nature take its course without interference with the normal processes of labor and birth. But when things did not proceed well, the midwives employed interventions of various nature and superstition to deliver the baby. Attempts to alleviate such complications were literally "fumbling in the dark," and well-intended interference inevitably led to infection, injury, or death.[9] Although men were basically excluded from the birth chamber, a midwife, in desperation, might summon a barber-surgeon who had the necessary tools to extract the baby. Even in these emergency cases, it was considered immoral and indecent for men to be present during childbirth. The story has been told that in 1522, a Dr. Wirtt of Hamburg posed as a woman to assist in a complicated birth and was subsequently burned at the stake.[10]

French author Jacques Gelis, in his *History of Childbirth*, stated, "The conditions under which childbirth took place ranged so widely among the different regions and milieu that it would be rash to attempt to create a model of childbirth for the France of olden times." [11] At times, women got by on their own, without assistance, and sometimes voluntarily gave birth in the fields. However, women in childbirth generally needed help, even when things were going well. Traditionally, women labored and gave birth in their own homes, in the "communal" room. Usually four to six women busied themselves by stopping up windows and doors and stirring up the fire to prevent cold drafts and the entrance of evil spirits. "Cold was a mortal enemy of women in travail."[12]

The women scattered straw on the floor of the birth chamber, in front of the hearth, where birth took place. The straw served the purpose of absorbing the secretions that accompanied the birth, and later was burned. The women attendants kept busy tending the fire, heating water, washing and drying linens in front of the fire, and pampering the mother-to-be.[13] The room of confinement hummed in tune with the woman's interludes of tension, cries, and relaxation as nature spun its magic.

Men's initial interest in midwifery in the sixteenth century seemed to arise from the belief that midwifery was in a poor state. The question of education arose, but there were no available schools for midwives. Moreover, it was frowned upon to print any details involving midwifery for reasons of modesty and indecency.[14] Nevertheless, efforts were made to improve the practice of midwifery, which began in Germany, with the publication of the first European textbook for midwives in 1513, written by Eucharius Rösslin. This book, called *Der Swangern Frauwen und Hebammen Roszgarten* (*The Rose Garden of the Pregnant Woman's Nurse*), was later translated into Latin by his son, Eucharius Rösslin the younger, in 1532. The name of the book was changed from *Roszgarten* to *De Partu Homines* and Rösslin became known as Rhodion.[15]

Sections of the book were taken from Moschian, of the sixth century, who had copied Soranus. However, the book was full of superstition, and sanctioned the crudest birth practices and interference, causing much harm to the fetus and mother.[16] At the request of some English matrons, Richard Jonas translated Rhodion's book from Latin into English in 1540 and the title became *The Byrth of Mankynde*. That same year, the book was again revised and published by Dr. Thomas Raynald, under a new title, *The Women's Book*.[17] This book became the standard work for nearly two hundred years.

The book was translated into nearly every European language in the next century and became the accepted guide by which midwives could gain any knowledge. Unfortunately, it was the wrong knowledge, full of the grossest blunders. He advocated "fomentations, bathing, fumigations, anointments, suppositories, pessaries, and the constant cruel manipulations, which poor women had then to undergo in cases of natural labour," and frightening mutilations in complicated labors.[18] This book certainly did not contribute to any advancement in the field of midwifery. There was basically no knowledge of the structure of the female reproductive system and the workings of nature. Interference in the natural process of labor only caused severe injury to the mother and her baby.

The first advances in the field of midwifery began in France. Ambroise Paré, born in 1509, was a barber-surgeon and had a keen interest in anatomy. He was famous for reintroducing podalic version, which had been taught by the ancient physician Soranus. Paré was educated by a parish priest, apprenticed under a barber-surgeon, and then perfected his surgical skills at the famous Hôtel-Dieu in Paris, where he opened a school for midwives. Paré wrote his first paper describing podalic version, which was published in 1551.[19]

Podalic version (reaching into the uterus to turn the baby feet down) was performed when labor was obstructed, prolonged, or if there was severe bleeding. Pare and others believed that this procedure would preclude the use of mutilating instruments, such as the crotchet, used at the time to extract an impacted fetus. It is possible that the reintroduction of podalic version might have saved some women from mutilation and death.

One of Paré's pupils (who was also his son-in-law), Jacques Guillemeau (1550–1613), wrote a book called *L'Heureux Accouchement des Femmes* (*The Happy Delivery of Women*), which was intended for instruction of midwives. A midwife, in his view, "was appallingly ignorant and self-opinionated, perpetrating many horrors on those in their care."[20] There is nothing that can compare to the horrors that the barber-surgeon inflicted on women. It would not be long before the barber-surgeons, and later the obstetricians, would label normal confinement and birth as pathological states and take over the field of obstetrics altogether. Not only did Guillemeau have disdain for the midwives, but it seems he even wanted to change the manner in which women gave birth. He advocated the reclining position during birth, for the comfort of the woman, so he claimed.[21] Would this position better accommodate the use of instruments? The reclining position works against the force of nature (gravity) that would help bring the baby to birth. Thus, a new way to manage birth had begun.

Advancements in midwifery were slower in England than they were in France. There was rivalry between the physicians and the barber-surgeons in England. Barber-surgeons, who were poorly trained, had difficulty achieving recognition. Physicians, who maintained a higher status than the barber-surgeons, were not eager to let them encroach upon their territory. Socially, the barber-surgeons ranked on par with carpenters, shoemakers, and other members of the trade guilds. After all, these men were first barbers, skilled in using the tools of that trade.

University-trained physicians were members of the Royal College of Physicians, who forbade its members from practicing midwifery. A rather perfunctory oral exam allowed admittance of barber-surgeons into the guild of barber-surgeons, which was officially founded in 1540.[22] There were no requirements for expertise in, or knowledge of, midwifery. It is interesting to note that during these times, men became organized. It is through organized groups of people in similar trades or professions that power is gained over those who are not organized. Most women midwives were not educated, nor were they organized. So women were at a disadvantage even though they had the empirical knowledge and skill to attend normal births.

Physicians did not interfere with the midwife's practice and surgeons only intervened when summoned to assist as a last resort. As stated earlier, the change from country life to city life affected women's health and pelvic structure. The poorly educated barber-surgeons did try desperately to save mothers' lives by extracting the fetus with whatever tools they had. However, their tools were destructive and painful. Women, afraid of childbirth to begin with, were exceedingly fearful of the barber-surgeons. Once in the hands of these men, mutilation and death during childbirth were almost inevitable. Needless to say, barber-surgeons were not very popular, but there were no alternatives when normal birth was hopeless.

The variation of tools used by the barber surgeons for extracting an impacted fetus included the hook, crotchet, lever, vectus, knife, fillet, and perforator. A crude bi-valve speculum was used to dilate the vagina so as to gain access to the impacted fetus. This vile instrument was apparently known to physicians as early as 400 BC.[23] The lever was a flat strip of metal that was inserted into the uterus to grasp the nape of the baby's neck. The other end was used as a lever against the mother's pubic bone, which probably ended up being broken. Hooks were blunt or sharp tools used to extract the baby. The crotchet, which also had a blunt hook on the end, and the fillet, were also used to extract the impacted baby. The tools were pushed up into the uterus and rotated so the hook would catch a part of the baby, such as the chin, mouth, armpit, or eye socket, then the baby would be pulled out intact or in parts.[24]

These tools obviously killed the baby (unless, hopefully, he or she was already dead), damaged the mother's tissues, led to bleeding, infection, and death or long-term injury and suffering. The vectus was an instrument superior to the fillet, used for the same purpose and probably designed by Peter Chamberlen in the 1600s, before he invented the obstetrical forceps.[25] The vectus was similar to a single blade of the forceps (which were not yet invented or known) and was used to extract the fetus. When these tools were ineffective in extracting the fetus, then the fetal skull was punctured with a scissors or perforator (sharp instrument) to "lessen the head" and evacuate the child's brain, so the fetus could be extracted using the other tools.[26]

As horrifying as these tools and techniques were, there were no alternatives other than letting the woman die undelivered. Podalic version may have been more effective if performed by a skilled surgeon, but most men knew nothing about this maneuver, nor did most midwives. Cesarean operations were recorded in the sixteenth century but were performed on women who were nearly dead or had just died, to hopefully save the child.[27] Cesarean deliveries were rarely performed on living women prior to the eighteenth century. One instance was the very unusual case in which Jacob Nufer, a Swiss sow gelder, who in desperation performed a cesarean on his own wife, in the year 1500.[28] It was miraculous that she survived, considering there was no anesthesia or antibiotics to fight infection. The baby lived 77 years and his wife went on to have five more vaginal births, including a set of twins.[29]

Scipione Mercurio, born in Rome in 1540, was a keen anatomist who introduced, in Italy, the cesarean operation on a living woman. Mercurio did not actually perform this operation, but advocated it as a life-saving intervention. In 1596, he published the first printed illustrations of the operation. Mercurio recorded that he had seen two women who had safely delivered by cesarean section in Touluse, France in 1571. Graham pointed out that this may have been a deliberate exaggeration to support Mercurio's theses.[30]

Without anesthesia, asepsis, or ways to control hemorrhage, it is unlikely that women could survive such a radical procedure. Except for the unusual case of Jacob Neufer's wife surviving the operation, there were no recorded cases of women surviving cesarean operations until the late eighteenth century. The first official documented case of a woman surviving a cesarean birth was performed by James Barlow in Great Britain, in 1793.[31]

Midwives continued to practice independently during the sixteenth century, although there were attempts to regulate them. English bishops oversaw midwifery mainly for the purpose of preventing witchcraft associated with birth and to assure loyalty to the decrees of the church.[32] The motives behind regulation were securing moral and religious control, rather than protecting the health of mothers and their infants by conducting standardized evaluations of competence.

A first attempt by church and state to regulate the field of midwifery occurred in France in 1560, during the reign of Henry III. A statute was passed to provide instruction, conduct examinations, grant licenses, and register all midwives. The regulations in the statute also specified conduct and character, reflecting the religious edicts of the times. For example, the midwives were forbidden to dispense medicine that could precipitate miscarriage.[33]

Some factors that led to this statute were the church's interest in baptism of all newborn infants, including stillbirths, and concerns regarding the welfare of women during childbirth. The regulations also specified education for the midwives. The nature of instruction included some theory in anatomy and an apprenticeship under appointed midwives of good reputation, who were known as *matrons juries*. The matrons were supervised by the King's barber-surgeons. Following a three-month apprenticeship, the prospective midwives received a certificate acclaiming good conduct and qualifications for practice, which were submitted to the King's chief barber-surgeon. The King's Assembly conducted oral questions to the midwifery students. If the students answered correctly, they took the midwife's oath, were presented with a diploma, and then permitted to practice in the community.[34]

This regulation was an early attempt to educate midwives. It demonstrated that midwives were valued in France. In the following centuries, French midwives continued to receive licenses to practice after completing private apprenticeships or courses of study at the Hôtel Dieu in Paris. France was the leader in midwifery education.

The famous Hôtel-Dieu, founded in A.D. 660, was originally intended as a refuge for the poor and homeless. The hospital grew to about 1200 beds by the sixteenth century. Conditions were abominable. Each bed held four to six patients, regardless of their age, sex, or condition. The hospital was filthy, vermin-ridden, and poorly ventilated. However, this was the first institution in Western Europe to open a school for midwifery. The famous French midwife, Louise de la Bourgeois, born in 1563, was the first graduate of the school and a student of Ambroise Paré's.[35] Her story will be told in the next chapter.

The intellectual awakenings of the sixteenth century led man to escape from the darkness, religious dogma, persecutions, ignorance, and superstitions of the middle ages. More men began attending universities and medicine emerged as a profession. While women were being murdered across Western Europe, medicine emerged as a profession and physicians began to gain status and recognition.

Women would remain the experts in childbirth in the centuries that followed. However, the time would come when men would view midwifery as a profitable enterprise and begin to compete with the traditional midwives, the noble women who had practiced their art from the earliest of times.

CHAPTER 4

The Seventeenth Century: Men and Their Instruments

The woman went into labor, settled down by the hearth, and told her husband to summon the women. "There were mundane tasks to be done: keeping the fire up, drawing water and heating it, holding the woman down later if necessary, then washing, sponging, drying linen before the hearth, looking after the child, preparing a cordial or broth.... Spontaneously the women got organized, with the mother, mother-in-law or aunt taking the leading role, as was to be expected."[1]

THE RITUALS AND ANCIENT CHRISTIAN and "pagan" beliefs that were played out during childbirth varied from region to region, but basically remained alive for centuries. As described in the previous chapter, birth usually took place in the woman's home by the hearth with several women (usually four to six) in attendance, turning the birth chamber into a "buzzing hive," humming around the parturient woman. If labor slowed or became difficult, talk of obtaining help from outside (physician or barber-surgeon) alarmed the woman.[2]

In the countryside, midwives were revered and respected for their empirical knowledge. The midwife was known as the "good mother," "wise woman," "wise mother," or "mother midwife." Her role was generally considered charitable and she was rewarded with presents of a capon, eggs, cake, or other goods. If midwives had taken courses, then they were expected to be paid money.[3]

Medical science continued to advance in the seventeenth century, as more became known about anatomy and the process of childbirth. Although most of the literature on the "new midwifery" had been written by men, there were some famous and highly educated midwives who wrote about the field. As stated in the previous chapter, Louise de la Bourgeois was the first graduate of the School of Midwifery at the Hôtel-Dieu. After graduating from the school, she received her license to practice midwifery, which was issued by the faculty de medicine. She was honored with the title of royal midwife in the court of King Henry IV of France.[4] Her influence overlapped into the seventeenth century.

When the King's wife, Marie de Medici, became pregnant in 1601, the King gave much thought about the choice of midwife, in whose hands would be the future King. Henry wanted an elderly widow. However, the Queen argued that the midwife should be pleasing to her mistress, young, alert, and experienced. The Queen won this round. The King obtained proof of Bourgeois' competence and good standing and so acceded to his wife's desire. Once engaged, the midwife was in constant attendance and advised the Queen on good health habits, such as what she should eat and good posture during birth.[5]

Bourgeois was the first woman midwife whose works were published. Her book, called *Observations diverses sur la sterilite, perte de fruict, foecundite, accouchements, et maladies des femmes, et enfants nouveuz naiz* (translated *Diverse observations on sterility, loss of fruit, fecundity, childbirth, and illnesses of women and newborn infants*), was published in 1609.[6] Based on the teachings of Ambroise Paré and on those of Jacques Guillemeau, Bourgeois' book described the management of birth, contributing greatly to the advancement of French midwifery. It was translated and published in England in 1659.[7]

Louise de la Bourgeois must have been ahead of the times, because she objected to bleeding, which was a common method of treatment during this era. Unfortunately, many midwives could not benefit from her book because they were illiterate. Also, she was not very popular with her less-educated fellow midwives because of her association with the male midwives at the Hôtel-Dieu.[8] Sadly, she lost both her reputation and position as royal midwife after the Duchess of Orleans died in childbirth.[9]

The seventeenth century was one of scientific discovery. It was the age of Hobbes and Bacon in philosophy, Napier in mathematics, Boyle in chemistry, and Harvey in physiology and medicine.[10] The "new midwifery" was labeled "scientific" because it opposed the traditional magic and religious explanations of labor and birth.[11] But midwifery was still a far cry from scientific. However, a better understanding of anatomy, physiology, and the mechanics of labor spurred the interest of some men in the field of midwifery.

The first Englishman who greatly influenced the study of midwifery was William Harvey, born in 1578. He was primarily a medical doctor and physiologist, best known for describing the circulation of the blood in 1616. His first book, *De Motu Cordes*, was published in 1628.[12] His main interest was the study of anatomy, but he also had a keen interest in obstetrics, particularly the function of the reproductive organs. Another of his books, *De Generatione Animalium* (*On the Generation of Animals*), was published in Latin in the year 1651. The chapter titled "Of the Birth" provided insight into the process of childbirth. Harvey wrote and taught the structure of female anatomy and the mechanisms of labor and birth. His book was translated into English and republished in 1653.[13] "The immortal Harvey was the first to rescue English midwifery from the age of darkness."[14] Known as the "father of English midwifery," Harvey discouraged meddlesome interference, contending that Mother Nature should be left alone to perform her magic.

Harvey's contemporary, Dr. Percival Willughby, encouraged midwives to follow Harvey's teachings and to refrain from meddlesome midwifery. Willughby was born in 1596, educated in Oxford, apprenticed to a barber-surgeon and subsequently set up his own practice in Derby.[15] He advocated Harvey's methods, but opposed those of Paré and Louise Bourgeous. Willughby's *Observations of Midwifery* described about 150 midwifery cases he had attended. He agreed with Harvey that natural labor should be left to the safe conduct of "the invisible midwife" [nature].[16]

Although Willughby can be commended for advocating non–interference, like many of his colleagues, he disparaged the midwives, blaming them for interfering with nature by rushing to get the stool at the first signs of labor. He wanted to banish the midwife's stool, preferring to have women birth in bed while kneeling on a bolster in a squatting position. He further believed that it was inappropriate for men to attend women in childbirth for reasons of modesty, unless there was urgent need. If he was called in to assist in a very difficult birth, it was said that he was obliged to crawl on his hands and knees into the darkened birth chamber.[17]

Perhaps the turning point in the history of obstetrics was the invention of the obstetrical forceps. This invention marked a revolution in the future ways that childbirth would be managed. Peter Chamberlen I, born in 1560, became a barber-surgeon, and was credited with inventing the first design in 1588, although a crude form of this instrument had been known since ancient times.[18] Arabian surgeons used a primitive forceps constructed with teeth in the inner surface, apparently to penetrate the head of a dead fetus to deliver it. Knowledge of this earlier form had been lost for centuries, and perhaps rediscovered by Peter Chamberlen I.[19]

The design of the forceps was in the form of two wide flat blades that were curved to fit over the fetal head. The handles were held together with tape.[20] The forceps were effective for delivering an impacted fetus that might be born alive. But no one can say what condition the baby was in following birth or even what the poor mother's condition was following the use of this crude instrument.

The Chamberlens were a family of barber-surgeons. Dr. William Chamberlen, a French Huguenot, fled with his wife and three children, Peter I, Simon, and Jane, from Paris to Southampton, England in 1569. Three years later, another son, Peter II was born. Peter the Elder (I) and Peter the Younger (II) were barber-surgeons who practiced in London and later became physicians. Peter I was granted a license in "physic" in 1607, without attending lectures, because he "was already in good practice and could use his time more profitably in attending to professional duties." At this time in history, physicians were allowed to practice surgery, but surgeons were forbidden to practice physic.[21]

Both Chamberlen brothers used the forceps secretly to attend women in complicated confinements. They would carry the forceps with them (along with their other instruments) in ornate carved gilded boxes and charge handsome fees for their services. The brothers were far from altruistic. For materialistic and self-righteous motives, the invention of the forceps was not shared with their colleagues, but instead kept a secret within the family for three generations (about one hundred years). In addition to profiting from their secretive innovation, they contrived other monetary schemes. Peter II, in 1616, appealed to James I of England with a proposal to instruct and govern midwives.[22] His intention was to head such a regulatory body and in so doing, he would aspire to gain status as well as financial reward. His proposal, however, wasn't accepted.

Peter the Younger (Peter II) had eight children. His eldest son, Peter III, born in 1601, also became a barber-surgeon and a physician. In 1628, he was made a Fellow of the College of the Faculty of Physic. In 1634, Peter III attempted to regulate midwives, as did his uncle, Peter II, back in 1616, and so advocated the establishment of a corporation, under the auspices of the Royal College of Physicians, to train and license women midwives.[23] This was a second attempt by a Chamberlen to control the practice of traditional midwifery.

Peter III's motives were the same as those of his uncle (Peter II) in that he would aspire to head this enterprise and gain both status and wealth. Fortunately, his plan too was rejected. The London midwives won this round by bitterly complaining and petitioning the bishops, who licensed both midwives and physicians in London.[24]

The midwives were appalled that this Mr. Chamberlen, who had no experience in midwifery, other than what he learned from reading, hoped to teach the art of midwifery.[25] They accused him of interfering with their business, stating "Neither can Dr. Chamberlane teach the art of midwifery in most births because he hath no experience in it but by reading and it must be continuall practice in this kind that will bring experience."[26] (Different authors spelled "Chamberlen" differently.) Chamberlen later sought his revenge by writing a pamphlet denouncing midwives whose "ignorance and disorder amongst some uncontrolled female arbiters of life and death."[27] Chamberlen was not the last man-midwife to paint this dismal picture. Barber-surgeons and midwives became embroiled with each other once these men began to invade the midwives' territory.

Peter III had 14 children. His eldest son, Hugh, born in 1630, and two other sons also practiced midwifery. Hugh also used the secret forceps. He held the Bishop of London's license to practice midwifery and was the man-midwife in attendance to the court of James II and Mary.[28] Mary was expecting her first baby in July 1688, and went into premature labor in June, while Dr. Chamberlen was out of town. The baby was delivered safely instead by the midwife, Mrs. Labany, who received a substantial fee.[29] If physicians weren't on time for a birth, women fared far better with their midwives.

In 1670, Hugh traveled to Paris to visit Francois Mauriceau, the famous French accoucheur, to whom he offered to sell the forceps, but without success. Mauriceau asked Dr. Chamberlen to demonstrate the use of the instrument on a badly deformed dwarf, who was well advanced in labor. Hugh's attempt to use forceps to deliver her baby failed after three hours and the woman died the following day. Mauriceau did not even see the forceps, but declined to buy them. Mauriceau claimed that upon autopsy, the uterus had been torn and perforated in various places, proving how inadequate a tool it was. Hugh translated Mauriceau's great works on obstetrics into English, which was said to have made a substantial contribution to the progress in midwifery in England.[30] Hugh Chamberlen also finally achieved his much-sought status and wealth.

Following Peter III's death in 1683, his wife hid the original forceps, along with the other instruments and letters, in boxes in the attic of their home, where they were not discovered until 1813. However, his son, Hugh Chamberlen, after 1683 settled in Holland and sold it to a Dr. Van Roanhuyze and his colleagues, who then sold the secret to other men-midwives or physicians who could afford it. Van Roanhuyze may have tried to swindle others. It is not entirely clear who sold what to whom. Dr. Chamberlen's son, Hugh Junior, born in 1664, was the last of the Chamberlens who practiced midwifery. He allowed the family secret to leak out before his death in 1728. A book written by a Dr. Chapman in 1733 made public the design and method of application of the forceps.[31] As the forceps became known, physicians had much to gain in the way of financial rewards and power.

Thereafter, forceps were widely used by physicians, who experimented with various shapes to fit the birth canal. Numerous applications were made and carried to France, Holland, Denmark, and Sweden. This invention marked the beginning of obstetrics. Townsend stated that "it seems incredible that such a marvelous invention, as the obstetric forceps, could have remained a family secret for more than a century."[32] Marvelous indeed! Once the secret was out, men were eager to try out these new instruments, which could be deadly.

Some men attempted to use forceps even in normal births. Indeed, a new, revised instrument replaced the more mutilating ones, but it also later became a weapon used by the men-midwives to usurp traditional midwifery. Forceps incurred much damage, particularly in the hands of unskilled practitioners, of which there were many. There were well-educated physicians and men-midwives, in addition to the women midwives, who were adamantly against "meddlesome midwifery."

Although some men were gaining ground in the development of obstetrics, midwives were still in power and were still needed. There were some well-educated female midwives; however, they didn't write or publish to the extent that men did. Men had greater advantages. Those who wrote and published became famous. Hence, history tended to favor the achievements of men over those of women. However, France valued all its midwives and encouraged their education.

The famous French male accoucheur, François Mauriceau, was born in 1637, and had an extensive private midwifery practice in Paris, and also at the famous Hôtel-Dieu. This hospital was considered to be the greatest establishment in Europe for lying-in women.[33] Mauriceau also was probably the first man to initiate the concept that all pregnancies (even those progressing normally) were pathological, claiming that pregnancy was a "tumor of the belly" caused by the infant.[34] Men later adopted Mauriceau's ideas of treating childbirth as an illness.

Mauriceau was renowned for advocating the reclining position for women during childbirth, which he contended was more comfortable for the woman and, he admitted, more convenient for the accoucheur. So be it; he substituted the bed for the birth stool, which was but another affront toward women and traditional midwifery. Mauriceau gave the cold shoulder to the midwives' stools, and recommended that women should give birth in their own beds.[35] In his book, *Traité des Maladies des Femmes Grosses et Accouchess (The Diseases of Women with Child* and Child Bed), published in 1668, Mauriceau declared that "the woman should lie on her back with her head and shoulders slightly raised and bearing down when they [pains] take her, which she may do by holding her breath, and forcing herself as much as she can, just as when she goeth to stool."[36]

However, his views were disputed by other accoucheurs for many years. Used since antiquity, the birthing stools were far superior to the reclining position. Sitting in front of the parturient woman seated on the stool, the midwife was better able to assist the birth, and it was less fatiguing for the woman at birth. Upright positions, such as squatting, crouching, or sitting are naturally adapted by women in labor. The holding of the breath while pushing, known as the valsava maneuver, is dangerous to the woman and her fetus. When the baby's head is descended in the mother's pelvis, it presses on nerves that give her the urge to push. It is nature's way, so it is not necessary for the woman to push "on command" and hold her breath. However, this maneuver, believed to shorten the second stage of labor, is advantageous to the accoucheur. Wealthy families had their own birthing stools, or midwives carried their own stools from house to house when they attended women who were not so well-to-do.

The "French position" (as Mauriceau's back-lying position became known) was not adopted in England after Chamberlen translated Mauriceau's works into English. The idea of reclining during childbirth was noted in a passage in an eighteenth century English translation of Aristotle's Experienced Midwife, written about 350 B.C. Other classical authors, however, did recommend an upright position for birth.[37] Women on their backs lost much control to their male attendants.

King Louis XIV of France supported the idea of this reclining position. It seems he had a perversion for observing women during birth and so had a better view.[38] The King also favored male accoucheurs.

The famous ancient physicians—Hippocrates, Soranus, and other Greek and Roman writers—advocated the upright positions during birth. Paré also advocated the sella perforata (birth stool) so that the sacral bones and pelvic ligaments would more easily yield and the birth canal would more easily dilate. However, Mauriceau disregarded their teachings. Louis de Mercado, court physician to Philip II of Spain, likewise advocated the sella obstetrica (obstetric stool), enumerating such advantages as: (1) the cervix is directed toward the outlet; (2) the weight of the baby aids expulsive pains by the force of gravity; and (3) the coccyx is free to move backwards. De Mercado further emphasized "the midwife's hands must be covered with a cloth into which the child is received."[39] It wasn't necessary to interfere when all was proceeding well. The role of the midwife was to support the mother and *catch* the baby as it was born!

Goodell, a nineteenth century physician, later wrote, "In our time eminent physicians are seeking to improve the obstetric forceps, so in those days learned men did not distain to perfect the sella [obstetric stool]."[40] Goodell criticized the use of forceps, while explaining the natural advantages of the upright position for women during birth.

There were other men who rebuked Mauriceau's views. The Dutch physician, Henrik van Deventer, advocated the birthing chair and presented a new model, in which the back of the chair provided more support to the woman, allowing more force from her abdominal muscles to be transmitted to the uterus. Van Deventer ridiculed Mauriceau's reason for women reclining in bed during birth, indicating how uncomfortable it would be for the parturient woman.[41]

Although Mauriceau advocated the reclining position during birth, he recommended ambulation during labor. In his book, *Traité des Maladies*, he wrote, "They have always worse labours if they be much on their beds in travail" and "the woman being on her legs, causeth the inward orifice of the womb to dilate sooner than in bed; and her pains to be stronger and frequenter that her labour be nothing near so long."[42] This is indeed true, but his recommendation was not followed by men in later eras.

Mauriceau at least recognized that the upright position allowed natural forces, such as gravity, and the natural physiological forces of the woman's body to do their work. These forces are healthier than any interference. Men who eventually took over the practice of midwifery didn't follow these laws of nature. These same principles apply to the second stage of labor (birth), which Mauriceau disregarded. Men altered these natural processes for their own convenience, profit, and control.

One famous English midwife, Jane Sharp, spoke out against the men midwives, proclaiming that midwifery belonged to women. Mrs. Sharp was the first English midwife to write a book about midwifery. *The Midwives' Book* was published in 1671 to "enlighten her sister practitioners," and also to direct "childbearing women how to conduct themselves." She described herself as "a practitioner in the art of midwifery above thirty years." Mrs. Sharp wanted to educate midwives and beseech them to be "both fearing God and faithful" and "exceeding well experienced in that profession."[43]

Mrs. Sharp acknowledged that men-midwives were educated, but that women, although lacking formal education, had experience and could much more easily care for women having natural births. She wrote that "though we women cannot deny that men in some things may come to a greater perfection of knowledge than women ordinarily can..., yet the Holy Scripture hath recorded midwives to the perpetual honor of the female sex."[44]

Mrs. Sharp contended that there were occasions when the services of a physician or "chyrurgion" was indicated, but that among "barbarous peoples, where there were no men of learning, women are sufficient to perform this duty; and even in our own nation, that we need to go no further, to assist ... women are fruitful and as safe and well delivered, if not much more fruitful, and better commonly in childbed, than the greatest ladies of the land."[45] Sharp was saying that when there were no men around, as in the countryside, women did better without them. Male intervention was unnecessary.

Midwives did have their remedies when labor and birth were difficult; the efficacy of these remedies was never doubted. For example, Mrs. Sharp described in her book a remedy for "sore travel" (severe labor pain), advising a woman to "wrap her back with a sheepskin, newly flead off, and let her lie in it; and to lay a hareskin, rub'd over with hare's blood newly prepared to her belly."[46] Superstition was still part of the picture. In her book, Mrs. Sharp wrote, "The eagle-stone held near the privy parts will draw fourth the child as the loadstone draws iron, but be sure, so soon as the child and after-birth are come away, that you hold the stone no longer, for fear of danger."[47]

Other remedies included heavily greasing the birth canal, stretching the cervical os, and giving ergot (a drug derived from a fungus that grew on rye and caused the uterus to contract) to help labor advance. Ergot is a dangerous drug that stimulates the uterus to contract, but can result in intense contractions that can last too long, leading to fetal and maternal death. From years of practice the midwives had a pretty good handle on the dosage. Although there were many skilled midwives, there were also those who were not as skilled. Some of the traditional remedies used by the midwives seem strange today, but doctors also had seemingly strange remedies, such as bleeding, purging, and administering dangerous remedies, such as mercury.

Childbirth was still women's sphere across Europe in the seventeenth century. Male midwifery developed more slowly in Germany than in France and England. Germany already had numerous highly skilled midwives, many of whom were educated. Justine Siegemundin, born in 1650, was the most celebrated German midwife. In addition to her extensive practice, she was also a consultant for difficult cases. At the age of 40, her book on midwifery, *Die Chur-Brandenburgische Hoff-Wehe-mutter*, was published in 1690.[48] Justine Siegemundin was as famous in Germany as Louise de la Bourgeous was in France. Siegemundin was appointed court midwife by Frederick III. The purpose of her book was also to educate midwives. It included discussions of pregnancy, labor onset, the process of labor and birth, useful medicines, and management of difficult labors. She advocated gentle manipulations to extract the fetus in difficult labors and emphasized not resorting to the "hook." Instead, she recommended Ambroise Pare's method of turning the fetus. She diligently observed all her cases and recorded her observations accurately.[49]

Obstetric science was still in its infancy in the seventeenth century. The instruments used by barber-surgeons to extract the baby, in addition to mutilating and killing the baby (if not already dead), also caused much damage to the mother's reproductive organs. If the mother did survive this ordeal, she often suffered from long-term trauma. Common conditions that followed traumatic birth were perineal tears that did not heal (they were not sutured) and vesico-vaginal or recto-vaginal fistulas (which are openings between the walls of the vagina and urinary bladder or rectum). These debilitating ailments caused uncontrollable leakage of urine from the bladder or fecal matter from the rectum into the vagina, which caused vaginal irritation, infection, pain, and foul odor from the putrid vaginal discharge. Sexual intercourse became painful, humiliating, and sexually repelling to her husband. The physical and emotional pain these poor women had to endure generally lasted for years or a lifetime.

There were no recorded statistics of maternal or fetal mortality in those days. However, Harvey Graham, in his book *Eternal Eve*, stated that "many women died in childbirth and that infantile mortality rates were extremely high." According to Graham, in restoration England sometimes half the children died in the first few weeks of life.[50]

Men-midwives were dangerously intervening, and some began to discredit the traditional midwives as being ignorant, superstitious, and unskilled. To the contrary, it was the men who were ignorant and unskilled. As obstetric science continued to evolve, men began to invade what was traditionally the role of women. Some men thought they could do better because they were more literate and more published. However, there were also some famous and educated midwives who were quite literate, wrote, and also spoke out against the threat of men invading their territory. Male midwives developed birthing techniques different from those of midwives, and were improving and inventing new tools. By the end of the seventeenth century, women still held their own in the field of childbirth, but the power they held would be challenged in the next century.

CHAPTER 5

The Eighteenth Century: Men and Science

The twenty-five-year-old woman was in labor with her second child. "Her first had come in that natural smooth way.... In this second labor, however, the head of the child stuck in the passage; and was so far advanced, that the Doctor told her, whether in jest or earnest I cannot say, that he could discern the color of its hair. Her pain, though extremely great, had not however hindered her observing the Doctor rummaging for his instruments." He convinced her that her child would die if he didn't expeditiously extract it. "The fatal instrument was struct into the brain-pan of the child," who had then died.[1]

UNQUESTIONABLY, CHILDBIRTH WAS A WOMEN'S sphere in the eighteenth century, but more men began to engage in the field. Their methods and use of instruments were not safe. An English physician, Dr. Mawbray, said, "It is indeed indifferent whether man or woman practices this art, so the practitioners be properly adopted and duly qualified for the purpose of so great a work." Another eighteenth-century physician, Dr. Chapman, contended that there were far more births than men practitioners could ever attend. Therefore, male practitioners were not inclined to monopolize the field.[2]

Although medicine began to advance in the eighteenth century, obstetrics lagged behind. However, medical education began to include courses in midwifery and more men became interested in the field. As knowledge in the field of anatomy and physiology advanced, so did a greater understanding of the reproductive process. What men learned about childbirth was mainly from reading and attending lectures, not from hands-on experience. Those men who achieved a university education gained status. In spite of women's expertise in the field of midwifery, men-midwives believed in their own superiority over women mainly because of this education.

As scientific discovery advanced, so did man's perception of his authority, which was "based on a superior model of rationality," and so not amenable to accepting as expert any non-scientific voice.[3] There was in fact minimal scientific discovery. The discovery of the obstetrical forceps was perhaps a technological advancement, but far from scientific. Although some men were gaining knowledge of reproductive processes, they were still ignorant about natural birth processes, having only limited experience during complicated confinements.

The eighteenth-century English midwife, Sarah Stone, contended that more women had died in the hands of barber-surgeons, who had just completed their apprenticeship, than in the hands of the most ignorant midwife.[4] Stone and other midwives advocated reform and regulation of their own practice. Sarah Stone wrote a book, *A Complete Practice of Midwifery*, published in 1737. In it, she described the consequences of some cases of complicated births that were mismanaged. Stating that "it is not improper for all the profession to see dissections and read anatomy as I have done," she suggested that midwives should apprentice for at least three years "with some ingenious woman in practicing this art."[5] Unfortunately, Sarah Stone's advice met with obstacles created by the men entering the field.

The obstetric forceps were becoming more widely used, and empowered the new professional men. However, the majority of barber-surgeons who were beginning to use them didn't know how to safely apply them and had little understanding of reproductive anatomy and physiology. Use of the forceps still frequently inflicted severe injury to the fetus, such as crushing his or her skull, and to the mother, tearing her soft tissues, or causing hemorrhage or infection. It is questionable whether this instrument was even clean, and of course, there was no such thing as sterilization.

Dr. Thomas Denman described the first variety of forceps as having sharp protuberances (like teeth) on the internal surfaces for grasping the head of the child and then extracting the child with likely injury. Other forceps were of "unnecessary length applied before the head of the child had descended very low into the pelvis" and were very strong thereby "exerting great pressure, so as to lead to injury of the child and the mother."[6] Forceps were used by some men to shorten the time of labor, contending that by so doing the time of the woman's suffering would be shortened. This notion appealed to some women, giving men-midwives an advantage. Women-midwives were not licensed, nor were they inclined to use forceps or any other instruments.

The use of the dirty forceps increased the likelihood of puerperal infections (those connected with childbirth). Birth was a dangerous event and men were trying to rescue women from these dangers. The notion of risk was one factor that men began to attribute to all births, whether complicated or not. What men didn't realize or acknowledge was that they were often responsible for many of the dangers of childbirth.

French science and English forceps came together in the eighteenth century. As forceps were used more widely, men began experimenting with different shapes to better fit the birth canal and the baby's head, so there were hundreds of modifications to the forceps by the next century. William Smellie, a man-midwife born in Lanark in 1697, was a pioneer in the use of the obstetric forceps. He began practicing medicine in Lanark in 1720 and shortly thereafter included midwifery in his general practice.[7] The midwives ridiculed Smellie, only allowing him to assist in complicated births. Because he didn't have the opportunity to attend normal confinements, he moved to London and then Paris to study normal labor.

After spending a year in Paris, Smellie returned to London to practice and teach midwifery. He set up his practice in an apothecary's shop about 1730 and soon began offering courses in anatomy and midwifery. Outside the shop, Smellie hung a shingle, which was actually a paper lantern, with the inscription, "Midwifery taught for five shillings."[8] Smellie used a wooden dummy covered with leather to simulate a woman's pelvis. He also contrived a wax doll to demonstrate various fetal presentations and to demonstrate a birth. The English midwives hated Smellie and his instruments. A famous and quite outspoken midwife, Elizabeth Nihell, made fun of his "machine which served him for a model of instruction to his pupils," exclaiming that the "wooden statue, representing a woman with child whose belly was of leather" could not compare to the firsthand experience on the many hundreds of births attended by midwives.[9]

Smellie wrote several books and adopted much of William Harvey's theories. The first book, *A Course of Lectures upon Midwifery*, was published in 1748 and the next, *Treatise on the Theory and Practice of Midwifery*, was published in 1752. He wrote much about the obstetric forceps and was accused by his critics of using them too frequently.[10]

Smellie disapproved of using high forceps, changing the existing ones by mid-century to twelve inches in length, with the widest part of the blade measuring about one and five-eighths inches.[11] He experimented with different sizes and shapes, attempting to improve the existing ones.

He tried wooden ones (which didn't work well) and then tried covering the steel ones with leather.[12] One can only imagine the tearing of flesh when these forceps were used. Elizabeth Nihell not only rebuked Smellie's use of instruments, but also his large hands, which she described as "raw-boned coarse clumsy hands, that no forceps he could invent of iron or steel, being more likely to hurt than his fingers, he had, at least, that excuse for recommending instruments."[13]

Smellie advocated cleanliness and so advised his students to wear "commodious dress, namely a loose washing nightgown, which he may have in readiness to put on when he is going to deliver."[14] Nihell couldn't resist such a target. "It is not too presumptuous for me to offer so learned a gentleman as the Doctor a hint of improvement for his man-practitioner's toilette, upon these occasions, I would advise, the younger ones, a round-ear cap, with pink and silver bridles, which would greatly soften anything too masculine in their appearance on a function which is so thoroughly a female one."[15] Nihell made no bones about her dislike of Dr. Smellie and other men-midwives.

Smellie made some significant contributions to the study of midwifery. He was the first to describe the mechanism of the baby moving down through the birth passage and the first to measure the pelvis and recognize that it was contracted.[16] However, he was injudicious about midwifery and so left himself open to ridicule from that camp. Midwives had been rightfully fearful of the threat to their ancient art.

Elizabeth Nihell was obstinately opposed to men-midwives and their instruments. Born in London in 1723, she adopted the profession of midwifery at an early age. She spent two years studying midwifery at the famous Hôtel-Dieu in Paris. She then practiced as an apprentice, during which she claimed to "have delivered gratuitously, and in pure charity, above nine hundred women."[17] She was well educated and experienced in the art and wrote several volumes of her *Treatise on the Art of Midwifery: Setting Forth Various Abuses Therein, Especially as to the Practice with Instruments*, published in 1760.

Nihell assailed men-midwives. She wrote that women may "fall into the hands of one of the common men-midwives, either of that multitude of disciples of Dr. Smellie, trained up at the feet of his artificial doll, or in short of those self-constituted men-midwives made out of broken barbers, tailors, or even pork-butchers."[18] Nihell was caustic in her attack against men's instruments. She wrote, "The substitution of men more especially of their iron and steel implements, is attended with greater danger, greater mischiefs, than those which that substitution is pretended to prevent or redress."[19] She believed men's rationale for the use of their instruments was based on false principles. She claimed that all their instruments caused the death of more children, and hurt, damaged, and even murdered some mothers.[20]

Midwives were the safest and most skilled practitioners. According to Nihell, midwives have natural aptitude, tender feelings toward the sufferings of their own sex, and the patience to remain with women as long as necessary. If the baby were in an abnormal position, a midwife would know how to manipulate with her hands to extract the baby. Men do not have such patience and too quickly resort to their instruments.[21] Nihell further proclaimed that all instruments were useless, dangerous, and often destructive.[22]

There were some male practitioners who sided with the midwives and cautioned against the inappropriate or over-use of the obstetric forceps. Dr. Thomas Denman, born in England in 1733, urged young and inexperienced practitioners to refrain from using the forceps, limiting their use to only "those who are experienced and have acquired dexterity." Denman advised that the "*os uteri* [neck of the uterus] be perfectly dilated, and the membranes broken" before applying the forceps. He advised that the head of the child should have descended into the mother's pelvis and have rested "for six hours, as low as the perinaeum ... before the forceps are applied, though the pains should have altogether ceased during that time," giving nature a chance before employing other interventions.[23]

Denman strongly advocated non-interference in normal labors, acknowledging that natural labors were not well understood by "scientific men [who were] not being formerly engaged in the management of common labours, had not opportunity of making observations upon them."[24] At least he agreed with the midwives on this point. He was against hastening the birth process by any artificial means and also against having the woman hold her breath to push vigorously as the French accoucheur, Mauriceau, had advocated. Denman described four types of labors he identified as: (1) natural—the baby's head presents and labor is completed in 24 hours; (2) difficult—labor prolonged beyond 24 hours; (3) preternatural—if any other part than the head presents; and (4) anomalous—circumstances that require assistance.[25] There were many male midwives who did not heed Smellie's or Denman's advice and went on fumbling in the dark.

Nihell simplified the descriptions of childbirth as natural, or "that in which the fetus comes out in the most ordinary way, when it presents the head foremost." She defined "preternatural" as "when the fetus presents in the passage any other part as the head."[26] Denman's definitions were based on artificial criteria in regard to time limits, refuting nature's greater flexibility. Instead of being in tune with nature, obstetric science sought to control women's bodies, implying that childbirth was a dangerous event, salvageable only by obstetrical interventions.

The natural versus preternatural dyad, believed to be objective and transferable to each case, was firmly in place as a "fundamental element in knowledge production" by the late eighteenth century.[27] Denman, Smellie, and other male practitioners of these times had good intentions, but didn't explore the effective methods used by traditional midwives for centuries. However, there were some men who did advocate safe methods and prudent use of instruments.

There were some circumstances that required men's tools and interventions in saving lives of childbearing women and their unborn infants. Ancient writings from European, Egyptian, and Far Eastern scholars referred to abdominal operations to save the life of the baby after the mother had died. The cesarean operation (Latin meaning "to cut") received its name from the Roman law, Lex Caesarea, which required that if a pregnant or parturient woman died, the baby should be removed and buried separately.[28] Cesarean operations were rarely attempted in the eighteenth century. Most any operation frequently resulted in death due to infection, hemorrhage, and shock. Shock resulted not only from hemorrhage, but also from the excruciating pain, since anesthesia was not yet used. Of the dozen or so reported cases, the women died, but some babies survived.[29]

Since cesarean deliveries were not yet an option, men-midwives used forceps and other instruments to intervene in obstructed births. However, they also interfered unnecessarily, in spite of Denman's advice to the contrary. Men even used instruments to forcibly dilate the cervix (neck of the womb) to hasten labor. Actually, several methods of forcible dilation of the cervix had been used since the sixteenth century for purposes of inducing labor, shortening a slowly progressing labor, or facilitating the use of instruments.[30] These methods, known as accouchement force, frequently led to infection, cervical lacerations, and hemorrhage. Later, men used the rationale that shortening the length of labor would ease a woman's suffering. Actually, men could attend more cases in a shorter period of time for a more profitable enterprise. Interference didn't benefit the birthing woman, but it did work to the advantage of the physician or man-midwife.

Other operative interventions were introduced in the eighteenth century. The man-midwife, Fielding Ould, born in Dublin in 1710, described the operation of episiotomy. Ould became assistant master of the new Dublin Lying-In Hospital in 1745 and master in 1759. In his *Treatise of Midwifery, in Three Parts*, published in 1742, Ould wrote about the mechanism of normal labor and birth, recommended the use of opiates and rest for prolonged labor, and advocated the operation of episiotomy.[31] This operation (cutting of the perineum from the vaginal opening toward the rectum) was supposedly performed to prevent tearing of the perineum, which he believed was due to the tightness of the vaginal opening that prolonged labor. This operation gradually became accepted obstetric practice. What Ould and his followers never considered was that in most instances it was unnecessary if the woman remained in an upright position. In the reclining position, it is easier for the attendant to use forceps and an episiotomy better accommodates the use of forceps.

Ould was a firm believer in the avoidance of "meddlesome midwifery" and wrote that "the less the parts are handled the better," but if necessary, "let it be done with all the delicacy and tenderness ... rather than using any violence." So why did he advocate the operation of episiotomy? He criticized other accoucheurs for proceeding blindly in difficult situations, stating that "many of their schemes are like those of some navigators and geographers who never made use of a compass, but in their closet."[32] It seems that Ould had mixed messages in his advocacy of avoiding "meddlesome midwifery."

Ould contributed to obstetric science by explaining the dysfunction of labor, using women's normal physiology as the cause of prolonging the birth process. He wrote, "It [the baby] cannot however come forward, by reasons of the extraordinary constriction of the external orifice of the vagina, so that the head ... thrusts the flesh and integuments before it, as if it were contained in a purse."[33] Ould wanted to rescue women from the dangers of childbirth by shortening their labors and easing their suffering. There were better ways. Midwives used oil to lubricate and massage the woman's perineum to prevent tearing. Some tearing frequently occurs with or without episiotomy. As we have seen, none of the new interventions established by obstetric science were necessary in the normal events of birth. Obstetrics sought to rescue all women from the afflictions they believed were inherent in childbirth.

It is important to mention William Hunter, born in Lanark, England in 1718, who contributed greatly to the advancement of obstetrics. He was primarily a surgeon and anatomist. He was appointed physician and accoucheur to the Middlesex Lying-In Hospital in 1749. His greatest contribution was in describing the physiology and pathology of parturition. Hunter established a school of anatomy with his brother John Hunter and another physician, William Hewson, in 1768. Hunter's book on *The Anatomy of the Gravid Uterus*, which he worked on for thirty years, was published in 1774. Like Denman and Ould, William Hunter was conservative and denounced operative interference even in desperate situations. He contended that the "more ignorant the operator, the more willing was he to employ his instrumental armamentariam."[34] Although Hunter was not as keenly interested in clinical midwifery as he was in anatomy and pathology, he was relatively wealthy because his practice included royal and aristocratic clientele.

Hunter applied for admission as a Licentiate to the College of Physicians in 1756, but was disappointed that he was turned down, even though he had prestige as royal accoucheur to the Queen.[35] In Hunter's time, there was not just rivalry between male and female midwives, but also between the rich and not-so-well-to-do accoucheurs, and between doctors of physic (medicine) and surgeons. Men-midwives and surgeons were not eligible for election to the Fellowship of the College of Physicians.

The competition between all of the various practitioners is portrayed by a publication, written by a Dr. Frank Nicholls in 1755, which, on her deathbed, Mrs. Kennon, a royal midwife to George II's Queen Caroline, was delighted to read. Nicholls wrote, in his *Petition of Unborn Babies,* "The babies complained that their mothers through ignorance and fear had relied upon ignorant man-midwives and hired them at extravagant rates to distress, bruise, kill, and destroy." Hunter responded to this petition, claiming it as a violent attack on the practitioners of midwifery by a madman and that the reason is that "we get money, our antagonists none."[36] The pioneers of the infant field of obstetrics received their rewards.

Another way for men to gain experience in midwifery was to house laboring women in lying-in hospitals. The establishment of these facilities proliferated throughout Europe during the eighteenth century. This concept was not a new one, since the first one was established centuries before in the famous Hôtel-Dieu in Paris. The growth of lying-in hospitals evolved from the notion that women in labor should have the opportunity to receive hospital treatment if things went badly for them. But these hospitals also served obstetrics well by providing readily available patients for clinical practice.

The first lying-in hospital established in the United Kingdom opened in Dublin and was founded by Bartholomew Mosse in 1745. Mosse, a licentiate in midwifery, formed a committee to establish a place for the confinements of his poor patients who lived in "conditions of squalor." This establishment, the Dublin Lying-In Hospital, was originally a fifteen-room, three-story house that was replaced with a new building in 1757 renamed the Rotunda. Another establishment, the General Lying-In Hospital, opened in 1752 outside London and became the Queen's Lying-In Hospital in 1791 (under the patronage of Queen Charlotte) for "poor pregnant women as well as married as unmarried."[37]

From the middle to the end of the eighteenth century, eight lying-in hospitals opened in England, eight in Scotland, and three in Ireland. Most of these establishments were for poor women. The Middlesex Hospital, which opened in England in 1747, in its book of *Laws, Orders and Regulations*, promulgated in 1770 that (among other laws) men-midwives eligible for practicing there must have a degree of doctor of physic and "none but married women, or widows of newly deceased husbands may be admitted to lying-in at this hospital." [38]

Most women gave birth in their own homes, attended by midwives and other women. They also had options about where to give birth and who their attendants were. However, poor and desolate women had little choice. Their options were lying-in wards or any shelter they could find. Some desolate women chose to birth alone, rather than in the lying-in hospitals where they would be experimented on and die from disease, which was rampant in those establishments.

The filthy, overcrowded maternity wards were fertile ground for the spread of puerperal fever, better known as "childbed fever" or "lying-in fever." This disease was first discovered in Leipzig in 1652. It then spread throughout Germany, into France in 1664, into London, and back into Germany in 1770. Of the 17,876 women who gave birth in the Hôtel-Dieu in Paris between 1776 and 1786, 1,142 women died from the fever. No European country escaped these epidemics in the seventeenth and eighteenth centuries.[39]

The industrial revolution, which began in England about the middle of the century, saw an influx of people moving from the countryside into the cities. After 1750, most poor women living in industrial areas, and some middle to upper class women, were attended by men-midwives.[40] The lying-in hospitals marked the beginning of hospital births, mainly for poor women. The middle or upper class women who chose men-midwives gave birth in their own homes. These women believed they would be safer in the hands of these new professionals. They weren't. Meddlesome interference and the use of instruments greatly increased the risk of injury and infection.

The cause of infection was unknown, so nothing was sterilized and more than likely not even clean. However, the risk of infection was not nearly as high when birth took place in the home as compared to the lying-in hospitals. Although there were no national statistics on maternal, fetal, or infant death rates before 1838, estimates of deaths from childbirth were recorded from various sources from the sixteenth to the eighteenth centuries. Maternal deaths were classified into two categories: associated or puerperal deaths. Associated deaths were those that occurred during or after birth, but were not directly related to the pregnancy or birth, such as pneumonia or typhoid fever. Puerperal deaths were those that were directly related to childbirth or occurred during the lying-in period. Puerperal deaths were further divided into puerperal fever or accidents of birth. Records of these deaths were kept in the lying-in hospitals or private practices.[41]

The men-midwives made the diagnosis of the cause of death. Because the causes of the various diseases weren't known or agreed upon by these new professionals, the accuracy of the statistics was questionable. It could have been easy enough to record that the death was due to an associated cause. Symptoms of puerperal fever varied as the disease progressed; in the disease's final stages sepsis raged throughout the body and could very well have been misdiagnosed as pneumonia.[42]

Maternal mortality statistics were also derived from the number of baptisms kept in parish records and from Bills of Mortality, which included women who had died in childbirth, as reported by the next of kin. Parish records of maternal mortality could be misleading because if the mother had a stillbirth, her death did not appear on the register. Yet in these cases it was likely that the mother also died in childbirth or soon after. Estimates from various districts in England indicate that between 1657 and 1700, deaths attributed to "childbed" ranged from fourteen deaths per one thousand total births at their lowest rate to fifty-nine per one thousand total births, averaging to about twenty-one maternal deaths per one thousand births.[43]

It has been speculated that the rates during the last half of the seventeenth century were even higher than those during the middle ages because "meddlesome midwifery" became more common by the end of the seventeenth century. Estimates of maternal mortality rates from the register of St. Botolph in the sixteenth century were 23.5 deaths per one thousand baptisms from 1583 to 1599. So there did not seem to be much change in rates from the sixteenth to the seventeenth centuries. The most dramatic death rates undoubtedly occurred in the lying-in hospitals in the eighteenth century.[44]

Other statistics cited by Loudon (1986), based on London Bills of Mortality, were 16.7 maternal deaths per one thousand births in 1760 and fifteen per one thousand in 1781.[45] Estimates of maternal deaths in three Northern England parish registers were (per 1000 stillbirths) 137 from 1629 to 1729, sixty-four from 1664 to 1675, and down to fifty-seven from 1700 to 1750.[46] The number of women who died following the deaths of their unborn babies was much higher than the number of maternal deaths following all births. Women who had such difficulties as a deformed pelvis were more likely to die in childbirth and so was their unborn child.

Conditions that were likely to result in death related to childbirth included hemorrhage, pelvic contraction or deformity, abnormal presentation of the fetus, infection, or eclampsia (convulsions due to what had been known as toxemia of pregnancy). The use of forceps, other instruments, and forcible dilation of the cervix resulted in severe injury, hemorrhage, and even possibly rupture of the uterus. In the event of a contracted or deformed pelvis, the uterus continues to contract so forcibly that it finally ruptures, causing massive hemorrhage and death. Infections result from bacteria invading the birth canal, proliferating in the lining of the uterus, particularly where the placenta is attached, and spreading through the reproductive organs, into the abdominal cavity and throughout the body, causing septicemia and death.

Puerperal fever was recognized by Hippocrates, but was infrequent when midwives, who generally practiced without interference, were the only attendants during childbirth. William Harvey described the symptoms of cases he saw of high fever and offensive vaginal discharge following apparently normal births. Other symptoms included diarrhea and pelvic pain. The mortality rates were so high in the lying-in hospitals in Paris, Vienna, and other countries that there were periods of time when twenty percent of the women died within a week following their births. It was estimated that about two hundred epidemics of puerperal fever occurred from the middle of the seventeenth to the middle of the nineteenth centuries in European countries, the worst having occurred in 1772 and raging across Europe for three years.[47] The men-midwives and physicians were alarmed. Their own credibility and esteem were threatened in the wake of these horrendous epidemics. Poor women knew if they entered these hospitals they wouldn't come out alive, but had little alternative but to give birth in the alleys, which some chose to do.

Male practitioners never considered themselves responsible for the spread of the dreaded disease, although some did acknowledge the contagiousness of the fever. Numerous theories were offered. The disease was blamed on a "putrid atmosphere" in the lying-in wards or birth chambers, stagnation of the lochial discharge (normal bleeding following birth), and other such theories. Blame was even directed toward the (women) midwives and nurses, whom, it was believed, carried the contagion from one infected woman to another. The fever was also attributed to a woman's lifestyle during pregnancy, such as the squalid living conditions of poor women or women's manner of dress, such as the "tightness of stays and petticoat bindings" that press the womb and constrict the intestines and so prevent "exclusion of the excrements," according to Charles White of Manchester.[48]

Charles White, born in 1727, a surgeon and man-midwife residing in Manchester, was consumed with finding the cause and cure of puerperal fever. He described the disease as an absorption fever and a putrid fever. He recognized it as a contagious phenomenon and was the first to recommend absolute cleanliness, isolation of infected women and adequate ventilation in the lying-in ward or chamber.[49] White believed that the fever resulted from the lochia stagnating in the folds of the vagina and womb, becoming putrid and then being absorbed by the lymphatics. He was close to describing the actual pathology, but declared that the disease was "conveyed from one to another by putrid miasmata lodging in the curtains, bed cloths, furniture, and by the necessary houses."[50] White also acknowledged that the risk of disease could be greater by the use of instruments or manual manipulations to extract the child. He didn't imagine the presence of microscopic organisms spread by human hands and the tools that these hands held.

Another man-midwife and friend of White's, Thomas Kirkland, born 1722, concurred with White that the fever was a putrid disease that spread from the coagulated blood in the uterus.[51] Both White and Kirkland agreed that putrid matter was absorbed into the body, but they could not define what this matter was. These men did, however, advocate a clean environment, and clean and fresh-smelling curtains, bedclothes, and attire worn by the attendants. White also specified that the woman should sit up in bed a few hours after birth, and as often as she can afterward, to prevent the lochia from stagnating in her vagina and uterus.[52] This did make sense and continued to be a standard of care if women developed an endometrial (lining of the uterus) infection.

White claimed that of all the lying-in patients he delivered he never lost one, but further stated that he spoke only of natural parturitions, not preternatural ones such as those of "floodings" (hemorrhage) or convulsions.[53] It seems as though with such claims he absolved himself from any responsibility of maternal morbidity or mortality. The men-midwives of these times were able to describe the symptoms and even the pathology because of what they observed from the dissections performed on the women who died from puerperal fever. They described widespread inflammation of the peritoneum (membrane that lines the abdominal cavity), abundant putrid matter, and sticky glue-like matter on the intestines. They saw massive abscesses and adhesions. Women had to endure so much pain and misery prior to their deaths. White was the first man to recognize the contagiousness of this disease and advocated sensible preventive measures. But he never recognized that men (because of their meddlesome interventions) were most responsible for the spread of childbed fever.

There were other men who also recognized the contagiousness of the fever. Alexander Gordon went a step further than White, denying that puerperal fever was due to a noxious constitution of the atmosphere, but was more likely due to a specific contagion "readily communicated as that of small pox" and that it "seized such women only, as were visited, or delivered by a practitioner, or taken care of by a nurse."[54] This was the first time anyone alluded to the possibility that the attendant could be carrying the contagious matter from patient to patient. Nurses and midwives may also have been responsible, but nurses never, and midwives rarely, performed any invasive methods and they didn't use instruments. Still, Gordon and his colleagues didn't know just what this contagion was.

Gordon proposed some preventive measures, in addition to those White had proposed. He recommended fumigating the attendants' and the patients' apparel. Unfortunately, other male practitioners denied theories proposed by Gordon, White, and Kirkland and ignored their advocacy for cleanliness. The epidemics raged on into the next century. For two hundred years women sacrificed their bodies and their lives to obstetric science.

By the end of the eighteenth century, obstetrics, though still in its infancy, was growing in pace with advancements in the field of anatomy and pathology. Childbearing women living in crowded, filthy cities were not as healthy as those living in rural communities, and had more complications and greater difficulties during childbirth than before. More men became interested in the field of midwifery and sought to save women from the dangers of childbirth. Therefore, in this century, it is easy to see why the new men-midwives and male doctors *perceived* the developing science of obstetrics as beneficial, in juxtaposition to the traditional and more natural practices of female midwives. These men were actually contributing to the dangers of childbirth.

As men struggled to find the cause of puerperal fever and save women from death in childbirth, obstetric science became established and paved the road that would later change the path of the traditional ways of childbirth.

CHAPTER 6

The Nineteenth Century: Men and Disease

Eliza's pains began on a gray and dreary day in March of 1870. Living alone and desolate, Eliza, who didn't even have enough money for food, couldn't afford a midwife. She was admitted to the Rotunda Lying-In Hospital on the 12th of March. After laboring for eighteen hours, Eliza was given an enema and a dose of ergot to stimulate labor. When she still didn't progress, the doctor gave her a dose of chloroform and delivered her baby by forceps. The following morning, Eliza developed a high fever, a rapid pulse rate, and complained of pain in her pelvic region. The doctor ordered a turpentine stupe and a drink of wine to ease her pain. Her vagina was syringed with a solution of potash and beef tea. For sixteen days she was in and out of delirium. On the fourteenth day, her vagina began to slough. She died two days later. A post-mortem examination was performed. Her entire abdominal and pelvic cavities were inflamed. Her uterus was discolored, black, and ulcerated. In fact the inflammation and ulceration were so extensive over the cervix [neck of the uterus] that it had separated from the uterus.[1]

IN THE NINETEENTH CENTURY, most women were still in control of their own childbirth and were attended by midwives. In 1843, the London Medical Gazette reported that "a larger proportion of the 500,000 English women who give birth every year and have any attendance at all are attended by midwives."[2] Like Eliza, indigent women living in the crowded cities gave birth in lying-in hospitals, attended by men-midwives or students. Following the industrial revolution, families began to move from the country to the overcrowded cities to find work. Poor women, who lived in overcrowded tenements, or those who were homeless, couldn't afford any attendants at all during their confinements. They were left with little choice but to have their babies in lying-in hospitals or charities.

The death rates of lying-in women and their babies were usually due to epidemics of childbed fever. Most women who entered these hospitals never left alive and those who did survive, often did not leave with a living baby. Well into the nineteenth century, physicians continued to search for the cause of puerperal fever. As late as 1870, Sir James Young Simpson spoke of "morbid matter" entering the woman's circulation following childbirth.[3]

As women were dying, the medical profession was losing credibility at a time when men-midwives were struggling to achieve esteem. There was no public condemnation when such fever occurred in the home, but the epidemics that raged in the lying-in hospitals caused much alarm and posed a political threat to the medical establishment.[4] Yet men-midwives didn't connect their methods of practice or the filthy, overcrowded conditions in these hospitals with the epidemics. All kinds of theories were still being generated. For example, Joseph Clark, Master of the Rotunda Hospital in Dublin, blamed the epidemics on the wretched circumstances of the working-class women who entered the Rotunda Hospital, contending that the fever did not occur among the upper-class women who birthed at home.[5]

Epidemics of puerperal fever escalated in the nineteenth century and were the major cause of maternal deaths in that era. Other causes of death during childbirth were hemorrhage, obstructed labor, and convulsions of pregnancy, but puerperal fever remained the main killer.

Throughout Europe and America, medical men continued to search for answers to the cause of childbed fever, but continued to scoff at the notion that they were in any way responsible. They blamed the atmosphere, overcrowded environment, the ventilation, the nurses, the midwives, and so forth. Some men, however, were on the right track. For example, Robert Collins, Master of the Rotunda Hospital in Dublin, had each ward, in rotation, thoroughly cleaned and fumigated with chlorine gas and the floors and woodwork covered with chloride of lime in 1829. In his *Treatise* of 1835, he wrote that after cleaning and fumigation "until the termination of my Mastership in November 1833, we did not lose one patient by this disease."[6]

After Collins retired as Master of the Rotunda, new epidemics occurred in 1835. Apparently the use of chlorine, a strong disinfectant, was effective in stemming the spread of the infection, but Collins never mentioned anything about the men washing their hands. In France, early in the nineteenth century, Auguste Cesar Baudeloque perceived that the introduction of the attendant's hand into the parturient woman's vagina and the use of instruments were possible causes of spreading puerperal fever.[7] Yet, many men still could not conceive of the notion that they could be the transmitters of this disease. Methods of cleanliness that had been proposed by White, Kirkland, and Gordon in the previous century that had demonstrated some positive effects were either ignored or forgotten. However, two brilliant and persevering men who lived in different parts of the world were determined to find the answer.

Ignaz Philip Semmelweis was born in Buda, Hungary in 1818. He was educated in Pesth and later in Vienna, where he was awarded the degree of Master in Midwifery in 1844. That same year, he was appointed assistant to Professor Johann Klein at the Great Free Vienna Lying-In Hospital. Founded in 1840, it had two parts—the First Division in which men-midwives were the birth attendants and the Second Division where only women midwives attended. This First Division was devoted to the instruction of students.[8]

Prior to Johann Klein's professorial appointment in 1841, Professor Lucas Boer had introduced Charles White's methods of practice at this hospital. During Boer's tenure the maternal death rate had been 0.9 percent. When Johann Klein took over, he did not follow Boer's or White's methods of cleanliness, and his method of teaching students was to teach and demonstrate in the dissecting room, then go straight to the maternity wards of the First Division to attend to women during labor, birth, and postpartum.[9] As Jessica Mitford so bluntly pointed out in her book, *The American Way of Birth*, "Doctors and students would leave the dissecting rooms having performed autopsies on women who died from puerperal fever and then go directly to the lying-in wards where they would poke their dirty fingers up the vaginas of women in labor."[10] As puerperal fever spread and the death rate climbed, the male attendants just shrugged their shoulders.[11]

Semmelweis, a brilliant doctor, teacher, and researcher, could not shrug his shoulders. It took him several years and much encouragement from his close colleagues to write his treatise, which was finally published in 1861. In it, Semmelweis explained how women wept and begged to be assigned to the second clinic or be allowed to die at home rather than be assigned to the other clinic. He described "heart rending scenes when women, wringing their hands, begged on bended knee ... for their release, ... to seek admission to the Second Division."[12]

The maternal mortality rate in the First Division remained constant from 1841 until 1847 (during Professor Klein's tenure) and was, on the average, three times greater than that of the Second Division. In 1841 there were 237 maternal deaths out of 3,036 total births (7.7 percent) in the First Division compared with 86 maternal deaths out of 2,442 births (3.5 percent) in the Second Division. Semmelweis puzzled over the wide discrepancy. Of course the answer was obvious, but it took several more clues before he put all the pieces together. He wrote that the death rate was probably even higher because women who were dying from puerperal fever were transferred to the general hospital where these death rates were entered. There were many other women who had such a rapid course of the disease that they died before they could be transferred, so they were counted in the death rates of the first clinic.[13]

Semmelweis kept accurate records. Some women gave birth on their way to the hospital, in the street, in doorways of houses, or other shelter. After these so-called "street births," the women then proceeded to the lying-in hospital with their baby in their arms. Semmelweis observed that these women "became ill noticeably less often than those delivered in the hospital." He asked himself what protected these women "from the destructive effects of the unknown endemic agents active within the First Clinic."[14] He also observed that although the second clinic, run by the midwives, was more overcrowded than the first, the death rate in the second clinic was much less than in the first. He concluded that midwives did not practice the invasive procedures as did the men-midwives and students in the first clinic.

The newborn death rate was also greater in the First Division than in the Second. So Semmelweis reasoned that this was related to the increased incidence of puerperal fever among the women who gave birth in the First Division. He further analyzed that there were no differences in the conditions in the two Divisions, in regard to ventilation, condition of the linens, cleanliness, food and other factors. Semmelweiss's conclusions were based on his own scientific observations, not on speculations proposed by others.

The pieces began to fit together when an unfortunate event occurred in March of 1847. Semmelweiss's colleague, Professor Kolletschka, professor of forensic medicine, died from a disease having similar symptoms and pathology to the women who contracted puerperal fever. A student accidentally cut the professor's finger while participating in an autopsy on the cadaver of a woman who died from the fever. Semmelweis then realized that the disease was transmitted from the cadaver to his colleague, but he did not know what substance was actually transmitted. He observed that even when the birth attendants washed their hands following autopsies, they still carried the "cadaveric odor, which the hand retains for a shorter or longer time, ... the hand contaminated by cadaveric particles is brought into contact with the genitals of these individuals, ... and by means of absorption, introduction of cadaveric particles ... into the vascular system..., and by this means the same disease is produced in these puerperae ... [women who had given birth], which we saw in Kolletschka."[15] Semmelweis had the answer and he acted upon his conclusions.

Semmelweis instructed his students to wash their hands in a solution of chlorinated lime prior to examining and attending any patients. This practice began in March 1847 following Kolletschka's death. There was a significant drop in the maternal mortality rate in the First Division. The rate in May, of 12.24%, decreased to 2.38% by June. By the following year, the rate in the First Division again decreased to 1.27%, compared to 1.33% in the Second Division.[16] Semmelweis had proven his theory, but Professor Klein remained unconvinced and rebuked the idea that he or other men-midwives were responsible for transmitting the disease. In fact, Klein became so jealous and hostile toward his young assistant, that he dismissed him from his duties. Semmelweis, distressed and disillusioned, left Vienna.

Other physicians also disregarded Semmelweis's evidence with suspicion and jealousy and so ignored his teachings. In 1851, Semmelweis returned to Pesth where he was appointed obstetric physician at St. Rochus Hospital. While there, he continued to practice and teach cleanliness and hand washing. As a result, over a period of five years the maternal mortality rate was reduced from 15% to the unheard of rate of 1% at St. Rochus Hospital.[17]

Carl Braun, who succeeded Semmelweis as first assistant at the Vienna Lying-In Hospital, postulated that puerperal fever was caused by any number of factors ranging from cadaverous infection, shock to the nervous system from birth, milk secretions, the ventilation, the woman's diet, to their emotional disturbances. He speculated that cadaverous material contained "germs" that were conveyed through the air and into the open wounds of the woman's reproductive tract. However, Braun vehemently opposed Semmelweis's postulate that the matter was conveyed through the hands of the accoucheur.[18]

Semmelweis was so close to finding the actual cause of the disease, but didn't have proof of what the particular matter was that was transmitted to women from their attendants. However, instead of being recognized for his achievements and the subsequent reduction in mortality rates, he was ridiculed by his colleagues, who disregarded his evidence. Semmelweis led a disappointing and unhappy life. He suffered through the years from manic depression and was committed to a lunatic asylum in 1865. Prior to his commitment, he accidentally cut himself while performing a surgical procedure. He developed septicemia and died in 1865 from the very disease he fought so hard to conquer.[19]

Semmelweis never lived to know what the "cadaveric particles" actually were, but his theory was accurate. Years after his tragic death he became famous for his discovery.

About the same time that Semmelweis was in Vienna, another man on the other side of the Atlantic Ocean had also been seeking answers to the enigma of puerperal fever. This American was the famous physician, poet, and essayist Oliver Wendell Holmes, who was born in 1809 in Cambridge, Massachusetts. He was graduated with a law degree from Harvard University in 1824 and then abandoned law for medicine. He was graduated from Harvard Medical School in 1831. After a short span in private practice, he assumed the position of professor of anatomy and physiology at Harvard Medical School in 1836.[20]

Holmes was a physician, not an obstetrician, but he was troubled by the ravages of puerperal fever and sought to find the cause. Like Semmelweis, Holmes also recognized the contagiousness of the disease and believed that it was conveyed by the birth attendant's hands, instruments, and clothing. As in Europe, American physicians also scoffed at the theory of contagion and some were even known to have intentionally refrained from washing their hands when attending women in childbirth. Holmes read or heard about a story of a doctor in Edinburgh, who assisted at an autopsy of a woman who died of the fever, and brazenly carried her infected uterus in his pocket to the classroom. Later that evening, this physician attended a woman in childbirth without first changing his clothes or washing his hands. The woman subsequently died.[21]

Holmes was a distinguished lecturer and better able than Semmelweis to eloquently state his views. So when he presented his famous essay, "The Contagiousness of Puerperal Fever," to the Boston Society of Medical Improvement in 1843, he did so with such clarity and compelling logic that he was heard.[22] Holmes explained to the doctors attending the Boston Society conference that doctors went from post-mortem exam rooms to the lying-in wards to attend healthy childbearing women without washing their hands or changing their clothes. These women then contracted the disease. It was about this time that Semmelweis conducted his investigations and came to similar conclusions.

Like Semmelweis, Holmes was also savagely attacked by his peers. Two prominent physicians who led the attack were Hugh Lennox and Charles Meigs of Philadelphia. Holmes was clever enough to counterattack by deriding these men on their archaic methods of treating all illnesses, which included bleeding, purging, and heroic doses of calomel (mercury), quinine, and opium (which are poisonous in large doses).[23] Holmes added an introduction to his paper, which was republished in 1855. One statement read as follows: "I ask no personal favor, but I beg to be heard in behalf of the women whose lives are stolen, until some stronger voice shall plead for them."[24]

Many physicians were still skeptical, but proof was soon forthcoming. The microscope had already been in existence and bacteriology was a developing science in the nineteenth century. It is not clear who actually invented the microscope, but a Jesuit Monk, Athanasius Kircher, in the seventeenth century used a microscope through which he saw microorganisms. Then in the next century, Anton van Leeuwenhoek perfected the existing microscope and discovered bacteria and protozoa (one-celled animals).[25]

Back in Vienna, another physician, Dr. Carl Mayrhofer, second assistant at the lying-in hospital, also investigated the cause of puerperal fever. He actually obtained some discharge from the uterus of a woman suffering from puerperal fever, which he observed under a newly devised microscope. He observed many different kinds of microorganisms, which he called "vibrions," and found that one particular form was more abundant and regularly present in the discharges of women suffering from puerperal fever. He then conducted experiments on animals. He injected the discharge from infected women into the genitals of rabbits. He was not surprised that the rabbits got sick and died. Upon autopsy, the same pathological findings were found in the rabbits as had been found in the women who died from the disease.[26]

Mayrhofer concluded that microorganisms caused infectious diseases. He presented his research in a lecture in 1862 and also published his findings. Initially, his research was received favorably, but was undervalued. He suffered from health problems and disappointments in life and so was unable to pursue further research.[27] Mayrhofer's research and conclusions were phenomenal during this time in history, but were unrewarded. Unfortunately, he wasn't better known or sufficiently credited for his achievements. Throughout Europe and America women continued to die from puerperal fever and medical men continued to deny their own responsibility in its spread.

Semmelweis didn't live long enough to know what the "cadaveric particles" were, but Oliver Wendell Holmes did. Louis Pasteur added the last piece to complete the puzzle. Pasteur was born in 1822 "into a filthy, plague swept, disease ridden world."[28] He was a scientist who had investigated the process of fermentation and discovered that microorganisms played a role in this process. His research on fermentation and germ theory was published in 1865.

Pasteur also wanted to find out what the relationship between germs and disease was. His research in this relationship began when one of his lab assistants was troubled with multiple boils. At one point, his assistant was so troubled that he had to stay home from work. Annoyed that his assistant had to stay away from his job, Pasteur began to ponder over what caused these boils. So he took a sample of pus from his assistant's boil and he cultured it in beef broth. While observing the culture under his microscope, he saw multiple clusters of little spheres that resembled a bunch of grapes. On another occasion, while he was observing the surgery of a child who had osteomyelitis (bone infection), he saw pus pour out of the bone. He was able to obtain a sample of this pus, which he then cultured. Looking through his microscope, Pasteur discovered that these organisms were the same as those he had cultured from his assistant's boil. The bacteria he discovered were later given the name "staphylococci."[29]

Pasteur was familiar with the writings of Holmes and Semmelweis and set out to solve the mystery of puerperal fever, still rampant in America and Europe. The Paris Maternité Hospital overwhelmed by the epidemic, was forced to close in 1856. When it reopened again the following year twenty-eight women died from the disease out of 103 births and yet the Académie de Medicine pondered over the cause as though they never heard of Holmes or Semmelweis.[30]

In 1877, Pasteur was able to procure some purulent discharge from a woman dying of puerperal fever, which he cultured. However, what he observed under his microscope was different from the other colonies of bacteria he had previously observed. On another occasion, he pricked the finger of a woman suffering from the fever, obtained a sample of her blood and in the same manner as previously, he cultured the sample and observed under his microscope the same small chains of bacteria that he had previously observed from the sample taken from the diseased woman's discharge.[31] He had observed another kind of bacteria that caused puerperal fever, later given the name "streptococcus." This was the turning point in the history of the nineteenth century epidemics.

Pasteur demonstrated his earlier discovery when, in 1879, he attended a lecture given by a distinguished physician addressing the Académie de Medicine, who was speaking about the causes of puerperal fever. Pasteur stood up, interrupted the speaker and proclaimed, "None of those things cause the epidemics. It is the nursing and medical staff who carry the microbe from an infected woman to a healthy one."[32] Pasteur then walked to the blackboard and drew a chain of small circles to show what the microorganisms that caused puerperal fever looked like. Louis Pasteur provided the proof of what Semmelweis's "cadaveric particles" actually were.

The germ theory was proven, but it would take awhile longer before it was accepted throughout the Western world and before aseptic technique was actually practiced. Men needed to open their minds to the fact that they were responsible for the epidemics. Most had disregarded the teachings of Charles White, Alexander Gordon, and the others who had advocated cleanliness and the discoveries made by Ignaz Semmelweis and Oliver Wendell Holmes.

Now that the cause of puerperal fever was known, the next question was how to prevent the epidemics. One answer of course was cleanliness, but this wasn't sufficient in itself. Joseph Lister, born in London in 1827, added the final link that would establish the principle of asepsis. "Sepsis" is the term given to the presence of disease-producing microorganisms. So the term "asepsis" refers to absence of disease-producing microorganisms. Lister was a skillful surgeon and teacher, who was appointed professor of surgery at the University of Glasgow in 1860. He was deeply troubled over the many people who died following surgical operations.[33]

Lister studied the writings of Semmelweis, Holmes, and Pasteur. He pondered over Pasteur's discussion on putrefaction, which occurred in the presence of certain living microorganisms. Agitating over one particular young patient, whose leg was rotting as he was dying from hospital gangrene, Lister considered that suppuration (production of pus from an infection) must be caused by microorganisms invading living tissue, which then leads to putrefaction.[34] He set out to find a way to destroy these microorganisms before they could destroy living tissue. Familiar with various chemicals, Lister contemplated experimenting with carbolic acid, which he knew was used as an effective deodorant for sewage.

In March of 1865, Lister first used this chemical during the surgical repair of a bone fracture by painting the ends of the fractured bone and the wound with carbolic acid. Unfortunately, his patient died from infection anyway, as had so many others. In August of that year, he made a second attempt, except he used more carbolic acid around the wound. He also soaked all of his instruments and suture material in a strong solution of carbolic acid and used clean linens and dressings that had been boiled prior to surgery. Furthermore, he had the operating room sprayed with vapor of carbolic acid. His patient survived and so did all but four of the forty others whose amputations he performed between 1867 and 1869.[35] Lister presented his work at the annual meeting of the British Medical Association and also published his methods in the *British Medical Journal* in 1867. Lister became famous for the discovery of asepsis. By the late 1880s, the germ theory was finally becoming more accepted by physicians, as Lister's findings spread to other western countries across Europe and the United States.

The war against infection following childbirth and from operative interventions was finally won. But there was one more hurdle—the unbearable pain from any surgical procedure. The discovery of anesthesia in the nineteenth century paved the way for greater advances in surgery, ameliorating the agonizing pain and suffering from any surgical procedure. However, the use of anesthesia during childbirth raised other issues and met with controversy among physicians, theologians, and much of Victorian society. Women welcomed it. The fear of pain associated with childbirth was a close second to the fear of death.

The discovery of anesthesia was not a single or sudden spark of enlightenment. Primitive people accidentally discovered the pain-relieving properties of certain plants, which they used to dull the pain resulting from various ailments and operations. Early pain-relieving remedies included alcoholic agents, opium, Indian hemp, and juice of mandrake. Mandrake (*Mandragora officinarum*) was probably one of the oldest known remedies for ameliorating pain associated with amputations and other surgical procedures, popular during the Middle Ages. Because the roots of the mandrake plant resembled the human body, much superstition surrounded its use.[36]

Opium was considered the most potent pain-relieving remedy used before the discovery of anesthesia. The resin of the opium poppy (*Papaver somniferum*) has long been smoked for its narcotic effect. Morphine, the main active constituent of opium, was first isolated in the laboratory in 1803. The hypodermic syringe arrived in America in 1856. Doctors soon used the injectable form to relieve the severe pain from surgeries, painful chronic diseases, and also pain in childbirth. Initially, these narcotic drugs were legal and easy to obtain, consequently leading to high addiction rates among Americans during the late 1800s.[37]

These remedies were not sufficiently effective in relieving the agonizing pain and torture sustained during surgical procedures. Surgeons worldwide sought better ways to relieve such pain. It is difficult to say how and when anesthesia was first discovered, but many individuals were involved in its discovery. It appears that ether, which is inhaled, was the first chemical found to relieve the pain sustained during surgical procedures. During the eighteenth century, an English physician used ether to treat lung diseases because of its pungent and penetrating odor.[38]

In the early nineteenth century, Michael Faraday began experimenting with various gases while performing surgery on animals. He discovered that certain gases produce artificial sleep and insensibility to pain. He wrote about the intoxicating effects of ether in 1819.[39] When these effects became known, young medical students held "ether frolics," whereupon they inhaled ether to the point of intoxication. One such young man, who participated in these frolics as a student, was Dr. Crawford

Long of Georgia who had sustained bruises on his body yet did not remember injuring himself. After he completed his medical education and began his surgical practice, Long began to experiment with ether on himself and on a young slave. Then in 1842 he used ether to anesthetize a man during surgery for the removal of a tumor from his neck. Upon awakening, the patient claimed that he felt no pain.[40] Long, however, didn't place a great deal of significance on this event and so didn't publish his discovery. He did tell his friend, Dr. William Morton, about his experiments.

Dr. Morton had set up a dental practice with Horace Wells in the 1840s and together they became engaged in the manufacture of false teeth. But their business wasn't doing very well because before the plates could be placed the roots of broken teeth had to be removed. This was an extremely painful procedure, so people were reluctant to seek their dental services.[41] Morton remembered Crawford's work with anesthetic agents, but realized he needed more scientific knowledge. So he enrolled in Harvard Medical School in 1944 and became a physician, but thereafter continued to practice dentistry. Morton was able to obtain some ether from a chemist he knew and began to experiment with it on animals and then on himself.[42]

In 1846, one of his dental patients consented to being given ether during a tooth extraction. After inhaling the ether vapor, the patient fell asleep and upon awakening, he said he had felt no pain.[43] Morton wrote about his research, his success, how to prepare ether in its purest form and how to administer it safely. His paper, "On the Physiological Effects of Sulfuric Ether and Its Superiority to Chloroform," was published in 1850.[44] Morton demonstrated how to use ether safely and effectively and so was credited with its discovery, although he did not actually discover it.

Ether soon became known to the world. Dr. Walter Channing, professor of obstetrics at Harvard Medical School, was the first to use ether during childbirth. In 1848, Channing wrote his treatise on pain relief during labor and birth.[45] He contended that women were demanding pain relief during their confinements. Many physicians who resisted using anesthesia during childbirth still believed that women should suffer for their original sin. These men didn't seem to consider that they caused much of women's sufferings. Dr. Charles Meigs of Philadelphia believed that the pain of childbirth was necessary. He was concerned about the safety of anesthesia and resisted using any dangerous drugs in the course of labor and birth.[46] This was a valid concern because men weren't sure of safe doses of the anesthetics, thereby threatening the well-being of the baby and the mother.

The man who achieved much esteem and received the major credit for the discovery of chloroform anesthesia used during childbirth was Sir James Young Simpson, born in Scotland in 1811. At the age of fourteen, Simpson enrolled in Edinburgh University, became a professor of midwifery and then chair of midwifery at Edinburgh Medical School in 1840.[47] Simpson first used ether on a woman during her confinement in 1847, while other physicians in Europe and America were also beginning to offer it to their patients. This same year, a Cambridge, Massachusetts physician, Dr. Nathan Cooly Keep, gave ether to Fanny Appleton Longfellow during her confinement. Her husband, Henry Wadsworth Longfellow, held the ether-soaked handkerchief over her nose. Fanny gave birth to a healthy girl without pain.[48]

Dr. James Simpson also was a well-known skilled surgeon. He was deeply troubled by the agony people had to endure during operations, as were other surgeons of his time. When as a student, he observed a woman in agony undergoing a breast amputation without anesthesia, he was appalled and almost abandoned medicine. But he completed his medical education and, after he became established in surgical and midwifery practice, he began experimenting with various anesthetic agents. He obtained a sample of chloroform from a chemist in Edinburgh and began to experiment on himself and three other assistants. Simpson and his assistants would sit around his dining room table and inhale varying amounts of chloroform. He later wrote how the men first became very talkative, then incoherent, and that one of the men passed out. After this episode, Simpson proclaimed that chloroform was a better and stronger anesthetic agent than was ether. He then tried it out on a fellow physician's wife, during her confinement. This woman expressed delight over her painless birth.[49]

Simpson wrote his treatise, "Account of a New Anaesthetic Agent, as a Substitute for Sulphuric Ether in Surgery and Midwifery," published in 1848.[50] Simpson claimed that the advantages of chloroform over ether were that chloroform had a more agreeable odor, its action was more rapid, and a smaller quantity was needed to produce the desired effect. Chloroform was also less expensive than ether. Of course, there were the usual moral and religious objections. The Church of Scotland still outrageously contended that women should suffer in childbirth. There were medical concerns as well, such that the anesthetic agent might cause bleeding, convulsions, or other dangerous side effects.[51]

Simpson's most powerful opponent, Charles Meigs of Philadelphia, didn't believe chloroform was safe to use and that pain during childbirth served a biologic purpose.[52] These objections were swept aside and chloroform began to be widely accepted by those women who could afford the services of male physicians or men-midwives. Women who couldn't afford to engage private physicians to attend them continued to be attended by midwives in the traditional ways of childbirth, without having anesthesia.

Another nineteenth-century physician, Dr. John Snow of London, also experimented with ether and chloroform on animals and on himself and then began using chloroform on his patients during surgery. His first attempt to use anesthesia during childbirth was in 1853 when he administered chloroform to Queen Victoria during her confinement with her eighth child. The Queen was so pleased with the outcome that she endorsed the "blessed chloroform."[53] Unfortunately, Snow died of a stroke at the young age of 45 and was not recognized for his achievement.[54] His success was attributed to the Queen's endorsement.

In spite of the proclaimed advantages of chloroform over ether, chloroform was found to be much less safe than ether. In 1863, 123 maternal deaths were reported in Britain, attributed to the use of chloroform anesthesia. There were similar reports in Germany. Heart failure was believed to be the cause of death. There were also reports of fetal deaths from chloroform anesthesia. Another adverse effect of chloroform was that it slowed down labor, so physicians had to resort to the use of forceps and other interventions to speed up the course of labor.[55] However, Simpson denied the reports that chloroform was unsafe. He declared that the women were wrongly diagnosed and he continued to proclaim the safety of chloroform anesthesia.

Simpson's claim for the discovery of chloroform was not completely accurate. The agent had first been discovered in 1831 by two chemists, one in France and the other in Germany.[56] Simpson's claim to have been the first to use ether on a woman during her confinement in 1847 was also exaggerated, because about that same time Dr. Channing of Boston and Dr. Keep of Cambridge used ether during childbirth. Simpson claimed to be unaware of this.[57]

Nineteenth-century women embraced the promise of pain-free childbirth. Middle-class Victorian women didn't lead the same healthy and active lives as their grand-mothers did. Because of their more sedate lives and mode of dress with their tight corsets, Victorian women were more likely to have complications during childbirth. Women who could afford the services of a male practitioner chose to do so not only because of the prospect of pain-free childbirth, but also because they believed that their births would be safer in the hands of these practitioners. So, choosing male practitioners soon became the fashion.

Victorian women did, however, have conflicting feelings because of the indelicacy of being attended by men. However, their belief that they would be safer in the hands of men and the appeal of anesthesia overrode their modesty. Simpson's prediction that the "patients themselves will force the use of it [anesthesia] upon the profession" proved to be true.[58] The use of anesthesia for childbirth was certainly advantageous to both the specialists in midwifery and the general practitioners. It became more profitable for doctors to incorporate midwifery into their general practices.

Although the practice of midwifery was a risky and time-consuming business, anesthesia was the key to success and was therefore embraced by the obstetricians and general practitioners.[59] The competition between specialists in midwifery and general practitioners, and between both groups of medical men and the traditional midwives was intensifying. The discovery of anesthesia gave male practitioners an edge over traditional midwives who couldn't offer anesthesia for the birthing women they attended. Men were rapidly gaining ground in the field of midwifery toward the end of the nineteenth century. Simpson was right on target. Anesthesia, as well as instruments, gave men more power.

Anesthesia was indicated when childbirth was complicated, necessitating instrumental and operative interventions, which caused a great deal of pain. However, anesthesia during the course of normal labor and birth posed different issues. Did the benefits of painless birth outweigh the risks and disadvantages of anesthesia use? It was already established that chloroform was dangerous to the women and their unborn babies. The fact that chloroform anesthesia slowed down the progress of labor ultimately led to the use of other interventions to speed up labor. Furthermore, if women were not awake during childbirth, then they no longer had any control of their own confinement, birth, their bodies, their environment, or their babies.

The next issue was whether operative obstetrics was performed out of necessity or for the convenience of the practitioner. Without anesthesia, instruments or operative procedures caused women unbearable pain. The duration of labor was a concern to midwives only when women labored tediously, over a very long period of time, fearful that complications would arise. The element of time took on a different perspective as obstetric science advanced. If men could hasten the process of labor and birth, they could attend more women in a shorter period of time, thereby increasing their productivity. The use of anesthesia helped to pave the way for operative obstetrics, which also became a profitable enterprise. Thereafter, men began perfecting their tools and inventing new ways to speed up the process of labor and birth.

One method of speeding up labor and birth was the use of ergot, a medicine that had been used for centuries by midwives and medicine men. Ergot is a fungus that grows on rye and has the property of causing the uterus to contract. If the dose of ergot is too high, it is poisonous. The uterus can rupture, causing fetal death. The drug constricts blood vessels, leading to high blood pressure, stroke, and maternal death. Ergot derivatives used today for the treatment of postpartum hemorrhage are never used prior to the birth of the baby. So, as we will see, nineteenth-century physicians invented manipulative and surgical methods to accelerate labor and birth.

Soon, physicians established limits on labor. Professor James Hamilton of Edinburg estimated that normal labor should last no longer than fourteen hours. Beyond this time frame childbirth was no longer considered safe, at which point Hamilton recommended terminating the labor by artificially dilating the woman's cervix and extracting the baby with forceps.[60] One method used to do this was to insert a sponge into the cervical opening, instill water into the vagina to keep the sponge wet, and then insert larger sponges until dilation was complete.[61]

Other methods included use of an elastic bag, fiddle-shaped dilators, inelastic rubber cones inserted into the opening of the cervix, and a conical balloon. This last method was accomplished by opening the woman's vagina with a speculum, grabbing the lip of her cervix with a hook, and then forcing the balloon into her cervix. The physician would then pull on a tube that was attached to the balloon to open her cervix to its full extent. In describing this procedure, Dickinson wrote, "Anesthesia is required only in the hysterical or hyperesthetic [woman]." He also advised manual dilation in cases of an extremely rigid cervix, using a knife or metal dilator.[62]

An instrument called the "Bossi dilator," described as a "four-branched uterine dilator with a strong screw on the handle," was used to empty the uterus in about twenty to sixty minutes in cases in which delivery was urgent.[63] These procedures were painful, invasive, caused much damage to the woman's tissues and only heaven knows what damage was inflicted on the baby. However, in the minds of most male practitioners, this was progress in obstetric science.

Generally, once the woman's cervix was sufficiently dilated, forceps were used to deliver the baby. However, Dr. Hardin of Ulster recommended the use of long forceps on a rigid cervix to hasten birth in "tedious cases even before the os uteri [opening of cervix] is dilated and the head still above the brim [above the pubic bone]." Hardin also recommended that young practitioners should begin using forceps because "many a parturient woman may be saved from hours of thriftless labour and pain and the child not seldom from the dreadful alternative of craniotomy."[64] (Craniotomy was the procedure by which the fetus's skull would be pierced to decrease its size so it could be extracted, which was an earlier crude method.)

Hardin admonished the authorities of forty or fifty years before on acting upon Denman's dictum that only short forceps should be used and only when absolutely necessary. Certainly Denman's methods were more conservative and safer. These so-called "long" forceps, recommended by Hardin, were later referred to as "high" forceps, which were dangerous to the baby as well as the mother. Inserting any forceps into a cervix that isn't completely dilated tears the cervix and surrounding tissues. Ironically, at that time women still believed they were safer in the hands of male practitioners.

Other nineteenth-century physicians applauded the forceps. An American physician, Dr. Clark, claimed, "The whole armory of our art furnishes few instruments that are so useful in saving life and in lessening suffering."[65] Clark mistakenly maintained that the dangers were attributed to young physicians' fears and anxiety related only to the horrible consequences told to them by their teachers. In actuality, forceps, other instruments, and manual maneuvers, as explained earlier, were downright dangerous, causing lifelong damage to women's reproductive organs.

In most instances artificial dilation is not indicated. Physiologically, normal labor proceeds at its own pace. Chemical and physical mechanisms of the body take place that allow the cervix to dilate naturally as the fetus descends the birth passages. Artificial dilation was legitimately attempted to induce premature labor in cases of obstructed labor. The alternative to these artificial methods in true cases of obstructed labor is cesarean birth, which without the benefit of asepsis, was still, for the most part, fatal to mother and her baby. Some women had such severe cases of deformed pelvises, that the pelvic cavity was almost obliterated.

Dr. Thomas Radford of Manchester, England, born in 1793, recommended inducing premature labor by artificial cervical dilation, but only out of great necessity and by more gentle and gradual means than those described above. Radford recommended vaginal douching to wash away the mucus plug and preparing sponges that would easily pass into the cervix to effect dilation. He wrote in his treatise, "Observation on the Caesarean Section, Craniotomy and on other Operations," published in 1865, that "forcible dilatation without preparation, is at all times most mischievous."[66]

In his treatise, Thomas Radford also advocated that the cesarean operation be performed sooner, in cases of obstructed labor, rather than later. Radford collected seventy-seven cases in the United Kingdom before 1865, in which only fourteen percent of the mothers and fifty-nine percent of the infants survived. Radford blamed these tragic outcomes on the fact that the operations were performed as a last resort and strongly advocated to perform the operation sooner, rather than later, in cases of obstructed labor. He described the preparation for the operation and how it should be conducted. He believed chloroform was dangerous and recommended using a local anesthetic to be sprayed on the area where the incision was to be made or ether, which was safer than chloroform.[67]

In 1882, Max Sanger, a German physician, hailed the "antiseptic era" and wrote about the classical cesarean operation, advocating incising the abdomen and the uterus and then suturing each separately.[68] In previous cesarean operations, only the abdominal wall was sutured. Of course the uterus didn't heal well, resulting in the likelihood of the uterus rupturing in succeeding births. Once asepsis was practiced and anesthesia was used, cesarean births became a much safer option.

There indeed was a need for skilled physicians and surgeons to manage childbirth in women who had complications related to pregnancy and birth, but the management of normal birth was best left to the midwives. As men continued to pursue the field of midwifery, the competition between them and women-midwives intensified. Traditional midwives were still in business, but medical men continued to disparage them, contending they weren't educated and that they were ignorant and incompetent. Women-midwives wanted to be recognized for their expertise and empirical knowledge. They also wanted to seek further education to improve their status in society.

Charles Dickens's portrayal of Sarey Gamp didn't favor the image of the midwives. Sarah Roddry, a midwife who delivered over five thousand babies between 1817 and 1840 wrote to the Committee of Manchester Lying-In Hospital that "it affords me unspeakable pleasure to certify that I have never lost a mother."[69]

In countries throughout Europe, there were some forms of instruction for midwives. Some midwifery instruction had been ongoing in the lying-in hospitals in several cities and large towns in England, but most English midwives didn't have any education. Concerned about the high infant mortality rate, the Obstetrical Society of London made attempts to improve the condition of midwives. As early as 1813, the Society sought to persuade Parliament to pass an enactment to control the practice of midwifery, but was unsuccessful. Finally in 1869, the Society appointed a committee to investigate the causes of infant death. They first investigated the ratio of the number of births attended by midwives and of those attended by medical men. They found that midwives attended between thirty and ninety percent of poor women living in villages and in large provincial and manufacturing towns. They also found that most of the midwives lacked any form of education.[70]

The Society recommended a plan to regulate and license midwives. They established criteria that midwives must meet in order to be eligible for a diploma. These included being of good moral character, being between the ages of 21 and 30, having attended lectures, having practiced in a lying-in hospital or charity for at least six months, and having attended at least twenty-five labors under the supervision of someone approved by the board of examiners. The midwives then had to take both an oral and written exam covering reproductive anatomy, symptoms and course of normal labor, management of normal labor and birth, and recognition of signs of complicated labor and birth.[71] The idea was that midwives would care for women in normal labors and births, but would be able to recognize the need to consult with a physician. Midwives had already known when births were not following their normal progression.

Dr. James Aveling was a staunch advocate for education and elevating the status of midwives. Aveling was the first chairman of the board of examiners, set up by the London Obstetrical Society in 1872. An act of Parliament was finally passed to train and regulate midwives. In 1881, Dame Mary Rosalind Paget, British nurse and midwife, co-founded the Midwives' Institute, which later became the Royal College of Midwives. It was the first organization for midwives in England.[72] These landmarks did help raise the status of England midwives. Aveling acknowledged that the midwife's mission was to care for women in normal childbirth, "especially in attending to the wants and comfort of her patient, the actual labour being a physiological process to be watched rather than interfered with."[73] Unfortunately, this wasn't the prevailing mindset of male midwives or obstetricians at that time.

Aveling supported midwifery education, but he didn't know how to accomplish this because of the vast number of midwives scattered across the country. He considered ways in which other countries had adopted educational programs for their midwives. He described three modes. First, there was a "midwifery missionary system," in which a teacher traveled to different areas to provide practical instruction. A second mode was "oral instruction in a small institution and clinical tuition at the houses of patients." Thirdly, Aveling recommended erecting such institutions in London and other large towns.[74] A dual system eventually became accepted across most of Europe, where midwives were recognized in their role as practitioners in the care of women in normal childbirth. It took longer in England than it did in other European countries. Attitudes toward midwives were different in America.

CHAPTER 7

Childbirth in
Early America

On April 5, 1795, Sally Downing had "gone to bed." By the follow-
ing evening, she was still "in afflictive pain, tho unprofitable ... being
rather worse, before four o'clock Jacob went for Hannah Yerkes [mid-
wife], after breakfast we sent for Dr. Shippen, he felt her pulse ... he
din'd stay with us, and as Sally did not wish his stay, he left us ...
would return in the evening.... [Sally] suffer'd much to little purpose,—
when the Anodoyne was given, two Opium pills [given] ... but poor
Sally who instead of being compos'd grew worse. The Dr was call'd,
when he came I quited the room ... with a fluttering heart I went
upstairs.... It was mercifully born, ye Dr blowing in its mouth and
slapping it, it came to and cried—The Doc then told us, that a wrong
presentation had taken place ... by good management he brought on
a footling labour, which 'tho severe, had terminated by devine favour,
I trust, safely."[1]

This account of an eighteenth-century birth in America was an entry
in Elizabeth Drinker's diary, describing her oldest daughter's confinement
and birth. The doctor had performed a successful podalic version (turning the baby and delivering him feet first). The prominent Drinker family had settled in Philadelphia in 1677. By the eighteenth century, male
physicians were taking on midwifery, attending some middle- to upper-
class women in childbirth, who began to believe it was safer to be
attended during childbirth by an educated male practitioner.

In the beginning era of colonial America when the first settlers
arrived, the childbirth practices were just the same as they were in the
European countries from which the people had emigrated. Midwives or

other women were the only birth attendants. Although childbirth was a frightening event, it was also a social event. Women were in control; men stayed behind the scenes. The early American midwives who practiced midwifery in their native lands brought their traditions with them to the New World. However, there were very few midwives in the early colonial times. So the midwives were much in demand, valued, and highly respected.

The earliest known colonial midwife was Bridget Fuller, who landed at Plymouth, Massachusetts in 1620. Mrs. Fuller was believed to be the midwife who assisted the births of the three babies born on the *Mayflower* or her sister ship, the *Speedwell*, which landed on Plymouth Island on August 5, 1620. Mrs. Fuller was the third wife of Deacon Samuel Fuller, who also practiced as a "physition" and "cherugen" (physician and surgeon).[2] Mrs. Fuller was invited by the town of Rehobeth in 1663 to be the "official midwife to answer the town's necessity which at present is great."[3] Other notable midwives were Alice Tilley of Boston and "old widow Wait" of Dorchester, Massachusetts, who attended over 1100 births before she died at the age of 94.[4]

The most famous colonial midwife was Anne Hutchinson, who emigrated from England and arrived in Boston in 1634, at the age of 34 as the mother of 15 children. Mrs. Hutchinson had practiced in England and had considerable experience in healing and in midwifery. She was considered to be highly intelligent, and was held in great esteem as a midwife. However, in addition to midwifery and healing, Anne pursued other missions. A devout Christian, she organized weekly meetings in her home with a group of women who expressed different interpretations of the Bible, focusing on inner faith as opposed to outward piety. Anne's views contrasted with those of her pastor, John Cotton, and therefore caused some suspicion of heresy.[5]

By 1636, Anne's prayer sessions had grown to include up to eighty women and men, a sizable number in a community of one thousand persons. She further alienated the men in her community, because at her gatherings, she sat in the only chair with a back support, one which was usually reserved for the male leader.[6] Mrs. Hutchinson's career came to a sudden and tragic end when, on October 17, 1637, she and another midwife, Jane Hawkins, were called upon to attend the birth of Mrs. William Dyer. Mary Dyer gave birth to a stillborn, anencephalic monster. John Winthrop recorded, "So monstrous and misshapen as the like has scarce been heard of: it had no head but a face, which stood so low upon the breast, as the eares (which were like apes) grew upon the shoulders."[7]

Following this tragic event, Anne Hutchinson was accused of witchcraft, excommunicated from her church, and banished from Massachusetts.

With her family and several of her followers, Anne settled in Rhode Island, a small colony founded by other dissidents. After her husband died in 1642, Anne moved with her six youngest children and a small group of followers to a remote area in New York. While there, in 1643, all but her youngest daughter were killed by Indians.[8]

Anne Hutchinson was succeeded by Ruth Barnaby, who practiced midwifery into old age. Another midwife who practiced midwifery in Massachusetts and was also accused of witchcraft was Margaret Jones, because she had auxiliary breasts. She was hanged in 1648. Another midwife, Jane Hawkins, who refused to leave Massachusetts with Anne Hutchinson, was accused of "notorious familiarity with the devil."[9] Magical rites had always been part of midwifery, but because magic undermined religious doctrine, those using magic in healing or midwifery were accused of heresy and witchcraft. Protestants wanted birth to be a religious event.[10]

Medieval beliefs in witchcraft were carried over to the new colony of Massachusetts, but were short lived. Because there were no logical explanations for the mistakes of nature, disease, and tragic outcomes, these were attributed to the workings of the devil, evil spirits, or witchcraft.

In America, the witch fever was fueled by belief in the supernatural, political feuds, and the isolation of colonial Massachusetts. The witch craze, which reached its height in 1692 in Massachusetts Bay Colony, never approached the multitude of murders in western Europe during the sixteenth and seventeenth centuries. There were different circumstances in the New World. However, those who came to America with hopes of a better world brought their fears and frustrations with them. The Puritans who immigrated to Massachusetts were rigid and dogmatic in their beliefs. The witch fever that arose in Salem Village didn't emanate from the abhorrent misogynistic nature of the inquisition in medieval Europe. What happened was motivated by fear, power, and politics. Also, the more rigid a group is in its own values and beliefs, the more intolerant it is to others with diverse beliefs.

Salem Village was developed from grants of land to the north and south of the mainland of Massachusetts Bay Colony near rivers and inlets. The colony itself had been settled in 1635. Salem Village developed because of the need for more farmland, but was isolated from the mainland.[11] By 1689, the village had its own church and pastor, the Reverend Samuel Parris, a failed businessman, who was obsessed with the "sinfulness he saw everywhere and with his own importance and status."[12]

Life in the village was rigid and monotonous. There were no books other than the Bible, and no arts or entertainment. Young people had nothing to occupy their minds other than going to church only to hear about dying in hell for human sins. Terror and shame were used to encourage conformity. A group of young girls, including Parris's daughter Betty and niece Abigail Williams, began meeting together in a type of "club" to escape from the many threats in their lives, such as dying in hell from their sins, Indian attacks, and serious illnesses. Their fears, rebelliousness, and rage had to be repressed. The group of girls, daughters of prominent families of the village, began to develop strange fits in January of 1692. They accused certain women (later a few men) of causing their fits and inflicting pain. The accused were identified as witches. The leading Puritans of the community, including the Reverend Parris, faced with increasing commercialism and individualism that were a threat to the original Puritan ideals, were far too ready to believe the girls' accusations.[13]

So the accused witches were examined, imprisoned, and tried. Most of the accused had either risen or fallen in social status or were enemies of the accusers, who had competed for land or engaged in other such hostilities. In all, nineteen accused witches were hanged and one man was pressed to death under rocks. Fourteen women and six men died in the dungeons during their long imprisonments, and "well over a hundred languished for months in cramped, dark, stinking prisons, hungry and thirsty, never moving from the walls they were chained to, unsure if they would ever go free."[14]

After his own wife was accused, Governor Phipps forbade any more imprisonments or trials. A special court convened and pardoned all the remaining accused. The prisoners were then freed after paying for their prison "room and board." Before the Salem witch trials, there had been isolated events in other parts of Massachusetts and Connecticut, involving one or two suspects. The Salem trials ended in May of 1693 and fortunately, the witch fever never reached the other American colonies.[15]

In earlier American times, women were valued and respected because their contributions at home and on the farm were equal in status to those of men. Women's roles were childbearing and rearing, making commodities in the home, and farming. All family members contributed work of equal importance to the family's survival. Although American women were more valued than their European sisters, there were still inequities among the sexes, such as in education, church affairs, politics, and property rights.[16]

Colonial midwives were held in high esteem and rewarded for their services. For example, a New Haven Colony record dated January 28, 1655, read as follows: "It was ordered by the whole town that while the Widow Bradly continueth in the town, and is employed a midwife wherein she hath been very helpful, specially to the farms, and doth not refuse when called to it, she shall have a house and home lot, which may be convenient for her rent free."[17] Several New England towns provided rent-free houses. In New Amsterdam (which later became New York), one of the first houses was constructed for Tryntje Jonas, a widow who had earned her credentials in midwifery and nursing in the Netherlands. Midwives living in New Amsterdam were considered servants and were supposed to receive a large annual salary for attending the poor but were not always paid.[18]

Historical records from the colony of Virginia revealed that midwives were rewarded for their services, but not always monetarily. For example, "Goodwife Thorpe, a midwife, had a regular fee of 100 pounds of tobacco for her services, and the Widow Hollis was paid twelve hens for her services in 1634."[19] Midwives were well treated by the women they attended. For example, a diary entry, written January 7, 1701 stated: "My wife treats her midwife and women; has a good dinner, boiled pork, beef, fowl."[20]

Women held the monopoly in midwifery in early America and continued to practice their art in the traditional ways of their ancestors. Women labored and birthed in the "borning room," which was partitioned off from the living area.[21] Men were excluded. The midwives didn't interfere with the normal processes of birth, but let nature take its course. They were left to their own resources even if complications arose. Herbal teas were used to lessen pain, and ergot or other herbs were used to speed up labor and birth. Rum was given liberally as a muscle relaxant. Magical rituals were also practiced. For example, a sharpened ax would be placed under the birthing woman's bed to make her birth easier or burning corncobs were placed on the doorstep to her house to discourage evil spirits from entering.[22] Good luck charms, saint's relics, and eagle stones were used along with prayers for a favorable outcome.

Some midwives were highly skilled, while others were illiterate and superstitious. Midwifery was still a risky business since a significant number of women died from complications of childbirth. About one-fifth of the pregnant women in New England died giving birth over the course of their lives. Cotton Mather advised pregnant women that "preparation for death is that most reasonable and seasonable thing, to which you must now apply yourself."[23] However, the occurrence of extremely difficult births due to an impacted fetus was not nearly as prevalent as it was in the crowded European cities during the same era. Most early American women lived in rural environments and were relatively healthy with strong bones. They worked hard both in and out of doors. Women spent nearly all of their childbearing years either pregnant or nursing their children. Maternal and infant death was mainly attributed to infection.

There were no regulations for midwives during seventeenth-century America, unless the baby died or was expected to die. As in England and other European countries, it was expected that a minister supervise the midwife so that the child could be baptized. Certain rules and regulations were adopted from England. Some of the qualifications were that the midwife had to have given birth to children of her own, that she had observed a number of births, and that she was talented.[24]

Women were also the healers, just as their European sisters had been. Medical care was all but non-existent, but what did exist was based on ignorance and superstition. "Anyone with the inclination and audacity could present himself as a healer of the sick."[25] The death rate was staggering and was due to such illnesses as scurvy, beriberi, infectious diseases and injuries that were left untreated. There were no medical establishments outside the home for nearly 150 years after the first colonial settlements were developed.[26]

In the later part of the seventeenth century, establishments did start to be developed for the care of the homeless, indigent, infirm, and insane. Prisoners were housed in the same institutions. These people were not cared for with the idea of curing, only to house them until they died. They were attended by prisoners and paupers. These early establishments were known as almshouses and were ravaged by filth, pestilence, and epidemics. A better descriptive was "house of horrors." The West India Company established the first of these facilities in New York in 1658 and named it Bellevue.[27]

There were few men who practiced medicine in early America. Some had been clergymen in England. The elite European physicians did not immigrate to America because they were well established where they were. They enjoyed financial and professional status and so had no incentive to come to America. Those American men who did take up the practice of medicine learned the trade through apprenticeships. This was the only medical education in the colonies. Following their apprenticeships, men called themselves "doctors." There were no state or church regulations, so there were no controls on anyone practicing medical care. In essence, anyone could practice medicine at will. Medical care was quite dubious and medical science was very slow in reaching the colonies. Methods of treating disease were archaic and based on theoretical premises. The death rate was appalling.[28] In contrast, empirical observation was the basis for women healers and midwives.

Women continued to monopolize midwifery in the early centuries in America. Men took no part in it nor were they expected to, as it was against all principles of modesty and tradition. When a woman went into labor she called her women together while the men waited outside.

Women feared childbirth and the possibility of death, but their strength came from shared support and bonding together with other women. They shared their experiences with one another and gained the strength to endure. This network empowered women to determine their own course.[29]

Childbirth was also a festive event. During the early stages of labor, the women often feasted on roast beef, mince pies, cheese and tarts, gossiped, and told bawdy jokes.[30] After a successful birth, the celebration resumed for days. As the mother rested and healed, her women cared for her, her newborn and her other children. If childbirth ended tragically, her network of caring women provided love and support.

Midwives continued to practice unimpeded by competition throughout the seventeenth and most of the eighteenth centuries. There were no regulations governing midwives. The first ordinance passed in New York in 1761 was not instituted for the purpose of regulating the abilities of midwives, but chiefly concerned with ethical matters. This ordinance stipulated that the midwives take an oath before the mayor, stating "She will be diligent and ready to help any woman in labor, whether poor or rich; ... that she will not administer any medicine to produce miscarriage."[31]

Men gradually began to enter the picture in early America for the same reasons they had done so in Europe, which was to intervene in complicated births. Even though the presence of men in the birth chamber was adamantly opposed in colonial America, there were rare occasions when a male physician was summoned as a last resort. There were no barber-surgeons as there were in England nor were there any male midwives. So in extremely complicated cases, a doctor or clergyman might be called upon. If the fetus was impacted, men resorted to the use of destructive instruments or other mutilative means in an attempt to save the mother. But it was rare that the mother or her baby survived.

One of the first men known to have practiced midwifery in the colonies was William Avery of Massachusetts, who died in 1687. Dr. John Moultrie of Charleston practiced in the early 1700s.[32] He included midwifery in his practice after he had been called upon in "cases of extremity."[33] An obituary of "John Dupuy, M.D. and Man-Midwife" appeared in *The New York Weekly Post Boy* on June 22, 1745.[34]

American doctors who began to incorporate midwifery into their medical practice early in the eighteenth century, knew nothing about childbirth and in fact, knew very little in regard to medical practice in general. There were no universities or medical schools until late in the eighteenth century, with the exception of Harvard University, which was founded in Boston in 1636. Medicine was not taught at Harvard until the next century. By the end of the seventeenth century twenty-seven of the men who graduated from Harvard practiced medicine, but none had any medical education and none achieved a degree in medicine.[35] A medical degree was not required to hang up a doctor's shingle.

After 1700 most so-called doctors received what education they had by apprenticeships. Some men who had the financial means traveled to Europe in the eighteenth century to pursue a medical education. The most prestigious schools were in London, Leyden, and Edinburgh. Schools of midwifery were established, in conjunction with the medical schools in Leyden in 1724, in Edinburgh in 1739, in Vienna in 1748, and in Strasbourg in 1751.[36] Those doctors who obtained medical degrees from these European schools were not necessarily more skilled than the "regular" doctors (who trained under apprenticeships), nor did they practice differently. They did, however, achieve greater status because of their university education.[37] A Boston doctor declared in 1753, "There is more danger from the Physician than from the Distemper."[38] Historically, medical men, including those who engaged in midwifery, gained prestige and power because of social and cultural acceptance, not because of their skills in doctoring.

Except for Harvard, other colleges in America were not established until the late eighteenth century. The College of Philadelphia was founded in 1765 and Kings College in New York was founded in 1767.[39] Initially, medicine was not included in the curriculum of these earlier colleges. American men who could not afford to travel to Europe for a medical degree attended American colleges and then learned medicine by apprenticeships. Medical practice was based on ad hoc theory rather than theoretical principles based on any scientific foundation. A legacy of medical secrets was passed on by an eighteenth-century Dutch physician, Boerhaave, who advised, "Keep the heal cool, the feet warm, and the bowels open."[40] Colonial doctors adopted this legacy and purged everyone for any ailment, including puerperal fever. The popular treatments of this era were purging with castor oil, calomel (mercury), Epson salts or rhubarb. Ipecac was used to loosen coughs. Bleeding and blistering were favorites.[41] Mercury is poisonous and ipecac is a nasty medicine that induces vomiting. Between purging and bleeding, it is a wonder that anyone survived the resulting dehydration and shock.

John Morgan and Benjamin Rush, the famous revolutionary doctor, adopted these methods, which became standard treatment protocols in the eighteenth and most of the nineteenth centuries. Rush theorized that all illnesses were caused by tension of the blood vessels. Binger described Rush as "devoid of insight and so given to noble rationalizations of his behavior."[42] His "heroic" methods of treatment were sometimes carried to extreme.[43] Science was slow to reach America because scientific study was not a priority. The pioneering demands and patriotic goals of the colonists required a practical approach to serve its people, so there was little time to pursue scientific knowledge.[44]

When doctors began to include midwifery in their practice, they used the same methods of treatment that they were accustomed to in their general practice. They knew nothing about the management of natural, let alone preternatural, labor and birth. There were some men who did take a special interest in midwifery. One such man was Dr. William Shippen of Philadelphia, born in 1736. Shippen was awarded a bachelor's degree in 1754 from the College of New Jersey. He then traveled to Europe for further education and received a medical degree from Edinburgh.[45] He spent 1759 to 1762 in England studying mostly under William Hunter, from whom his interest in anatomy and midwifery were inspired.[46]

When Shippen returned to Philadelphia in 1762, he began offering a series of lectures in anatomy for young gentlemen engaged in "the study of physic in this and the neighboring provinces, whose circumstances and connections will not permit of their going abroad for improvement to the anatomical schools in Europe; and also for the entertainment of any gentleman who may have the curiosity to understand the anatomy of the human form."[47] Shippen soon began to conduct his lectures in a house located on the corner of Locust and Spruce Streets in Philadelphia. Twelve students attended his first course. He added lectures in midwifery three years later. His intentions were to also offer his midwifery course to women because of the "appalling care given by local midwives."[48] Shippen blamed midwives for the high maternal mortality.

Shippen advertised his course in the *Pennsylvania Gazette* on January 1, 1765. In it he wrote: "Dr. Shippen, Jr. having been lately called to the assistance of a number of women in the country in difficult labors, most of which were made so by the unskillful old women ... in order to instruct these women who have virtue enough to own their ignorance and apply for instruction, as well as those young gentleman now engaged in the study of that useful and necessary branch of surgery, who are taking pains to qualify themselves in practice in different parts of the country with safety and advantage to their fellow citizens."[49] However, few midwives were able to attend his course because they couldn't afford it and most were illiterate. Those who did attend were separated from the male students because it was against all moral principles for both sexes to be present during discussions of anatomy, female reproduction, and female matters. The Puritan philosophy didn't encourage education for women.[50] Furthermore, many women themselves didn't see the need for formal education, particularly because of their long history of empirical wisdom and experience in the practice of midwifery.

Shippen initiated a clinical component to his course by offering free lodging to a few poor women who agreed in turn to allow students to examine them and observe them during childbirth. This idea was the impetus for the later establishments of lying-in hospitals in America for indigent and homeless women.

Medical schools were just beginning to be established in America. William Shippen and John Morgan initiated the establishment of the first medical school in America, The Medical School of the College of Philadelphia, in 1765. Morgan's goal was to train physicians "to practice in the best London tradition."[51] Dr. Morgan was elected professor of theory and practice of medicine and Dr. Shippen was elected professor of anatomy and surgery.[52] Because of hostilities that developed between Shippen and Morgan, when organizing the faculty, Morgan omitted having separate chairs for midwifery and surgery. These disciplines were included in the curriculum, but weren't separate departments. Shippen would have certainly included these separate chairs had he been included in the planning.[53]

Other eighteenth-century physicians took an interest in midwifery. Samuel Bard, who graduated from Edinburgh in 1765, founded the Kings College of New York in 1767. At age 28, Bard chaired the department of theory and practice of physic. The first medical degrees were conferred in 1769. About this time only about four hundred men, out of 3,500 who practiced medicine in the colonies, had medical degrees.[54]

In America, male physicians only intervened in childbirth when there were complications. When doctors were summoned for emergencies or for consultation, they generally charged substantial fees. Some of the physicians, who were educated in Europe where male midwifery was already established, became interested in practicing midwifery in America. Physicians, who practiced in middle- and upper-class urban areas, benefited by incorporating midwifery in their general practice. Once a doctor attended a woman's first birth, he generally continued to attend her other births and those of all the other women in the family. There were many fertile women in one family. If the doctor continued to be that family's long-term trusted physician, he did well.[55] For example, William Shippen attended the entire Drinker family, a well-to-do prominent Philadelphia family going back to the seventeenth century. The women in this family felt fortunate to be able to afford an educated and prominent physician instead of an uneducated midwife.[56]

Women were afraid of childbirth. They anticipated either dying in childbirth or being permanently disabled. Well-to-do women believed they were safer if attended by an educated physician than by a midwife. So, in spite of puritan values, women invited these men into their homes to attend them in childbirth. Midwives were agents of tradition, whereas male physicians "represented the new, untried challenge of the future."[57] It soon became fashionable among wealthy women to engage physicians instead of midwives to attend them during childbirth.

The second half of the eighteenth century marked the first break in traditional midwifery in America. Physicians told women about the dangers of childbirth. Physicians used this propaganda to attract upper-class women away from midwives and the traditional ways of childbirth. Men spoke of childbirth as a disease and that even uncomplicated childbirth was a pathological state that only they could fix. Medical students were taught to do something while attending births, not to just stand around and wait. This was Dr. Walter Channing's dictum.

American doctors used whatever technology they had to speed up the process of labor, as practitioners were doing in other countries. Their favorite interventions were still bloodletting, purging, and administering ergot to speed up labor. Doctors were eager to try forceps, even though Dr. Dewees spoke of the "mischief" caused by them.[58] Although there were several professors who warned against the dangers of using forceps, students and doctors attempted to use them anyway. These instruments were particularly dangerous in the hands of inexperienced practitioners and because they were inserted blindly under the skirts of the parturient woman. Because of women's delicacy and modesty, it just wasn't proper for men to look at a woman's genitalia.

Forceps, as well as the older instruments, such as the crotchet, caused much damage to the woman's soft tissues. Women sustained horrible lacerations that didn't heal, often leading to vaginal fistulas, as described in Chapter 4. Women who suffered from these horrible sequelae took to their beds. Women-midwives were not sanctioned to use instruments, so it was rare that such injuries occurred when they attended births. Men used their instruments, not only when necessary to save a woman's life, but also to expedite labor and birth to their own advantage.

In her diary, Elizabeth Drinker revealed compelling accounts of her four daughters' confinements. Dr. William Shippen attended most of the Drinker women. Mrs. Drinker's youngest daughter, Molly, went into labor on June 14, 1797. Molly's labor was long and tedious, lasting several days. Her baby was in the breech position and was not born alive. Dr. Shippen didn't attend Molly, because he was elsewhere attending her sister Sally Downing. Shippen's pupil, Dr. Way, attended Molly. Molly's birth injuries didn't heal and she was left with an opening between her vagina and rectum. She was given daily laxatives to treat her "disordered bowel." Two years after this confinement, Elizabeth described Molly "as not being fit to be around people.[59] Molly was only 23 years old. Many other young women had similar outcomes.

Elizabeth Drinker described the sixth birth of her daughter, Sally Downing, in October 1799, as difficult, as were most of the Drinker women's births. Because Sally's labor was long and painful, Dr. Shippen gave her eighty to ninety drops of laudanum (an opium derivative). Sally was still unable to sleep during her forty-eight hours of labor. The doctor then bled her, taking a total of fourteen ounces of blood, and gave her more opium. When these didn't work, he went to get his instruments. When Sally heard the instruments jingling in his pocket, she was finally able to birth a healthy son.[60] So, fortunately, Sally was able to give birth naturally without the use of force or the tragic trauma that her sister Molly had been left with.

By the end of the eighteenth century, midwives still attended the majority of women in childbirth. Traditional ways of birth remained unchanged for the most part and midwives let nature take its course. Birthing women were pampered, fed, and nurtured as in times past.

Women who chose male physicians still had much control, since birth took place in their own homes. Generally, other women and perhaps a midwife were present for support and comfort, and to even help in decision-making. The doctor generally was obliged to obtain permission from his patient before he used any interventions. So, as long as birth took place in the home, women still had control of their own birth experience. It wasn't until women gave birth in hospitals that they lost it all.

CHAPTER 8

Nineteenth-Century America: The Birth of Obstetrics and Gynecology

Sixteen-year-old Bridget Logan gave birth at 5:00 A.M. on January 14, 1883. That evening and the next morning she was given douches of weak carbolic acid. But these treatments didn't prevent her from developing a fever, rapid pulse, and severe chills by the second day after she gave birth. During the next two days her abdomen became distended and painful; her cheeks were flushed and her eyes were sunken. During the next five days, she vomited off and on and she shifted from states of consciousness, drowsiness, to delirium. On January 23 her breathing became slow, labored, and finally ceased.[1]

Bridget Logan gave birth in a lying-in ward. She died of childbed fever. During the nineteenth century, medical schools and lying-in hospitals or wards were on the rise, fueling the fire of childbed fever epidemics. The nineteenth century brought challenges to the traditional ways of childbirth in America. Midwives still held the monopoly, but more doctors were becoming interested in the field. Some medical men began to include midwifery in their general practices; eventually, some specialized in the growing field of obstetrics. Midwives were beginning to lose some of the esteem they held in earlier years in America, as doctors began to compete for their clientele. But midwives were still very much in demand. There were some medical men who advocated education for the midwives. Although medical schools were on the rise, there were no schools for midwives, or for nurses—who also needed to be educated.

An advocate of midwifery education was Dr. Valentine Seaman, who was medical chief of the New York Hospital, which opened in 1771. Dr. Seaman was credited with opening the first training school for nurses in 1798. He also offered private instruction for midwives, whom he believed were ignorant. However, he also contended that midwives were indispensable and needed to be educated. He published his lectures in *The Midwife's Monitor and Mother's Mirror* in 1800. This was the first manual for midwives published in the United States and used in the nineteenth century.[2]

Dr. Samuel Bard was born in 1742 and graduated from Edinburgh in 1765, specialized in midwifery. He also taught midwifery and wrote the first truly comprehensive book, *A Compendium of the Theory and Practice of Midwifery,* which was published in 1812. This book was intended to train midwives in the nineteenth century. Bard was adamantly against meddlesome midwifery. He emphasized that the major role of the midwife was to let nature take its course. He scorned frequent vaginal exams and manipulations and condemned "the abominable practice of boring, scooping, and stretching the soft parts of the mother, under the preposterous idea of making room for the child to pass."[3] He did support women-midwives, believing that they were the experts in their field.

Bard's main objective was to teach the progress and management of natural labor, not medical interference. In the introduction to his book, he wrote, "There is some reason to believe there is greater safety in this branch of medicine from modest unassuming ignorance, than from a meddling presumption which frequently accompanies a little learning."[4] Bard decided not to include a chapter on instruments, as suggested by his associates, because he believed if he laid down the rules of birthing, which he hoped would be understood and practiced, there would be no need to use instruments.

Bard recommended the works of Charles White of Manchester and Thomas Denman of London, both of whom had previously advocated non-interference during birth. Bard was advanced in his wisdom. He understood the cause and the effects of rickets in deforming bones, particularly women's pelvic bones, which led to obstructive childbirth. To prevent the debilitating effects of rickets, Bard advocated adequate playtime in the out-of-doors for children and "a full but plain and simple diet" for young women.[5]

Bard's cautions were unheeded as were White's and Denman's in England. There were still many male midwives who continued to use their tools and hands as they chose to expedite labor and birth, more to their advantage rather than to the women giving birth. As described previously, doctors used drugs, instruments, other kinds of devices, and operative procedures to hasten the process.

In an 1885 issue of the *Journal of the American Medical Association*, an article appeared describing the consequences of "operative delivery." "The application of the forceps through an os [opening to the cervix] not completely dilated is an operation at once difficult, dangerous and seldom indicated." The author (unknown) cited a case in which as a result of this unnecessary operation, the vaginal wall perforated, through which the intestines escaped "through the vulvar orifice between the thighs [meaning through the vagina]."[6] Physicians claimed that by shortening the length of time a woman labored, the less she suffered in childbirth. In actuality, it was more productive for the physicians, who did not necessarily follow the wisdom of men like Dr. Bard. Yet some women were beginning to put their faith in male practitioners. Men accused midwives of ignorance, but it was the men who were ignorant in managing childbirth.

Doctors who practiced midwifery following medical school had little if any practical experience, and yet many were taught how to use instruments, such as forceps or the crotchet, and how to manipulate the birth process. Models and animals were used to teach anatomy and birthing techniques. There was no clinical instruction in the medical schools, since it was improper for women to expose themselves to men. Students were unable to observe midwives or physicians who attended women in the privacy of their homes. In fact, most young doctors who completed their medical education never even witnessed an actual birth. They didn't have the opportunity to practice using instruments, leaving them literally fumbling in the dark.

Drs. Thomas James and John Church, who conducted the first complete course of lectures in midwifery in 1802, recognized this dilemma and sought to find a way to add practical instruction to their course. By 1805, they were successful in establishing a lying-in ward in the Philadelphia almshouse. Students were sold tickets to gain entrance to the lying-in ward and observe women during labor and birth.[7] The women who were admitted to these wards were desolate, homeless, and had no other place to go to have their babies. Many were immigrants who did not know the language and did not know what was happening to them. Furthermore, there was no such thing as informed consent. Lying-in wards or hospitals were the answer to the need for clinical instruction in medical education, but were detrimental to women.

Lying-in hospitals began to open in other almshouses in America. They were filthy, infested, and disease was rampant. Rooms were overcrowded with more than one person occupying a bed. Linens were filthy because there were no facilities to wash or dry the bedding. The wards were open for everyone to see what was going on with the other patients. Screens for privacy were too costly. The average stay for lying-in women was fifty-two days (if they survived). Patients who had died were left in coffins within the sight and smell of other patients.[8] Most deaths were due to childbed fever. Filth and disease permeated these wards.

The Boston Lying-In Hospital opened in 1832 in a small brick house. Drs. Enoch Hale and Walter Channing, the leading physicians in Boston who specialized in midwifery, were the birth attendants in this hospital. Six hundred babies were born between its opening in 1832 and its closing in 1856. "Every hospital in America was avoided by all except the wretched and destitute."[9]

Conditions in the lying-in ward in New York City's Bellevue Hospital were depicted in an engraving in *Harper's Weekly* in 1860. The inscription that appeared with the illustration reads, "We give herewith a picture of the beds in Bellevue Hospital in this city, in one of which the newborn child of Mary Connor was eaten by rats on Monday morning, April 23.... The building's swarming with rats, as many as 40 having been found in the bathtub one evening, and Mary Connor herself mentions that in her agony, she felt them running over her body."[10] These places of horror were where doctors could obtain their practical experience. The women who served as "material" for the medical students sacrificed their dignity, their bodies, and in many cases their lives, for science.

Midwifery was evolving into a medical specialty in America and was gaining equal status with medicine and surgery early in the nineteenth century. Philadelphia was the hub of this specialty and many prominent physicians set up practices there. One such famous physician was William Potts Dewees, who was held in high esteem by the medical community. Dewees received his medical degree from the University of Pennsylvania in 1806 and, in 1810, was offered the chair of midwifery at that university.[11] He was credited with bringing science to midwifery, but in so doing, did not regard childbirth as a normal event. In an example of how "scientific" Dewees was, while attending a woman in protracted labor, he bled her, taking more than two quarts of blood. The doctor later wrote that everything seemed better after she fainted.[12] This was an example of the heroic treatments, without scientific basis, in those times.

Dewees contributed two important innovations to obstetrics. He introduced pelvimetry (a method of measuring the diameters of the pelvis) and he also was the first to advocate prenatal care. However, he perpetuated the notion that childbirth was pathological. He taught that birth could best be accomplished with the woman lying on her back with her knees drawn up upon her chest.[13] Basically, this position doesn't utilize the natural forces of gravity and is uncomfortable for the woman giving birth, but it is easier for the doctor to use his instruments.

Another prominent physician from Philadelphia who specialized in midwifery was Charles Meigs, a professor of obstetrics and diseases of women and children at Jefferson Medical College in Philadelphia. Meigs was a prolific writer and also was well known for his dramatic style of teaching.[14]

As was discussed in chapter 6, during this period of time Ignaz Semmelweis and Oliver Wendell Holmes had published their works on the causes of puerperal fever. Meigs was one of the physicians who denied that this disease was spread by the dirty hands of physicians or the use of contaminated instruments—there was still little or no understanding of germ theory. Meigs avoided any mention of Holmes's writing about the transmission of puerperal fever in his second book, *Obstetrics: The Science and the Art*.[15] He disputed all the evidence that Holmes had demonstrated. Meigs was also adamantly against the use of anesthesia during labor and birth. He believed it was God's will that women should endure pain during childbirth. Meigs practiced the old "heroic" methods of bleeding, purging, and blistering in treating all diseases, as well as complications of pregnancy and childbirth.

Midwifery was taught in medical schools along with lectures on anatomy and physiology, diagnoses, hygiene, conception, abortion, and natural and unnatural birth. Students were also taught what to carry in their bags, such as laudanum, emetics (drugs that caused vomiting), drugs for purging, a lancet (for bleeding), silk thread (for sewing up what they tore), and forceps (for dragging out the baby). They were advised to respect the delicacy of women, to use good manners, and that the birth chamber was no place for "do nothing management."[16]

Medicine and midwifery was practiced more traditionally in the southern states than in the North. Life in the South was more relaxed and, generally, southern women, living in a rural environment, were healthier and had fewer complications in childbirth. Also, political and social issues in the antebellum south were different from those in the North. The southern states were more rural and slaves worked in the homes and large plantations. Trained physicians and doctors of any kind were scarce, so women, both white and black, became the healers and midwives. Although childbirth was difficult for most women, slave women were less likely to die giving birth. Because of hard labor, these women were generally more fit that white women. Moreover, the slaves didn't wear tight corsets nor were they subjected to "heroic" medical treatments. However, the slaves' infants died at twice the rate of white babies, because of their mothers' poor nutrition and poor prenatal care.[17]

Black midwives and healers had an excellent reputation for their skills and knowledge of herbal remedies, birth control, and abortion, which they brought from their native African countries. It is speculated that the abortifants used were tansy, rue, pennyroyal, and the roots and seeds of the cotton plant.[18]

Doctors kept records of their cases in their daybooks, including such accounts of the miles they traveled, weather conditions, the time they spent with their patients, and the social milieu. The birth chamber was usually crowded. Greater than two-thirds of a physician's cases might be slaves. It was to the advantage of the owners to take good care of their slaves. Some slaves had a choice in their doctoring; most chose their granny midwives over male doctors. Some southern physicians acknowledged the presence of midwives as experienced attendants and often accepted help and advice from them.[19]

Although there were some women who chose male physicians for their birth attendants, most, whether in the North or South, were adamantly opposed to the idea of male attendants, because it was offensive to female modesty. Consequently, there were conflicting feelings in regard to trusting physicians' credibility over that of traditional midwives. As it was with European society, a compromise was reached. Male attendants were expected to examine women, if they must, by "touch" without looking at their private parts. Consequently, male attendants performed their examinations "under the voluminous skirts of the mother, her private parts thus shielded from the prying masculine eyes."[20]

So it was that young men, having completed their medical education without the benefit of clinical practice, went on to practice midwifery, using their tools blindly to deliver babies. Dr. Dewees devised manikins for teaching students how to perform manual exams and insert forceps, "unsighted." Some professors were even embarrassed to teach about childbirth. For example, one of Dr. Thomas James's students revealed that Dr. James blushed and could not even look directly at his students while teaching on the subject.[21] It is difficult to use instruments during birth; to do so blindly is even more tricky and dangerous.

The issue of men attending women during childbirth was not only against moral principles, but actually caused outrage among some folks. For example, in 1851, an anonymous defender of female midwives questioned men's motives for practicing midwifery, asking "what can induce physicians to make frequent examinations with the finger, or the speculum, where the highest medical authorities have declared such examinations generally unnecessary, or often hurtful." [22]

Another outspoken man was Samuel Gregory, who was vehemently against men attending women in childbirth. Gregory was a graduate of

Yale University, but he was not a physician. He was a woman's advocate and preached that women should be attended by those of their own sex during childbirth or for any other women's ailments. Gregory acted on his beliefs and established a three-month midwifery school in association with the Boston Female Medical College in 1848. Twelve women attended this course, which was repeated six more times between 1848 and 1851.[23]

Gregory also conducted lectures and wrote about such topics as "Licentiousness, Its Cause and Effects" and "Facts and Important Information for Young Men on Self-Indulgence of the Sexual Appetite."[24] Gregory's views and teachings caused a loud uproar among the medical establishment. Many doctors were afraid they would lose credibility. Nevertheless, doctors did survive this threat and continued to practice and tout their credibility in the field of midwifery. The Boston Female Medical College expanded its curriculum in 1853 to include obstetrics. Reforms were introduced by Dr. Marie Zakrzewska, who had trained to be a midwife in Berlin before she immigrated to the United States. She was graduated from the Cleveland Medical School in 1856.[25]

Dr. Thomas Ewell of Rhode Island was another leading physician who also opposed male midwifery because it was offensive to women's modesty. Others shared Ewell's views. An anonymous author wrote in a pamphlet in 1851 that "twenty women now die in childbed, and a hundred are tortured with instruments, where there would not be one, if only women officiated as midwives; in fact, the very instruments were never invented or required until the assumption of man as midwife."[26] This author was right on target in describing what was happening.

Unfortunately, many men did continue in their pursuit of midwifery and used whatever manipulations and instruments that they believed were best to manage childbirth. The spread of childbed fever was due to unsterile examinations, instruments, and manual manipulations. There was much less risk of infection if nothing entered the woman's vagina during childbirth. In the lying-in hospitals, women were in proximity to one another and doctors didn't wash their hands between patients. Midwives attended women in their own homes, so there wasn't close contact; plus midwives probably washed their hands between visits. There were times when midwives did manipulate fetal positions to aid in the birth. There were sporadic cases of childbed fever connected with home births, but the deadly epidemics occurred in the hospitals.

Both midwifery and medical care were dangerous in the hands of most men. Men who practiced midwifery generally had little or no experience in the conduct of natural births. By mid-century, medical education was still poor and the lack of clinical practice was still being debated. One innovative professor of midwifery at the University of Buffalo Medical

College, Dr. James Platt White, broke tradition in 1850 when he demonstrated an actual delivery to his class of twenty students. He engaged a young woman of twenty-six years old, who was single and destitute, for this demonstration. White rescued her from the Erie County almshouse. The woman agreed to reside at the medical college and allow the students to observe her birth. Prior to her birth all twenty students listened to her baby's heart and performed vaginal examinations on her.[27] This humiliation may have been preferable to the almshouse.

While some medical men praised White for his innovation, others scorned him. "Sixteen medical gentleman" denounced White in scathing indictments in the *Buffalo Daily Courier* and in the *Buffalo Medical Journal*. White sued one of the local physicians, Dr. Horatio Loomis, for libel. Fifteen physicians testified that obstetrical demonstrations were neither necessary nor proper and were offensive to women's dignity. They contended that students could learn just as well by practicing on monkeys or other animals.[28]

By the 1870s there was a gradual acceptance of demonstrative delivery (observation of births). Lying-in hospitals, hospital clinics, and amphitheaters served this purpose. Although this practice was still condemned by some physicians and citizens, more medical schools incorporated clinical instruction into their curriculums. Physicians and professors could then demonstrate their manipulative techniques to students.

Dr. William Richardson, an instructor of obstetrics at Harvard Medical School, allowed his second-year students to visit the lying-in wards, where he demonstrated such techniques as podalic version (turning the fetus in the uterus) and manual dilation of the woman's cervix. Richardson was known for his dexterity. His teachings, however, encouraged less skilled practitioners to undertake these manipulations, which inevitably led to injuries of the genital organs, infection, hemorrhage, shock, and sometimes death.[29]

In spite of the opposition against male midwives and Victorian values of the times, male midwifery practice was gaining ground. Traditional midwives continued to practice throughout the century without the benefits of regulation, training, or elevating their professional status. Midwives who wanted to advance their status and seek educational opportunities were not accepted into colleges. Physicians fought against women's attempts for education, contending that women lacked the ability to become competent birth attendants.[30]

Physicians continued to emphasize the dangerous nature of childbirth and that only they, the experts, had the capability to provide the best care possible. Doctors proclaimed that midwives were not capable of safely managing childbirth because of the nature of their physiology, in that women were delicate, frail creatures, dominated by their emotions, and lacked intellectual capabilities. Moreover, many doctors proclaimed that midwives were "hopelessly dirty, ignorant and incompetent relics of a barbaric past."[31] Obstetrics advanced as a medical specialty in the second half of the nineteenth century and the doctors' campaign to replace traditional midwives accelerated. The introduction of anesthesia in America helped pave the way for doctors to overshadow the traditional midwives.

The first American physician to advocate anesthesia in childbirth was Dr. Walter Channing of Boston. Channing graduated from the University of Pennsylvania Medical School in 1809 and also studied and practiced obstetrics in London and Edinburgh before returning to the States. Through his work at the Boston Lying-In Hospital in the 1830s and 1840s, he was recognized as the ablest obstetrician in Boston.[32] After Queen Victoria was given anesthesia for her birth in 1853, middle- and upper-class women who could afford a male physician believed if anesthesia was safe for the Queen, then it would be safe for them. Women everywhere welcomed the idea of pain-free childbirth.

Although physicians who practiced midwifery were gaining favor among some upper-class urban women, medicine, in general, was still slow to advance. There was only gradual acceptance of the contagiousness of puerperal fever, which was still taking many young lives. There were still many physicians who didn't accept the germ theory. With the increasing number of lying-in hospitals being established, puerperal fever was still a huge problem. Epidemics continued until almost the turn of the century. About one in every two women who entered the lying-in hospitals became infected. In 1872, one out of every six women died in the epidemics that broke out in Bellevue Lying-In Hospital in New York. Because of epidemics, the Boston Lying-In Hospital had been closed for sixteen years until it reopened in 1873. During the next five years, five hundred mothers were infected with puerperal fever and fifty died.[33]

Medical education was still in a poor state. The apprenticeship system of medical training during the seventeenth and eighteenth centuries expanded to a proliferation of medical schools, which sprouted like mushrooms during the first part of the nineteenth century. Twenty-six schools opened between 1810 and 1840 and 47 more opened between 1840 and 1875.[34] It was easy to obtain the required legislative charters. All that was required to run a medical school was a lecture hall, a professor, a dissection room, and interested students. Medical schools were privately funded business ventures and there were no educational standards. Fees were paid directly to the professors so it was economically beneficial to keep classes large.[35]

Doctors who had attended these schools or had learned doctoring through apprenticeships and having learned centuries-old remedies, were known as "regular" doctors. The men who attended universities and medical schools in Europe brought back what they considered the latest science and cures and a newfound professionalism to America. By mid-century, the competition intensified between physicians, regular doctors, increasing numbers of quacks, and midwives, as well as female doctors.

America was a burgeoning capitalistic society; most doctors didn't have time to delve into research. They were more concerned with the commercial benefits of doctoring. They needed immediate cures and therefore were indifferent to scientific methods. Unlike European physicians, American doctors focused more on practical principles than they did on scientific discovery. They often made use of false principles, rather than delve into the search for truth.[36]

Theoretical propositions, such as tension of the blood vessels being the underlying cause of all diseases, including problems in pregnancy and childbirth, were the rationale given for opening a vein to bleed the patient. "Heroic" remedies used to treat illnesses and problems of childbirth included crawling leeches, purging laxatives, medicines to induce vomiting, mustard plasters to cause blistering, and mercury poisoning.

Even normal female physiological states, such as menstruation, pregnancy, childbirth, and menopause, were subject to barbaric treatments, almost designed, it seemed, to place women under a form of discipline and control.[37] Some people started to rebel against the orthodox medical system and sought alternative, more gentle approaches to care. Eclectic schools of thought began to emerge, such as homeopathy, hydrotherapy (water cures), mesmerism (a form of hypnosis), osteopathy, and Thomsonism.

The popular Thomsonian movement was based on botanic remedies and warm baths. Samuel Thompson, a New Hampshire farmer turned healer (he didn't have a formal education), believed that body heat was crucial to health. He patented his own package of remedies and literature. He had a large following of people traveling westward. Other unorthodox schools originated in Europe. The German physician, Samuel Hahnemann, introduced homeopathy, a method of using minute amounts of a drug to cure diseases. These drugs would often mimic symptoms of the disease being treated. Hydrotherapy, originating in Austria, was based on the curative powers of water. Hydropathic therapists advocated sensible dress, diet, and pure water. They also regarded pregnancy and childbirth as normal states, contrary to orthodox physicians' beliefs that these were pathological conditions.[38] Of course, all of these eclectic doctors, as well as other healers and midwives, were considered to be quacks by the regular and university-trained physicians.

Most orthodox medical schools were still of very poor quality. In the mid-century, there were still no national standards or regulations for medical practice or medical education and there were no incentives to raise standards. The proprietary schools—both regular and eclectic—opposed regulations for fear they would be closed down. Licensing exams were also a threat because there were still many students who were illiterate.[39] There were no changes in medical education or in the quality in medical practice until the next century; yet, the doctors who were graduated by these schools continued to denigrate midwives.

Only state and county medical societies had regulatory authority, but these societies enabled physicians to determine their own qualifications. A diploma from any medical school conveyed authority to practice. The first medical society in America was founded in New York in 1760 and the second in New Jersey in 1766. By 1830, all thirteen states had formed medical societies to raise standards in their states and also to raise income of their practitioners.[40]

Dr. Nathan Davis, a delegate to the New York State Medical Society, proposed educational standards in 1843. There followed in the next four years much discussion and disputes over this issue. Preliminary plans to establish a national medical organization were spurred by the New York State Medical Society in 1846. This effort was initially in response to protests against professors who licensed their own students.[41] Finally, in 1846, Congress passed four resolutions that addressed medical education standards and led to the formation of a national medical organization.[42] Even after the establishment of the American Medical Association (AMA) in 1847, the quality of medical practice and education didn't change. However, the organization gave physicians a stronger power base.

The purposes of the Association were to impose reform in the medical schools, to initiate registration of vital statistics, and also to improve sanitary conditions in the major cities. To say that conditions in crowded cities were unsanitary would be putting it mildly. Conditions among the poor, living in crowded tenement buildings, were rampant with filth, infestation, and disease. There was no public sanitation. The general public was apathetic to the problems and there was no help for the poor.[43] So the responsibility for addressing these issues was given to the AMA.

It wasn't until 1871 that Harvard University's president, Charles W. Eliot, proposed to extend the academic curriculum from four to nine months and to require a written exam. This proposal met with much criticism since, as Henry Bigelow, professor of surgery at Harvard explained, such improvements would destroy the school since half the students could barely write, let alone pass an exam.[44]

Belonging to the AMA gave physicians the status of belonging to a

strong professional organization. Members formalized entry requirements, which included the exclusion of women and African Americans.
The AMA became a "family of triumphant specialists and culminated in
the long power struggle of overtaking the midwife's hold on the practice
of obstetrics."[45] Medical men were organized; midwives were not.
Because traditional midwives didn't create an organization, physicians
didn't look upon them as professionals. Many midwives felt that they
didn't need a college education or a professional group to practice what
they had been successfully doing for centuries. Furthermore, many midwives were illiterate and practiced in isolation.[46] Forming an organization of their own was not yet feasible. Midwives who did want an
education were refused admission to medical schools, except for the few
that attended Samuel Gregory's Boston Female Medical College, which
was basically a school for midwives.

Midwives, however, remained in practice for the rest of the century
because most doctors were not willing to attend poor women living in
urban communities, nor were they willing to travel to remote rural areas.
In fact, midwives attended the vast majority of births up until the first
decades of the twentieth century.[47] Immigrants preferred midwives with
their long-established traditions who spoke their language, to attend them
in childbirth. Another advantage of midwives was the provision of additional services, unavailable from physicians, such as continuing to care
for the mother, her baby, and manage the household for days or even
weeks after the birth.

When male midwifery became a medical specialty, the field became
known as obstetrics. Physicians who practiced in this field were called
obstetricians and regular doctors continued to practice midwifery along
with their general practices. Women-midwives held on to their title. The
specialty of obstetrics gained greater acceptance and status among the
medical community after the founding of the first medical specialty journal, *The American Journal of Obstetrics*, in 1868, and the establishment
of the American Association of Obstetricians and Gynecologists in 1888.
These developments "advanced the tenet that obstetrics was a complicated specialty which only the physician was capable of pursuing."[48]
American obstetricians used propaganda and legislation to rule the field
of midwifery. They used propaganda to portray childbirth as dangerous
and pathological.

Physicians disregarded the fact that midwives had been the experts
in their field for centuries. With the increase of immigration in the late
1800s, the number of trained midwives also increased. Many immigrant
midwives were educated, having graduated from excellent European
midwifery schools. However, attempts to create adequate midwifery

training in the States were met with a great deal of resistance. There were a few schools that provided adequate training. The College of Midwifery of New York City was granted the right to confer a diploma to its graduates by the New York Supreme Court in 1883. This program included three months each of instruction and clinical practice. Other schools established in the 1890s were the Playfair School of Midwifery in Chicago and the St. Louis College of Midwifery.[49]

Dr. A. A. Henshe, who founded the St. Louis College and was a faculty member, established a monthly journal, *The American Midwife*, in 1895. This publication, which was printed in both English and German, was the only professional literature of value to midwives, yet it lasted only a year. Another trained midwife and faculty member of the St. Louis college criticized physicians for falsely portraying midwives as dirty and ignorant. She wrote about the aseptic techniques that midwives did employ and about the thousands of midwives who did read *The American Midwife.* [50]

However, midwives had more critics than proponents. As one New York obstetrician stated, midwives were "inveterate quacks." He urged the country to "form a vanguard in a war of extermination against the pestiferous remnant of the pre-antiseptic days, midwives and schools of midwifery."[51]

The attitudes against midwives were much stronger in America than they were in Europe. Most American men didn't believe women needed to be educated. In contrast, England and other European countries accepted dual roles, in which women were trained to manage normal births while physicians were trained to manage complicated births. This didn't happen in the United States. American obstetricians didn't want a dichotomy.

Male attitudes toward midwives were consistent with overall male attitudes toward women. American men believed that women were inherently inferior to men. Prior to the industrial revolution, women were valued for their share of labor on the home front. However, as men left the farms to seek employment away from the home, the division of labor within the family widened. Women became the master of the home but remained politically and economically subordinate. In a society of commodities, women were devalued. Their ascribed role was to care "for the home while men engaged in activities to reshape the world."[52]

Among the well-to-do families, women took on new definitions. Older definitions of usefulness and strength gave way to definitions of domesticity and frailty. These women became "creatures of solely decorative worth, possessing a beauty which rested upon their frailty, purity, delicacy, and even asexuality."[53] Their lifestyles were not conducive to health.

The Victorian ideal of womanhood was "angel in the house." Stereotypical terms describing women were intellectually inferior, delicate, gentle, self-sacrificing, morally superior, and also "passionless maiden."[54] This concept was totally opposite from the beliefs of the early colonial Puritans, who expected women to enjoy sex. The Puritans believed that a woman must reach orgasm to conceive, and babies were needed to populate the new colonies. Men even read sex manuals, such as *Aristotle's Master Piece*, to gain knowledge about arousal and foreplay. However, the Puritans believed that having sex too often "gluts the Womb and renders it unfit for its office."[55]

Women in the 1800s were perceived as sexually repressed. Childbearing and domesticity were women's most revered virtues. Because women were ascribed superior moral character, they weren't expected to participate in sexual activity for their own pleasure, but only for their husbands' satisfaction. Women's role in sexual activity was to conceive. This double standard allowed for promiscuity in men, but not in women. Harriet Martineu, a European writer and traveler, wrote about the discrepancy between the democratic ideals of American society and women's domestic subjugation.[56]

A famous physician and gynecologist, Marion Sims, was obsessed with fertility. He perceived copulation as a mechanical act "to get the semen into the proper place in the proper time."[57] He believed that women didn't experience sexual desire, that it wasn't their purpose in life. Sims's wife conformed to the expectations of the typical housewife. "She was a source of assurance, steadiness, restraint, buoyancy, and stability," ready to listen to her husband's frustrations, but never voice her own needs.[58]

Men considered it irrelevant for women to develop any mental abilities. Often, females in the home were forbidden to read any part of the newspaper except the fashion and "ladies' sections." There were some women who began to question their constricted place in society and rebelled against men's ascriptions of women's domestic role and their delicate, self-sacrificing nature. Women also began to react to the dangerous medical practice of treating disease as a "malevolent entity that must be bludgeoned, bled, defecated, poisoned, and puked out."[59] Women wanted practitioners of their own sex to treat their female disorders. Because of modesty, many women avoided medical attention for too long, leading to serious health conditions.

There were those women who also wanted freedom from constant childbearing throughout their reproductive lives. Some wanted an education and opportunities outside the home. Another reason women wanted to limit childbearing was related to economic issues and the fear of permanent disability or death from childbirth.[60] Birth control would be a giant step toward emancipation. Women nursed their babies for as long as possible to prevent conception. Abstinence was advocated by health reformers who felt children should be planned. They believed that excessive childbearing damaged a woman's health.[61] Many women doctors agreed.

There were some methods of contraception that women tried. Coitus interruptus (withdrawal before ejaculation) and douching with alcohol or vinegar were recommended, but were not very reliable. Some of these methods, however, did reduce the chance of conception. By the mid 1800s, women could send away for pamphlets on birth control and devices, such as pessaries, syringes, condoms, spermicides for douching, and pills that promised to induce abortion. Some of the pills were sugar pills and the birth control advice was dangerously erroneous. Although illegal, abortions performed early in pregnancy were another means of birth control. American households actually did begin to shrink, so that by the end of the nineteenth century, the birth rate had been cut in half.[62]

Some women sought to change their ascribed image of delicacy and moral superiority. They wanted control of their own property and the right to personal liberty, and they also wanted to develop political consciousness. Some women joined forces and became active in the reform movements of the times, which were health, temperance, and abolition.[63] By banning together to change their lives, women also gained organizational skills and leadership abilities. These early initiatives led to the first women's movement.

The first feminist rights movement began in England when Mary Wollstonecraft's book, *Vindication of the Rights of Women*, was published in 1791. Wollstonecraft advocated education for women, even co-education. Female literature, including novels and magazines, burgeoned with feminist views of double standards and sexual and economic exploitation of women, came on the market. The organized women's movement in America was launched by Elizabeth Cady Stanton who initiated the first Women's Rights Convention at Seneca Falls in New York in 1848. Stanton was "committed to unearthing and understanding the long history of women's oppression and impelled women to revolt against it."[64]

Stanton met her lifelong friend and fellow reformer, Susan B. Anthony, in 1851. Anthony, born into a conservative Quaker family, became involved in the temperance movement. While Anthony's mission was focused on the economic needs of women, Stanton's focus was on the sexual oppression of women.[65] Stanton traveled around the country in the 1870s giving speeches and lectures about women's issues. One particular speech about marriage and divorce in 1875 strongly signifies her passion. In her speech she proclaimed:

> I should feel that I had not lived in vain if faith of mine could roll off the soul of women that dark cloud, that nightmare, that false belief that all her weaknesses and disabilities are natural, that her sufferings in maternity are a punishment for the sins of Adam and Eve and teach her that higher gospel that by obedience to natural laws she might secure uninterrupted health and happiness for herself and mold future generations to her will.[66]

Men became threatened by these feminist views and sought to preserve traditional social relationships as they existed. They employed arguments to "rationalize traditional sex roles as rooted inevitably and irreversibly in the prescriptions of anatomy and physiology."[67] Physicians and physiologists formulated medical and scientific arguments about the natural differences between men and women. They proclaimed that the underlying causes of women's physical and emotional disorders were rooted in their reproductive organs, which shaped their personality, social role and intellectual capacities. Being emotionally uncontrolled was attributed to a disturbance of the uterus. (The Greeks coined the phrase "hysteria," meaning wondering womb.) Professional men believed, and so taught, that men were dominated by their brains, whereas women were dominated by their emotions.

In a lecture on "Some of the Distinctive Characteristics of the Female" at Jefferson College in Philadelphia in 1847, Charles Meigs told his students, "Woman is a moral, asexual, a germiferous, gestative and parturient creature."[68] Meigs implored his students to study women's reproductive organs, which "are capable of exerting, not on her body alone, but on the heart, the mind and the every soul of women."[69] Some physicians went as far as to relate women's sexuality to madness; so naturally the cure then was to remove her sexual organs. Physicians attacked women's desire for education because it would harm their health and reproductive capabilities. Physicians expressed concern about women's deteriorating health compared with their more vigorous and less nervous grandmothers.

Physiologic reformers proclaimed that women would be healthier if they were less coddled and participated in more strenuous activities such as housework than in educational pursuits. One woman physician stood up and refuted this argument, stating that "no one worked harder or in unhealthier conditions than a washer woman" and that the reason for poor health was more related to fashion, such as wearing tight corsets that cause "compressed viscera, tortured stomachs and displaced uteruses."[70]

Physicians also expressed concern about women wanting to limit childbearing. Men contended that contraception was unnatural and deleterious to women's health. One physician proclaimed that "sex, like all aspects of human bodily activity, involved an exchange of nervous energy ... without which the female partner could never find true fulfillment."[71] It is ironic that men contended that limiting childbearing was unnatural, yet argued that childbirth was an unnatural state. However, men used these arguments to discredit women's desires to take control of their own lives.

In 1871, Dr. Alfred Stille, president of the AMA, warned physicians that some women "seek to rival men in manly sports and occupations." He blamed women for attempting to castrate men in order to achieve perfection in their own right.[72] In 1870, The Reverend John Todd wrote about his fears that women who partook in masturbation, contraception and abortion would lead to extinction of the American people.[73]

Women did have "female" problems that required medical attention. Many of these conditions were related to frequent childbearing and injuries incurred during childbirth. So there was a market for specialists in female problems, leading the path to the field of gynecology. Some "female" conditions included: vaginal discharge; difficult, painful or absence of menses; pelvic cysts and tumors; "vaginismus" (extreme pain during intercourse); and prolapsed uterus.

Prolapsed uterus (dropping of the uterus in the pelvic cavity and protrusion of the cervix into the vagina) causes a very uncomfortable feeling of pressure. The pessaries used to treat this disorder, available from doctors or mail order, were equally uncomfortable. The cause was blamed on long-time wearing of tight corsets or unskilled doctors or midwives tugging on the afterbirth. The major and most horrible conditions were vesico- and recto-vaginal fistulas. During the first half of the nineteenth century, about one-fourth of middle- and upper-class women were "laid up sickly" as a result of this condition. Women became invalids and kept to their rooms, reclining in their beds or on couches.[74]

Physicians pondered the causes of women's unique conditions. They attributed them to various environmental factors, moral disorders, such as "lustful indulgence," excessive coitus or abstinence, masturbation, unsatisfied sexual appetite, depression, jealousy or other "vivid emotions of the soul." One surgeon declared that these problems "reflected the close sympathy said to exist between the brain and organs of generation."[75] Men didn't consider that the damage incurred during childbirth was responsible for many of women's chronic ailments. One author of an article in the *Journal of the American Medical Association* wrote, "While the majority of cases are generally attributed to traumatism, this may often in itself be the result of defective development, and inherited or acquired weaknesses or malformations."[76] In another article written in 1884 in the same *Journal*, the author wrote, "The gynaecologist is ready to offer his services in sewing up lacerations of the genital organs of maltreated and unfortunate women. Seldom do we hear the voice of any of them raised in behalf of preventive measures."[77]

Men sought to rescue women from their ailments just as they sought to rescue them from the perils of childbirth. Treatments varied from advising fresh air, nourishing foods, and hip baths to the more heroic methods of bleeding, purging, or calomel. As a result of too much calomel, mercury poisoning resulted, with symptoms of headaches and loss of control of the hands. Leeches were applied to the vulva, vagina, and rectum. Doctors might treat nervous disorders by injecting water, milk or linseed oil into the uterus.[78]

The late nineteenth century became an era of mutilative surgery to curb women's passions and treat conditions that men believed were rooted in their reproductive organs. So men removed these organs to cure a variety of afflictions, such as mental disorders or moral disturbances. Removal of the clitoris was prescribed for nymphomania or masturbation, and ovaries or the uterus were removed for anything from painful menstruation to overeating.[79]

There was no cure for the most dreaded maladies, vaginal fistulas (openings between the walls of the vagina and the urinary bladder or rectum), which resulted from birth injuries related to the use of obstetric instruments. By mid-century, one man set out to find a cure for this dreaded condition. J. Marion Sims, born in the back country of South Carolina in 1813, became interested in medicine at a young age. He first attended the Medical College of the state of South Carolina in 1833. Feeling the need to further his education, he traveled to Philadelphia in October of 1834, where he attended Jefferson Medical College, graduating with a medical degree in 1835. Sims was also interested in surgery and Jefferson was highly regarded for its instruction in surgery. Philadelphia was becoming the hub of medical education. Sims then returned to Lancaster, South Carolina to marry his beloved Theresa in 1836.[80]

Sims had little clinical experience, but he needed to make a living. Having little success in Lancaster, he set off to rural Alabama and became a plantation physician. His practice included attending women in childbirth. Since slaves accounted for greater than fifty percent of the population, many of his patients were slaves. There were many black midwives (granny midwives) who held a prominent place in childbirth, and who attended both their mistresses and field hands. They attended most all births, but physicians were called upon when there was difficulty.[81]

In June 1845, Anarcha, a slave girl of seventeen, was in labor for seventy-two hours when Dr. Sims was called upon. He applied forceps to the impacted head of the fetus, even though he had little experience using them. Five days later, Anarcha lost all control of her urinary and bowel function; part of her vaginal tissue had sloughed off. Later, her master brought her to Sims, hoping he could cure her. Upon examination, Sims diagnosed the problem as "an enormous fistula at the base her bladder ... destruction of the posterior wall of the vagina, opening in to the rectum.... The urine was running day and night ... with constant pain and burning. The odor from this saturation permeated everything ... her life was one of suffering and disgust. [82]

Betsy and Lucy were two other young slaves who gave birth to their first babies and who also suffered afterwards from the same ailment as Anarcha. They also were taken to Sims by their owner, but Sims was unable to treat them. A strange event occurred that same evening, when Sims was called to an emergency to attend a woman, Mrs. Merrill, who had been thrown from her pony, leaving her in severe back and pelvic pain. Placing her in a "knee-chest" position with her buttocks faced upward to examine her, he was able to visualize the entire wall of her vaginal cavity.[83] This case was the impetus that drove Sims to find a cure for vesico-vaginal fistula and into practicing gynecological surgery.

After doing what he could for the injured woman, excited about his discovery, he rushed home to examine Lucy in the same knee-chest position, using the handle of a pewter spoon as a speculum to visualize the walls of her vagina. He was able to see her fistula in plain view. Sims later wrote that he set out to "relieve the loneliest of all God's creatures of one of the most loathsome maladies that can possible befall poor human nature."[84] He saw himself, like Columbus, as an explorer and the discoverer of a new world—the "world of the vagina."[85]

Sims then sought permission from the owner of the slaves, Anarcha, Betsy, and Lucy, to house them on his own estate so he could find a cure. He was given permission, since slaves with such severe fistulas would be of little value in the fields or as "breeders." He housed them in a hut in his backyard where for four years, from 1846 to 1849, he repeatedly operated and experimented on these women. He experimented with various instruments and sutures that he invented or improved upon. Invariably he failed; the women's wounds didn't heal and ultimately became infected.[86] The women suffered through all these operations without the benefit of anesthesia. Sims held to the theory that blacks had a physiological tolerance to pain and so he never felt the need to anesthetize them. Sims claimed that the women begged him to continue the surgeries in hope of a cure. He did offer them opium, but only after each procedure. He required them to remain horizontal for two weeks.[87]

Eventually, Sims did find a suture material that didn't lead to infection. Sims's claim to fame was that he found the cure for the dreaded condition. However, he achieved his goal by means that were far from ethical by today's standards. It is not clear whether his patients were completely cured, but it was a beginning of the new field of gynecology, which Sims pioneered. Sims became famous and reaped the rewards for his innovations. But what price did the slave women pay?

His paper "On the Treatment of Vesico-Vaginal Fistula" was published in the *American Journal of Medical Science* in 1852. Sims went on to co-found the Women's Hospital in New York in 1855, the first hospital devoted to gynecology. He became president of the AMA in 1876, and president of the American Gynecologic Society in 1880.[88] Sims found the cure for the very ailment that men were probably responsible for in their management of childbirth. Sims and his colleagues continued to perform gynecological surgeries (most experimental), including repair of fistulas, clitoridectomies, incisions into the cervix, inserting probes into the cervix to keep it open, and removal of ovaries and uterus for various ailments, including nervous disorders and moral disturbances. He even experimented with injecting sperm into the uterus in cases of infertility. Gynecology was born and carried on without ethical considerations or respect for women.

The drive for power, in general, was more intense among American men than it was among European men for several reasons. The effect of democracy on American men and the unrelenting pressures of society influenced men's attitudes toward women, sexual beliefs and their treatment of women during the nineteenth century. According to G.J. Barker-Benfield, Alexis de Tocqueville, the French author and adventurer, saw American men as "cold and implacable" toward nature. America's drive for equality was not shared by all people; most men viewed native Indians, African Americans, and women as inferior.[89]

The ideals of freedom and citizenry in America did not extend to women. Even though about one-fifth of the female population was employed in industry from 1850 to 1900, female labor remained cheap and unskilled. The rise of capitalism contributed to the competitive nature of American men, who were viewed as pragmatic and technical. In contrast, women were sensitive, caring, loving, and more in tune with nature.[90] Therefore, American men saw their role as protector of women and needed to be in control. American doctors fought to take the reigns from women and continued to manipulate childbirth in their own best interests. They used their power and declared open war against the midwives in the next century.

CHAPTER 9

Early Twentieth-Century America: The "Midwife Problem" and Medicalized Childbirth

Joan Thompson's mother gave birth on November 3, 1932. Joan was her mother's second child, born at home on the remote island of Chincoteague off the coast of Virginia. The family lived on a houseboat. Her mother labored for twenty-four hours, without the assistance of other women. She was miserable because her labor was lasting so long. To ease her pain, she walked around her house and yard, ate when she was hungry, and went on a ride with her husband on a bumpy road "to shake it down." Finally, she sent her husband to fetch the only doctor in town at the local bar. She gave birth "the old fashion way, by squatting and holding onto a chair. She knew what to do." I asked Joan where her father was while this was going on. She responded, "He was probably taking a snort with the doctor." Her mother gave birth without any complications. Later, Joan's mother gave birth to her third child in a hospital, which she remembered as a horrible experience. "The doctor being catholic, didn't believe in pain medication and the nurse had no sympathy."[1]

The above scenario portrays the control women had in their own home births, although difficult, compared with hospital births that basically replaced home births in the early decades of the twentieth century. The scene played by the hospital birth is in sharp contrast to the milieu of the home birth.

A father wrote an article, "Our Streamlined Baby," published in

117

Reader's Digest in 1938, in which he described the birth of his daughter, who was born the "easy way." The date had been planned. Labor was started artificially with the drug, Pituitrin, at 10:45 in the morning. The woman's doctor told her she could have medicine to ease the labor pains. Her response was, "No, this is my first baby: I want to know something about it." Ignoring her wishes, her doctor gave her three capsules of Nembutal at 11:20 A.M. (Nembutal is a powerful sleep-inducing drug that crosses the placenta and causes central nervous depression in the newborn.) At 1:00 P.M., she was given a hypodermic of scopolamine, a medicine that causes memory loss and is also sedating. The Nembutal was repeated at 1:15 P.M. and the scopolamine was repeated at 3:27 P.M. Her baby was born at 6:47 P.M. The mother slept well until 11:00 P.M. and remembered nothing of her birth. The father praised the doctor and raved about his wife's easy birth.[2]

The father didn't describe what the baby looked like at birth and the mother wasn't awake to observe, either. In 1938, this "streamlined baby" was probably limp, blue and very sleepy because of all the sedating medication the mother received, which readily passes through the placenta and sedates the fetus as well. It took much effort on the part of the nurse to stimulate the baby to breathe and cry. The father was clueless. It is amazing that such large doses of highly sedating drugs were given to laboring women for much of the twentieth century. The mothers were in never-never land, while the nurse stimulated, suctioned, and oxygenated the baby.

In early twentieth-century America, childbirth was taken over by obstetricians and conducted in ways it never had been before. Middle-class and well-to-do women were beginning to seek medical services, although midwives continued to care for the poor, the immigrant populations, and those living in remote areas where doctors did not want to travel. The high infant and maternal mortality rates were blamed on the midwives. Physicians thought they could do better. The "midwife problem" or the "midwife question," as it became known, was more a question of whether midwives should be educated or abolished altogether. Midwives still didn't have the power base that medical men had. They still weren't regulated or educated (in the formal sense of the term), nor were they organized.

Many midwives were immigrants, speaking only their native languages and were scattered throughout the country, from crowded urban cities to remote rural communities. Many could not read or write, and so had no means of learning new discoveries, such as how to practice asepsis or to know that silver nitrate drops instilled in the eyes of the newborn baby would prevent blindness, which otherwise might occur due to gonorrheal infection in the mother. The midwives wanted to be educated and many public health professionals saw the need for training them. Many doctors, however, fought hard against midwifery education.

Physicians had advantages over the midwives, so they were better able to promote their own cause. They were organized and generally educated. However, medicine still struggled with the same problems it had in the last century. There were too many physicians in urban areas and insufficient numbers in remote rural areas of the country. Young men recently out of medical school still had little if any opportunity to observe or attend women in childbirth. Students continued to learn mainly from lectures, textbooks, and demonstrations on model equipment. They learned more about the dangers of childbirth than the normal aspects, and they learned how to intervene.

Members of the American Medical Association (AMA) began to be very concerned about the poor quality of medical education, particularly in the private schools that were mainly business ventures. There were too many students graduating and there were no effective licensing laws or regulations in many states.[3] Concerned about overcrowding in the medical field, the AMA wanted reform measures to limit the number of physicians and thereby decrease the competition. Licensing was also a mechanism to eliminate midwives, who competed for the clientele physicians wanted for themselves. These men also felt that the midwives stood in their way of achieving status in the field of obstetrics.

The AMA sought reform within the medical profession. In 1904, the Council on Medical Education was established by the AMA to develop minimal standards in medical schools in order to improve the quality of education.[4] A committee of one hundred physicians was formed to conduct a national survey of all medical schools in the United States in 1905. Abraham Flexnor was selected to direct the study.[5]

The results were published in 1910. Flexnor concluded that there was an "over-production of uneducated and ill-trained medical practitioners. He recommended the reduction of 155 medical schools in America to thirty-one, to be located in large cities across the nation and in proximity to adequate hospital facilities, which supplied "clinical material."[6] By "clinical material," Flexnor was referring to poor, indigent women who had no alternatives than to give birth in lying-in wards. Flexnor also recommended setting a minimum of two years of college before students were eligible for medical school and a licensing exam following graduation.

Between 1910 and 1930, the Carnegie and Rockefeller Foundations contributed over $300 million toward medical education and research and to finance medical school reforms. Between 1904 and 1915, ninety-two schools merged or closed their doors.[7]

Another issue of great concern was the high maternal and infant mortality rates in the congested inner cities. Physicians blamed the midwives. The real problem was the horribly unsanitary and crowded living conditions in large cities, resulting in disease and other major health problems. Public health officials, searching for ways to change this picture, came up with the concept of preventive health. The services of trained public health nurses and trained midwives were needed.

Dr. Sara Josephine Baker (1873–1945) was a pioneer in early public health initiatives. Baker, who preferred to be called Josephine, was the tomboy daughter of a well-to-do Quaker lawyer in Poughkeepsie, New York. After graduating from Women's Medical College in New York in 1899—a time when it was extremely difficult for women to be admitted to medical school—Baker interned for one year at the New England Hospital for Women and Children in Boston. She then interned for three months in an outpatient clinic that served the city's worst slum areas. Baker had goals and set out to achieve them. She was dedicated to saving babies and correcting the appalling living conditions in the slums of New York. After a few years in private practice, Baker was offered a summer position to attend sick babies in the tenements of New York City in 1902. She estimated that an average of 1,600 babies died weekly, mostly from dysentery.[8]

Baker believed that educating pregnant women before and after birth would make healthier babies. Toward that end, she conducted an experiment in the summer of 1908, in which she enlisted thirty off-duty school nurses to visit families in a neighborhood of recent Italian and Irish immigrants in the eastside neighborhood that had one of the highest infant death rates in the city. The nurses taught the mothers proper baby care, including proper nutrition, the importance of breastfeeding, frequent bathing, proper summer clothing, ventilation, and the necessity of fresh air in the park. By the end of the summer, there were 1,200 fewer deaths than there had been the previous summer. The death rate remained unchanged in other districts.[9]

In 1908, Baker was appointed the first chief of the newly established Bureau of Child Hygiene, under the Department of Health in New York City. Unlike most male physicians and some female doctors as well, she was a staunch advocate of the training, regulating, and licensing of midwives. She contended that "although the midwife is as old as mankind, she was something of an anomaly in an American Community."[10] As the new chief, Baker went to the state legislature to secure stringent licensing laws for midwives in New York City. The law stated that midwives needed a certificate from a doctor stating that they had attended twenty or more births under supervision. As a result of her efforts, four thousand midwives were licensed by the Department of Health of New York City.[11] The medical establishment was not happy about this outcome.

In 1910, midwives handled over forty percent of all births in New York City, primarily because of cultural preferences of the large immigrant population. Dr. Baker insisted that trained midwives were essential because immigrant women would absolutely refuse male birth attendants. Baker did believe that adequately trained obstetricians would be best, but acknowledged that these doctors would be too expensive.[12]

Baker was also instrumental in the establishment of the Bellevue School for Midwives in 1911. From then on, in New York City, licenses were issued only to midwives who had been graduated from Bellevue or from European schools of equal standing. According to Baker, "Its graduates knew more about delivering babies than three-fourths of the recently graduated interns entering medical practice in this country that year." She declared, "If I had a daughter who was going to have a baby, I would rather see her in the hands of one of the competent Scandinavian midwives who, in their own countries, work in squads under supervision of an obstetrician, rather than in the hands of the average general practitioner. A well-trained midwife deserves all possible respect as a practical specialist."[13] Baker blamed the distrust of and animosity toward midwives on the fact that the maternal mortality rates in America were higher than that of all other European countries.

From 1900 to 1910, there was no significant decrease in the maternal death rates in the United States. Yet there were reductions in these rates in England, Wales, Ireland, Japan, New Zealand, and Switzerland, where trained midwives attended the majority of births.[14] There was perhaps much variance in the statistics early in the century because not all states registered vital statistics. The U.S. Bureau of Census, which began publishing vital statistics in 1900, created a registration area that included all the New England states, New York, New Jersey, Indiana, Michigan and the District of Columbia. In this area, 10,010 deaths related to childbirth were reported in 1913. Of these, 4,542 were due to childbed fever, known to be preventable since the 1870s.[15]

England experienced its midwife controversy fifty years before it occurred in the United States. During those years, England also saw profoundly high maternal and infant death rates. However, England demonstrated how midwifery could survive and be effective. In the late nineteenth century, Florence Nightingale proposed that midwives be trained. Soon courses were offered to midwives in some private hospitals. In 1881, a group of English midwives formed the Matron's Aid Society, which later became the Midwives' Institute.[16] Midwifery regulations were proposed in 1892, after which several bills were drafted and rejected, until passage of the Midwives' Act of 1902. Sir Frances Champneys, president of the London Obstetrical Society in 1895, was instrumental in the passage of this act. Champneys stated, "The question is not whether midwives shall exist, but whether they shall be as good as possible."[17] This attitude had never existed among American obstetricians.

Other European countries had trained midwives by the early twentieth century. Clara D. Noyes, superintendent of the Bellevue School for Midwives, stated, "Excellent schools with courses varying in length from six months to two years, exist very generally in these countries, the laws of England and Denmark being particularly fine, and conspicuous for the class of women who enter the field."[18] As a result of midwifery training in most European countries, the maternal and infant death rates in Europe had remarkably decreased. Sweden, Norway, and Italy had the lowest rates. For example, in 1910, in Sweden, only one mother died out of every 430 babies born alive. In contrast, one mother died for every 154 live births in the United States.[19]

European countries, such as Finland, had schools for training midwives as early as the seventeenth century. Their first Finish teacher of midwifery was Dr. John von Hoorn, who received his obstetrical training at the famous Hôtel-Dieu in Paris and wrote the first textbook on midwifery, published in 1697. By the nineteenth century, the number of trained midwives greatly increased and the importance of their work toward the health of the population was widely recognized. Although there were obstacles to overcome, Finnish midwives have continued to practice autonomously into the twentieth century.[20]

France established a school in 1757 and a second in 1800. By the nineteenth century, French laws authorized three levels of obstetric practitioners—physicians, health officers, and midwives. French midwives had their own organization by 1913. From these early times and into the twentieth century, French midwives have continued to practice autonomously in private homes and under medical oversight in hospital births.[21]

Midwives in the Netherlands had long been accepted. The Dutch were more tolerant of new ideas than other countries and readily supported education for midwives. Books written by the famous French midwife, Louise Bourgeois, and German midwife, Justine Siegemundin, were translated by Dutch surgeons for the benefit of midwives. However, as obstetrics advanced in the nineteenth century, the academic doctors and obstetric surgeons began to infringe on the midwives' territory. But the Dutch midwives were able to take a firm stand against the medicalization of childbirth. The government, siding with the midwives, passed a law in 1865, which clearly defined the roles of the three practicing groups—the "doctors medecinae" (academic physician), the "obstetric surgeons," and the midwives—all of whom were recognized for their unique roles. The midwives continued to practice autonomously in normal births in private homes and hospitals.[22]

German midwives were also highly trained, regulated, and recognized as superior to most American doctors.[23] Throughout western Europe, trained midwives learned and practiced aseptic care, safe methods, and recognized early signs of problems necessitating medical intervention. Yet in America, physicians didn't acknowledge that there was a connection between trained midwives and a decline in maternal and infant mortality in other countries. Noyes declared, "Midwives asserted themselves against kings," but in America, midwives were "pushed into the background of the medical profession even though statistics have shown that midwives inflicted less birth injuries than medical doctors."[24] European midwives had the advantages of education, organization, and governmental sanctions to overcome obstacles from the medical establishment and they prevailed. American midwives didn't have these advantages.

At the turn of the twentieth century in America, there were no training programs for midwives until 1911, when Bellevue opened its school. For fifty years prior to 1912 attempts were made by states to control, restrict, or even abolish midwives across the United States. Laws had been framed and passed, but had not been systematically enforced. A report from the Child Hygiene Bureau of New York City, where statistics were gathered from thirty-three states, showed that by 1912, only thirteen states had laws regulating midwives. However, by this time the state of Massachusetts had banned midwives altogether. Nevertheless, midwives' signatures appeared on birth certificates, indicating that many midwives still continued to practice there.[25]

American physicians began an active campaign to eliminate midwives. The major dispute between obstetric specialists and proponents of midwifery education reached its height between 1910 and 1935. The obstetric specialists believed that better-trained physicians should replace the midwives, even though there were so few physicians qualified to do this and it would take years to accomplish the necessary training. Doctors argued that visiting nurses and free clinics could replace the other services traditionally performed by midwives after the baby was born.[26] What doctors didn't accept was that foreign-born women and their husbands didn't want male birth attendants nor could they afford their fees.

The standard midwife fee in 1917 was $7 to $10 for a home birth, including daily visits for at least five days. In contrast, physicians charged from $10 to $30 and only attended the birth.[27] Proponents for training of midwives believed that with education, midwives would be safe practitioners and would learn to differentiate between normal and abnormal births and, therefore, know when to call in the specialist, all of which would significantly reduce the mortality rates as it did in other countries.[28]

Midwives were still attending about fifty percent of births across the country by the end of the first decade of the twentieth century. These estimates varied by city. For example, about forty-two percent of midwife-attended births were reported in New York City, seventy-five percent in St. Louis, and eighty-two percent in Chicago. In 1911, Dr. Thomas Darlington, commissioner of health in New York City, wrote about the value of midwives. "For economic and traditional reasons, she will continue to be in demand; she cannot be eliminated.... She is a 'deeply rooted, world-old tradition.'"[29] Although Darlington also disparaged midwives as being dirty and ignorant, he realized they were an economic necessity and so he advocated for their training.

Dr. J. Whitridge Williams, professor of obstetrics at Johns Hopkins University in Baltimore, conducted a study in 1912 to address the high mortality rates. He sent questionnaires to professors in 120 medical schools to investigate the status of obstetric training in medical education. His premise was that the medical community had "failed to train practitioners competent to meet the emergencies of obstetrical practice."[30] Forty-three professors responded. After analyzing the responses, Williams concluded that many professors were themselves inadequately prepared to assist in childbirth, many were not competent to deal with obstetric emergencies, and that the teaching equipment was inadequate. A large number of respondents admitted that the average practitioner wasn't adequately trained.

Williams concluded that many a practitioner "may do his patients as much harm as the much-maligned midwife.... Each student on an average has an opportunity to see only one woman delivered, which is manifestly inadequate ... only nine [schools] have anything like adequate clinical material for the instruction of their students."[31]

Williams also addressed the "midwife problem" in his investigation. Eighteen respondents advocated regulation and education of midwives and fourteen recommended abolition of the midwives. One group regarded midwifery education as hopeless and another held that "they [midwives] may be entirely done away with by educating the laity, by extending lying-in charities, and by supplying better doctors and cheaper nurses."[32] These attitudes reflected men's bitter animosity toward the midwives and toward women in general. Williams blamed the medical community for failure to more adequately train physicians in the field of obstetrics. Therefore, he felt physicians were partly responsible for the unnecessary maternal and infant deaths and injuries.

Williams's solution to the problems was to replace the midwives with adequately trained ordinary physicians to manage normal births and specialists to manage abnormal cases. A flood of articles about the midwife problem appeared in professional literature. The physicians who wrote these articles attempted to convince other physicians that childbirth was pathological, encouraging them to intervene unnecessarily. Unfortunately, the ordinary doctors still had little skill in applying these dangerous methods.

The advantages of physician-attended childbirth and hospital births were also promoted in the popular literature. Articles appeared in women's popular magazines promoting the importance of pregnant women first consulting with their physicians about their concerns regarding pregnancy and childbirth. Doctors even cautioned women against consulting with other women "for fear of being exposed to 'old wives' tales."[33] Many women were influenced by this propaganda because they had long been afraid of dying in childbirth.

There were those physicians who advocated outright abolition and others who held that midwives should continue to practice, but under regulation and supervision. There were also a group who believed that education would elevate the midwife's role as a safe and competent practitioner, as had been achieved in other countries. In 1917, the president of the AMA criticized his colleagues for their animosity toward the midwives. He praised midwives, saying that reports showed that midwives were more likely to follow regulations, such as applying silver nitrate drops in the eyes of newborn babies. He indicated that doctors should be proud of midwives.[34]

Dr. Charles Ziegler, professor of obstetrics at the University of Pittsburgh, was among the group who adamantly opposed midwifery education and advocated abolition of midwives. He reasoned that the "great danger lies in the possibility of attempting to educate the midwife and in licensing her to practice midwifery, giving her, therefore, a legal status which later cannot perhaps be altered."[35] Ziegler made other scathing remarks about midwives. "If she becomes a fixed element..., we may never be able to get rid of her ... [she is] a menace to the health of the community, an unnecessary evil and a nuisance." Ziegler and his colleagues further propagated the view that birth was dangerous and needed intervention. He didn't believe that obstetrics could be practiced by "standing by while natural forces of labor complete the act as best they may."[36] "Standing by" is precisely how normal childbirth should be managed. But since the eighteenth century, doctors were taught "to do something."

Dr. Ziegler and others believed that women should give birth in hospitals. Ziegler also believed that standards should be set, stipulating who should and who should not practice. He wanted the same kind of standards in obstetrics that were held in the surgical specialty. He wrote, "Obstetrics is a brand of surgery; its successful practice is dependent upon surgical principles and surgical technique. The obstetricians of the country are the family doctors and the midwives, who know nothing about surgery."[37]

In addition to economic and status-seeking motives, obstetricians also competed with the midwives for their poor clientele, whom they needed for clinical practice. Zeigler asserted, "Another very pertinent objection to the midwife is that she has charge of fifty percent of all the obstetric material of the country without contributing anything to our knowledge of the subject."[38] This statement obviously shows how men degraded women by referring to them as "material"!

It is interesting that Dr. J. Whitridge Williams had complained about the lack of clinical experience of American medical students compared to European midwives who were required to attend at least twenty births under careful supervision.[39] At the same time, he never acknowledged that in those countries there were far fewer maternal and infant deaths and injuries than there were in the United States. He was still adamant about getting rid of the midwives in America, even though the system worked in other countries.

Clara D. Noyes strongly advocated against abolishing midwives and urged that they be educated, supervised, and regulated. She reasoned that it would take years to accomplish what physicians wanted, to substitute midwives with well-trained physicians, visiting obstetric nurses, free clinics, and enough hospitals. She refuted the doctors' fears that trained midwives would invalidate their profession. Noyes pointed out that trained English midwives were more likely to quickly recognize problems and seek obstetrical assistance early on. In this situation, there would be a greater demand for obstetrical services.[40] Many southern physicians also saw the value of midwifery education. There was a strong need for midwives among the rural poor, immigrants, and blacks in the southern parts of the country and those in other remote areas, such as Appalachia. There weren't enough physicians in these areas and many didn't want to attend poor women.

The high infant and maternal mortality rates and the horrible living conditions in poor, urban, crowded neighborhoods continued to be menacing problems. Something needed to be done. The pioneering leaders in social reform measures were women. A nurse, Lillian D. Wald, who was graduated from the New York Hospital, School of Nursing in 1891, experienced the horrible living conditions in the slums of New York City firsthand. On one occasion, while teaching a group of mothers in a tenement building, a young child sought help for her mother who was giving birth unattended. Wald set forth to change this picture. In 1893, Wald and her classmate, Mary Brewster, created the Henry Street Settlement House in New York City to provide nursing and social services for the indigent. This was the beginning of public health nursing in America.[41]

Public interest in child health led to the first White House Conference on Child Welfare in 1910 and two years later the Federal Children's Bureau was created. In addition to reporting all matters pertaining to child welfare, the Bureau was charged with reporting the incidence of maternal and infant deaths.[42] Dr. Josephine Baker testified for appropriation of funds. During one testimony, Baker related that a doctor from New England argued against funding, declaring, "We oppose this bill because, if you are going to save the lives of all these women and children at public expense, what inducement will there be for young men to study medicine?" The chair of the committee, Senator Sheppard, responded, "you surely don't mean that you want women and children to die unnecessarily or live in constant danger of sickness so there will be something for young doctors to do?"[43]

The first investigations conducted by the newly established Federal Children's Bureau brought to light the appalling infant death rates of 124 deaths for every one thousand live births. So the bureau formulated a plan in 1917 to initiate a program of care for pregnant women, whereby public health nurses would provide prenatal care and instruction.[44] This endeavor was on target with Baker's philosophy that healthy mothers would have healthy babies. However, funds were needed for this undertaking. So the chief of the Children's Bureau, Julia Lothrop, proposed federal aid, which led to passage of the Sheppard-Towner Act of 1921. It was with these funds that hundreds of nurses were employed to make home visits to pregnant women and new mothers. Passage of this act also enabled the establishment of health centers for pregnant women, infants, and preschool children.[45]

The Federal Children's Bureau also surveyed midwifery practice. In these early years, midwives were providing the majority of maternity care. Results from the survey showed that forty-five thousand untrained midwives were practicing. The Bureau set a priority to train these granny midwives. The Sheppard-Towner Act provided funds for each state to set up its own plan to improve maternal and child health care. New York City took the lead by establishing the Maternity Center Association in

1918, for the purpose of providing maternity care and instruction. In light of the excellent records of other countries where trained midwives attended most births, the Maternity Center Association sought to attain similar results in America.[46]

The reality was that the majority of physicians in the States weren't ready to take over the practice of midwifery. America didn't have the organized system that most European countries had, where well-trained midwives practiced under the supervision of competent obstetric specialists. Still in the 1920s, most American physicians were improperly trained and not very safe. As late as 1927, twelve states reported 2,652 maternal deaths (64.7 deaths per ten thousand live births). The causes of these deaths ranged from puerperal fever, toxemia, and operative deliveries, such as using forceps, mechanical dilation of the cervix, episiotomy, and cesarean delivery.[47] Doctors were causing these injuries, because they were the only ones allowed to use instruments or perform surgical procedures.

Although obstetrics was gaining status, midwives were still attending about half of the births across the country, fewer in urban areas, but just about all births in remote rural areas where there were few, if any, physicians. The idea of training nurses to be midwives came into focus with the establishment of the Frontier Nursing Service, founded by Mary Breckinridge in 1925. Breckinridge was a nurse who was graduated from the St. Luke's Hospital in New York City in 1910.[48] She studied public health nursing in the slums of Boston and worked for the Red Cross in Europe following World War I, where she was able to observe the excellent maternity care provided by French and English midwives. When she returned to the states in 1923, she worked for the Kentucky Health Department in Leslie County in the Appalachian mountains.[49]

There weren't any doctors practicing in these mountains, where the granny midwives had been practicing for centuries under medieval conditions. Breckinridge saw the need for superior midwifery services in the county, such as she had witnessed in England, France, New Zealand, and Australia. She traveled back to England for midwifery training and upon completing her courses, became certified by the Central Midwives' Board in 1925.[50] Breckinridge put her plan into action by recruiting trained midwives from England, since there were so few in the States. Because there were no roads, midwives traveled by horseback over mountains in wind, rain, or snow, to the eight districts in Leslie County, about seventy-eight square miles, to attend women in childbirth. These midwives also provided education and care to pregnant women and new mothers.[51] This project proved to be successful in lowering maternal and infant death rates. It also proved how competent well-trained nurse-midwives were in reaching out to this desolate and needy population.

The federal government finally saw the value of trained midwives. A report by a 1925 White House Conference on Child Health and Protection concluded that "untrained midwives approach, and trained midwives surpass, the record of physicians in normal deliveries."[52] Soon other states initiated some form of education for midwives.

Efforts were made to train the granny midwives in other areas of the country. There were documents in the Archives Honor Roll Files that paid tribute to the pioneers. Lalla Mary Goggans, a nursing consultant with the Children's Bureau, who worked with the Florida granny midwives, wrote a tribute to them. She wrote, "They could not read or write, yet they did the very best they could.... They walked many miles to attend training sessions, received little or no money for delivering so many babies ... and while I'm sure that many babies were delivered into hands that were not sterile, there's one thing I'm sure of, and that is that every baby was received into loving hands."[53]

Midwives were still very much in demand, as they continued to struggle to keep their vocation alive, while opponents of midwifery practice and midwifery education kept up their fight. Some physicians began to advocate hospital births as being safer than home births. This proposition was another strike against midwives, which would surely diminish their numbers. Abraham Flexnor, in his famous 1910 report, declared that hospitals were crucial to modern scientific medical education.

Another powerful and staunch opponent of midwifery and advocate for hospital births was Dr. Joseph B. DeLee, a prominent obstetrician and professor of obstetrics and gynecology at the University of Chicago and chair of obstetrics at Northwestern University. DeLee believed that childbirth was a pathological condition, which only physicians were qualified to manage. In a report to an Illinois sub-committee on prevention of infant mortality, DeLee stated, "If a delivery requires so little brains and skill that a midwife can conduct it, there is no place for him [physician]."[54]

In addition to writing and publishing medical and nursing textbooks, DeLee was most noted for his paper, written in 1920, advocating his prophylactic forceps operation. His protocol specified the medical conduct of labor and birth from the time a woman entered the hospital until after the birth of her child. He wrote that his operation was more than "routine delivery of the child in head presentation ... it is a rounded technique for the conduct of the whole labor, with the defined purpose of relieving pain, supplementing and anticipating the efforts of nature, reducing the hemorrhage, and preventing and repairing damage."[55] DeLee acknowledged that his routine interfered with nature and would be unjustifiable in unskilled hands. But his routine did become the model of how childbirth was managed whether in the hands of skilled or unskilled physicians.

His routine began with giving the woman medication to kill the pain of labor when her cervix was only two or three centimeters dilated. (This is the very beginning of true labor, when pain is at a minimum.) The prescribed medication and dosage was ⅙ of a grain of morphine and ¹⁄₂₀₀ of a grain of scopolamine and to repeat scopolamine, ¹⁄₄₀₀ in an hour and again in two hours. He then advised to give the woman gas (anesthesia) during the delivery. DeLee explained that when the baby's head rested on the perineum, an episiotomy should be performed, and forceps be applied to the baby's head to assist delivery. Finally, Pituitrin is to be administered to contract the uterus and the episiotomy incision is sutured.[56] (When birth was not interfered with, the baby was put to breast immediately and the mother's natural hormone, pitocin, was released in her circulation to contract her uterus naturally, and so prevent bleeding.)

The type and amount of medication that DeLee recommended was enough to knock the woman out for many hours, or even days, and what was worse was the dangerous effects on the newborn baby. The episiotomy is an incision cutting the perineum (pelvic floor) from the vagina almost to the rectum. When obstetricians sutured the incision, they often added some extra stitches "for the husband." The gas he spoke of was either nitrous oxide or ether, anesthetic agents that caused the mother to be totally unconscious during the birth and for hours after the birth.

What DeLee's routine accomplished was to remove the woman from taking part in her own baby's birth. No one told the woman about these effects. Her baby was also drugged because these medications readily cross the placenta. Forceps continued to be dangerous, particularly in the hands of unskilled practitioners. The perineal incision left women in pain for days, weeks, or even months afterward. Intercourse became a painful experience. "Routine" hospital care didn't end with the birth. The mother didn't see or hold her baby for hours, sometimes not until the next day, and then only at feeding time, which was about every four daytime hours. Breastfeeding was discouraged. The women were at the mercy of sterile hospital routines until they went home with their new little strangers.

As more women gave birth in hospitals, the number of practicing midwives declined. The number of hospital births increased, from five percent in 1900, to thirty percent by 1921.[57] There were many middle- and upper-class women who opted for hospital births. The medical profession convinced women that hospitals were safer places than their homes to give birth. Women were also attracted by the promise of pain-free childbirth and a short vacation from the responsibilities of home and their other children. However, childbirth in hospitals did not turn out to be the panacea that women thought it would be. Although they didn't realize it at the time, in their own homes women were in control; in the hospital they lost all autonomy.

DeLee's protocol was widely accepted by obstetricians in the years that followed. His protocol justified the need to routinize obstetric care in one central facility, which could only be in hospitals. Hospitals also supplied available clinical material. DeLee justified his routine by proclaiming that "only a small minority of women escape damage during labor, while four percent of babies are killed and a large indeterminable number are more or less injured by the direct action of the natural process itself."[58] DeLee's routine certainly couldn't be conducted in the home. In hospitals, physicians reigned and childbirth became medicalized. Childbirth no longer resembled the natural ways of the past.

Hospitals didn't turn out to be the safe haven that obstetricians had proclaimed. In 1925, Dr. Matthias Nicoll, Commissioner of Health of the State of New York, concerned about the 3,000 deaths in that year in the state of New York, sent questionnaires to physicians, in whose practices such deaths had occurred, and to various hospitals. A preliminary analysis of 696 replies revealed that of the 696 cases reported, 74 percent of these women gave birth in hospitals and about half of these women died. The other 26 percent delivered in their homes and later died in hospitals. Dr. Nicoll stated that 16 women were attended by midwives and of these, only one died. The attending midwife was later exonerated.[59] Dr. Nicoll did see the value of midwives and supported education for them.

Dr. Nicoll contended that "lack of reduction on maternal deaths was due in a large degree to bad obstetric procedures. ... there has arisen of late years a school of meddlesome obstetrics founded on the practice and teaching of certain unquestionable skilled obstetricians." (He possibly was referring to DeLee and his followers.) Nicoll added, "These men have little or no regard for the processes of parturition which nature has perfected and which cannot be improved upon in a vast majority of cases."[60]

The high maternal death rates continued into the 1930s. In 1915, the maternal mortality rate was 60.8 per ten thousand live births and actually increased to 67.3 in 1930. Meddlesome, unskilled obstetric interference and technology increased the risk of harm to both mothers and infants, including the risks of infections, overdosing, and mutilation from forceps.[61] The White House Conference on Child Health reported in 1933 that there was no decline in the maternal mortality since 1915 despite the increase in hospital births, the use of aseptic techniques, and the initiation of prenatal care.[62]

Between 1930 and 1933, an extensive investigation into every maternal death in New York City was conducted by the New York Academy of Medicine. The results were a scathing indictment of obstetric practice. Sixty-one percent of the deaths were due to the fault of the physician, 36.7 percent were due to patient problems, and only 2.2 percent were due to the fault of the midwife. The first reaction of both general practitioners and obstetricians was indignation, reminiscent of Oliver Wendell Holmes's conclusions in the cause of puerperal fever.[63]

Women sought the sanctuary of hospitals because they believed that they would be safer there than in their own homes. But women, once admitted to hospitals, lost their social, supportive network. They thought nurses would fill this role, but it didn't happen. The nurses were too busy following doctors' orders, monitoring their patients, assisting the doctor during examinations, preparing the woman for birth, and assisting the doctor during the delivery. Nurses were also responsible for caring for the baby and mother immediately after birth, cleaning the rooms, cleaning and sterilizing the instruments and equipment, setting up for the next case, and more. The nurses didn't have time to provide comfort or tender loving care to their patients. Medication was the answer to these needs.

When a woman entered the doors to the hospital, she entered a sterile world foreign to her and ruled by men. She left anything or anyone familiar and dear to her at home. She no longer had a say in her own care. She no longer birthed her baby; it was delivered. In hospitals, women were at the mercy of the hospital routine and rules. Women left their dignity at the doorstep. As soon as they entered the maternity unit, they were shaven in their most private parts, their bowels were purged; they were drugged, kept in beds with side rails up, and then left alone among strangers. They could no longer get up at will, move about, or drink or eat if hungry or thirsty. They had no choices in the management of their own births.

Hospital births climbed in the 1930s. Prior to 1920, women who gave birth in hospitals were primarily single or indigent. By 1936, thirty-seven percent of women had hospital births. This number increased to fifty-five percent by 1940 and ninety percent by 1951.[64] During the 1930s, a greater number of women living in the larger cities gave birth in hospitals. Hattie Hemschemeyer, director of the Maternity Center Association's School for Midwifery, estimated that ninety-five percent of maternity patients were cared for in hospitals in New York City by 1939.[65] Hospital insurance became available after the depression. Blue

Cross emerged in the 1930s, followed by other private insurance in the 1940s, so that more women were able to afford hospital births. The expansion of hospitals contributed to the demise of midwives, who were not given hospital privileges. However, many women, particularly those living in remote rural areas, had no access to doctors or hospitals, so were still able to remain at home to birth their babies. There were still women who held to their traditional ways, preferring midwives and having their babies at home, while others had been convinced that hospitals were safer. However, as mentioned before, hospitals weren't safer. As it turned out, hospitals were sterile, lonely, and controlling.

Hospital ways were certainly different from birthing in the comforts of one's home and physicians' ways were quite different from those of midwives. Midwives continued their struggle to survive and many wanted further training. The idea of trained nurse-midwives was beginning to materialize. A giant step in this direction was the establishment of the Maternity Center Association's midwifery school in 1931. The school needed qualified faculty. So the center sought the help of the Frontier Nursing Service, who sent Rose McNaught, a nurse-midwife who had trained in England. About twelve nurse-midwives graduated each year in the first few years of the school's existence.[66]

Some graduates traveled to the southern states to train and supervise granny midwives. One graduate, Mrs. Sara English, who resided in Kentucky, wrote to Miss Hattie Hemschemeyer, saying she had "delivered 1,400 babies, by lamplight, by candlelight, by sunlight, and on one occasion by moonlight, traveling by horseback over roads where it seemed the foot of man had never been." She added, "I never lost a mother, never had one with childbed fever."[67]

Although there was growing interest in the idea of the nurse-midwife, her role emerged on a different scale from that of the traditional or "granny" midwife. The traditional midwives worked for themselves and performed their duties independently. Nurse-midwives from the Association practiced under the supervision of physicians. The principles laid down by the new breed of nurse-midwives, who were employed by the Maternity Center Association, were: (1) patients were carefully selected for midwifery care after an initial medical exam; (2) abnormal patients were referred to hospitals under a physician's care; and (3) physician and midwife functions were clearly defined. The physician also designated what the midwife was allowed or not allowed to do in the care of her patients.[68]

The nurse-midwives gained valuable knowledge and were excellent practitioners, but they lost the autonomy enjoyed by their predecessors. In other areas of the country, such as in the mountains of Kentucky,

nurse-midwives and "granny" midwives continued to function independently because there were so few, if any, physicians who practiced obstetrics.

The nurse-midwives who graduated from midwifery schools were
already trained and registered nurses and had some years of nursing practice, particularly in public health. These nurse-midwives proved their
worth time and again. America borrowed the system of both medical and
nursing education from England and other continental schools, "but
never their system of training and utilizing the services of the midwife."[69]

Regardless of the successes of the nurse-midwifery schools and efforts
to train the grannies, midwives were losing their battle. Fewer and fewer
were practicing, mainly because of the expansion of hospitals and the
increasing number of physicians specializing in obstetrics. Also, the
decline in immigration during and after World War I contributed to the
decline in the number of midwives practicing.

In New York City alone, the 1,700 practicing midwives who attended
forty thousand births (thirty percent of all live births) in 1919, dropped
to 1,200 midwives attending only twelve percent of the births in 1929.
By 1939, their numbers decreased to three hundred and they attended
only two percent of all live births. The Bellevue School of Midwifery
closed its doors in 1932 because of the diminishing number of midwifery
students and because maternity care was moving fast from the home to
the hospital.[70]

The grand era of the granny midwives ended by the 1940s. They were
replaced by physicians who conducted childbirth as a medical affair. The
unrelenting hostility of the medical profession led to "the loss of a collective lineage of midwifery wisdom and lore" as laws in state after state
banned the lay midwives from practice.[71] The traditional midwives were
cast aside as dirty, ignorant, and incompetent and they were blamed for
the high maternal and infant mortality rates. But by far, midwives sur-
passed physicians in practical experience, skill without unnecessary intervention, patience, caring, and service that went far beyond just assisting
at birth.

The first challenge to medicalized childbirth came from Dr. Grantly
Dick-Read, who was born in England in 1890, received his medical degree
in 1912, and began his internship at the London Hospital, situated in the
heart of London's East End slums. He told the story about the cold and
rainy night in 1913, when he was called to attend a woman in labor, of
how he plowed through mud and rain on his bicycle at three o'clock in
the morning to find his patient covered only with sacks. He had brought
his own soap and a towel and a neighbor assisted him by bringing in a
jug of water and a basin. Dick-Read described this birth as peaceful and

the baby was born without fuss or noise. He had offered the woman chloroform, but she had refused. He was puzzled by her refusal and asked her why. The woman responded, "It didn't hurt. It wasn't meant to, was it, doctor?"[72]

Dick-Read grew up on a farm, loved animals and, being a naturalist, perceived childbirth as a natural life event. He witnessed many women who gave birth in the most natural way without apparent pain, particularly those he observed on the battlefields during World War I. But he also observed women who did experience severe labor pain and pondered why some women seemed to suffer more than others. After returning from service in 1918, he began to investigate the role that emotions played on the natural function of birth and concluded that fear caused the body to tense. He explained that tension "influences the muscles that close the womb and thus delay the progress of labor and create pain."[73]

Dick-Read witnessed many cases in which a state of calmness was the key to natural, and basically, painless childbirth. He kept notes, which, by 1919 at the age of thirty, he gathered into a manuscript, but received negative comments from his colleagues. However, Dick-Read's rewards came from his patients, whom he taught techniques of relaxation. Working from his manuscript, he finally completed his first book, *Natural Childbirth*, in 1930, published in 1933. After initial favorable reactions, he was charged with unprofessional conduct and was anonymously reported to the General Medical Council for advocating cruelty to women. Dick-Read was devastated by the reactions, but slowly his practice rebounded and he began receiving invitations to give lectures. After his book reached the United States, Dr. Joseph B. DeLee read it and wrote in 1938, "It will take several thousand generations before we can train women back to the state where Grantly Dick-Read speaks of as 'natural childbirth.'"[74]

Nevertheless, Dick-Read began writing his second book in 1939, but his views were disregarded by the majority of physicians. Discouraged, he hid it in a corner of his library; but it was later found by his wife, who encouraged him to finish it. *The Revelation of Childbirth* was published in England in 1942, and then in the United States in 1944 under a new title, *Childbirth without Fear*.[75] He won the adulation from women who wanted to take part in their own birth experience and received numerous letters from women thanking him for making their beautiful births possible.

Grantly Dick-Read had won the hearts of women, but not the hearts of medical men. Physicians wouldn't accept his views because they weren't willing to give back any control to their patients. At one meeting Dick-Read attended in New York, one obstetrician spoke out that women should be "kept in ignorance of the truth of childbirth, so that they would be unquestionably submissive to the recommendations and demands of the orthodox obstetric profession." Another obstetrician actually bragged that seventy-five percent of his patients were delivered by instruments and eighty-five to ninety percent were surgically or medically induced "at a time convenient to all concerned."[76] In response to Dick-Read's question concerning the fact that of the children who were born disabled, seventy percent of these disabilities were due to obstetric interference, a doctor responded that those children were the concern of pediatrics, not of obstetrics.[77] It is uncertain how much damage was inflicted upon the newborn babies and their mothers.

Grantly Dick-Read reached many women who wanted to have more natural births. While reading *Childbirth without Fear* in 1958, pregnant with my first child, I wasn't fearful and didn't have a painful labor. This is not to say that labor isn't painful. The experience of childbirth is indeed unique with every woman and with every birth. However, manipulations of natural births and absence of adequate support systems do contribute to more painful birth experiences.

Grantly Dick-Read became known as the father of natural childbirth. He believed childbirth to be a natural phenomenon, unnatural only if there were serious problems during labor or birth, or when men meddled when it was unnecessary.

By the middle of the twentieth century, childbirth was purely a medical event. The medical model of managing childbirth works against the laws of nature, but it worked for the convenience of obstetricians and gave them the power they had long sought. The first challenge to the medical model came from Dr. Grantly Dick-Read, whose message reached many women. He was a hero in an era when women had little choice in giving birth. Some women began to question the medicalization of childbirth, wanting more control of their own birth experience. During the next half of the twentieth century, women began to rebel against the medical ways. They wanted choices, as did their ancestors, before physicians made childbirth a medical affair.

CHAPTER 10

The Second Half of the Twentieth Century: Technology-Managed Childbirth

by Edna Quinn

It was 1961. Jan was twenty-two years old, happily married, and thrilled with her first pregnancy. It was fun to get together with her friends and trade maternity clothes and news, but it never occurred to any of them to read anything about pregnancy or attend childbirth classes. Jan was going to an obstetrician in Boston, about an hour away from home. He was very nice, but "rigid" and "fanatical about weight gain." To keep her weight down, Jan would "starve" herself for two days before each prenatal visit, and on the way home, she would treat herself to two ice cream sundaes!

After an uneventful pregnancy, Jan went into labor on a Friday night about midnight. She went to the maternity hospital a few hours later, and her husband, who was not allowed to go upstairs with her, dropped her off at the door. She was admitted to a labor ward, where there were about ten other women in labor, and was shaved and given an enema. By this time, her contractions stopped. On Saturday morning, an intravenous Pitocin drip was started. Soon contractions began and they were painful. She became uneasy when she heard other women screaming or swearing in labor. Six nursing students came into the room with their instructor, who asked if the students could feel her stomach when she had a contraction. Suddenly all hands were upon her and they were freezing cold. That was too much—Jan politely told them to get out. When her doctor's nurse came in and asked if she would like to go to a private room and have a private nurse, she readily agreed. (Later, her husband would be shocked by the bill.) At

*some point, she was given scopolamine and her father, who was a min-
ister, was allowed to be with her. She remembers very little after that,
except her father saying, "What? What?" She was taken to the delivery room (which was just like an operating room) on Sunday morning. After getting spinal anesthesia, she remembers all the strangers
in masks around her yelling "Push, push, push," and, afterwards,
clapping and yelling, "It's a boy!" She didn't see her baby until that
evening and her husband came during visiting hours and could only
look at the baby through the nursery window. Jan was kept in bed
until the third day. Breastfeeding was a terrible experience on a strict
schedule—nurses who were supposed to help were very impatient. Jan
was discharged on the tenth day. After trying to breastfeed for two
weeks, she gave up.[1]*

In the second half of the twentieth century, childbirth in America
was transformed by scientific, political, and social developments that created fifty years of dramatic change. Great battles were fought and gains
were made for family-centered/woman-centered childbirth, but the scene
shifted constantly, and ground gained yesterday was often lost.

The most persistent and ongoing influence on childbirth was the
growth of new technologies and procedures in obstetrical care. Since the
1960s, when the Apollo space program landed over a dozen men on the
moon, there have been no limits to America's faith in technology and
love affair with science. In the early fifties, childbirth was firmly
entrenched in the hospital, with physicians in charge of birth. Women in
the childbearing years were a full generation removed from midwifery
and home birth. Midwives were all but obsolete and alternatives to the
medical model were rare.

In the decades that followed, labor management protocols included
shaving the woman's pubic hair, administering an enema on admission,
intravenous infusion during labor while withholding food and liquids by
mouth, artificial rupture of membranes, the use of technological equipment, drugs for pain and to stimulate labor, episiotomy, and use of forceps to deliver the baby. It was not infrequent that these interventions
led to other interventions and operative births. In most hospitals, the rule
of nothing to eat or drink during labor, "in case" the patient needs an
emergency cesarean section, still prevails. In some settings, women in
labor were required to lie flat, despite the commonsense understanding
(and later research) that the upright position allows gravity to throw the
uterus forward and straighten the longitudinal axis of the birth canal,
enhancing the descent of the fetal head.[2] Women's confidence in their ability to give birth without medical interventions was seriously undermined

and women experienced helplessness in matters of self-care, as routine hospital procedures and policies gave little support to their belief in birth as a normal event.

In 1954, Dr. Emanuel Friedman plotted the average length of normal labor. Friedman defined the onset of normal labor as the time when a woman perceived that true labor began. False contractions, referred to as Braxton Hicks, do occur prior to the onset of true labor to prepare the uterus for the real thing and may be confused with the onset of true labor, which occurs when the cervix begins to shorten and dilate. Friedman concluded that in primiparous women (those having their first baby), the first stage of labor—ending with complete dilation (measured by the human hand at ten centimeters)—lasts about twelve hours. The second stage (pushing or birthing stage)—from ten centimeters dilatation until the birth of the baby—lasts about two hours, on the average.[3] The first stage of labor is further divided into two phases: first phase (early or latent) lasts longer than the second (active) phase and is said to end when the cervix dilates to 3.5 centimeters; then the second, more active phase begins and lasts until dilation is complete.

From his research of over one hundred women expecting their first child, "who presented themselves sufficiently early in their labors to permit adequate study," Friedman established that the latent phase lasts about an average of eight hours and the active phase lasts about an average of 4.4 hours. Friedman designed a curve, known as the "Friedman's curve," which became the hallmark for determining when labor was not progressing well. Terms used to diagnose this problem were dysfunctional labor, failure to progress, or uterine inertia. This determination was an indication to intervene, either by artificially rupturing the woman's membranes or/and administering oxytocin to stimulate labor. If it was believed that the baby could not be delivered vaginally, a cesarean birth would be indicated.

Friedman's curve defined normal labor with a variable range. Unfortunately, it was often applied as a rule, rather than a guideline, by some obstetricians eager to move labor along at a faster pace. Earlier in history, when there was no such thing as an average length of labor, experienced midwives recognized when there was trouble, but gave nature a fighting chance.

Medical technology exploded during the second part of the twentieth century. New technological advances in obstetrics included fetal diagnostic devices, such as ultrasound, amniocentesis, and electronic fetal monitoring. These also became institutionalized and routinely accepted practices. While often helpful and even life-saving, they contributed to the increased medicalization of normal childbirth and dramatically increased the cost of maternity care.

In the late 1950s, ultrasound became a useful diagnostic tool in obstetrics. It is sound that is pitched higher than the human ear can hear. Directed into the body, it produces echoes from points where different body tissues meet.[4] Ultrasound provides pictures of the fetus in the uterus. It became standard practice to use ultrasound scanning to determine gestational age and due date, to determine if there were twins or multiple pregnancy, and to localize the placenta. Early in pregnancy, ultrasound can provide absolute proof of pregnancy. Later scanning can determine if the fetus is growing normally or if abnormalities are present. It became common to do one or two scans during pregnancy, including one at approximately eighteen weeks, when abnormalities, such as nervous system defects (brain and spinal cord) and defects in the heart or kidneys, can be diagnosed. High-risk mothers—those with heart or kidney disease, high blood pressure, or diabetes, women who have had problems in previous pregnancies, or women who are bleeding in pregnancy—have more frequent testing to be sure the fetus is growing well and not in danger.

Although there is no evidence to indicate that the use of ultrasound is harmful, it has not been definitely proven to be safe, either. Doctors consider the risk of serious problems in pregnancy, if undetected, outweigh any risks associated with ultrasound, but opponents would like more evidence that its use is indeed safe.

Amniocentesis is an important prenatal diagnostic test, usually performed about the sixteenth week of pregnancy or earlier to evaluate an abnormal ultrasound or abnormal alphafetoprotein level (AFP test from a sample of the mother's blood), indicating possible neural tube defects, such as spina bifida, risk of Down's syndrome, and other defects. Amniocentesis involves using ultrasound to locate the placenta, fetus, and a "pocket" of amniotic fluid. A needle is inserted through the abdomen and uterus (local anesthesia is used) into the amniotic sac (avoiding the placenta and fetus) and a small amount of fluid is withdrawn for analysis. Results take four to six weeks. Because there is risk of miscarriage, informed consent is vital. The risk has to be weighed statistically against the potential benefits. For instance, a younger woman has a one in two thousandths chance of having a baby with Down's syndrome, but the chance of miscarriage after amniocentesis is one in two hundred. Her risk of having a Down's baby at 41 years increases to one in twelve. If she has strong reservations about terminating her pregnancy, regardless of the severity of the defect, she may elect not to have the amniocentesis, but there is considerable pressure for her to terminate.

In the 1970s, electronic fetal monitoring (EFM) became a popular means of detecting danger to the fetus in high-risk patients. EFM provides a continuous recording of the fetal heart rate via ultrasonic waves.

During labor, it can detect significant decreases in fetal heart rate or heart rate patterns that may signal impending complications associated with inadequate blood flow to the fetus. EFM has replaced the nurse's/nurse-midwife's standard technique of monitoring contractions by placing her hand on the abdomen and listening to the fetal heart with the fetoscope, a modified stethoscope with a metal headband to enhance the sound of fetal heart tones. The problem with using the fetoscope is the difficulty in hearing fetal heart tones during a uterine contraction. However, in 1991 the American College of Obstetricians and Gynecologists (ACOG) conceded that electronic fetal monitoring in low-risk women yielded no better results than the fetoscope.[5]

Fetal monitoring can be either external or internal. In the external mode, bands are placed around the pregnant woman's abdomen to secure the devices that display the fetal heartbeat and uterine contractions on a monitor screen, recording them as a continuous graph. If delivery is not anticipated or desirable, external monitoring is indicated, because the amniotic membranes surrounding and protecting the fetus must be ruptured before an internal monitor can be used. External monitoring was originally used during pregnancy and labor in high-risk patients only to detect abnormal changes in the fetal heart rate or premature labor. Since maternal movement in labor interferes with the recording even when the mother is reclining, the expectant mother is not free to move about once monitoring has begun.

Internal fetal monitoring, used only if the woman is in labor or labor is indicated, eliminates inaccuracies in the tracing caused by the mother's movements, and is preferred by most physicians, because of its increased accuracy. However, it is an invasive technique, requiring that an electrode be applied to the fetal scalp to record the heartbeat. A catheter is usually introduced alongside the fetus to measure uterine contractions. Obviously, the membranes surrounding the fetus must be ruptured before the electrode can be placed, and if they are intact, the physician must artificially rupture them.

Internal monitoring also limits the mother's mobility, though not as much as the external monitor. As mentioned previously, movement helps to enhance circulation so that optimum oxygen levels are delivered to the uterus, placenta, and fetus, which is comforting, and enhances labor progress. The uterus is composed of several muscle layers and any muscle that lacks oxygen due to decreased blood perfusion becomes painful. Physicians have actually chastised women for moving around in bed too much and disrupting the monitor tracing of the fetal heart rate.

The interference with ambulation is seen as a problem by normal birth advocates, since women normally change positions in labor frequently when unrestrained, and they are less likely to need medication for pain.[6] With all the equipment attached to her, there is little opportunity for a woman to get out of bed, walk about, take a bath or shower, and do all the things that would add to her comfort and help labor progress.

The practice of fetal monitoring quickly spread to low-risk mothers during labor and became a part of routine care in most hospitals for all patients in the labor room. EFM definitely surpasses the fetoscope in accuracy and it is universally recognized that it is important to evaluate the health status of the fetus during labor. The need for continuous fetal monitoring in normal labor is controversial. Another issue is that both external and internal monitoring can result in false readings (especially if evaluated by inexperienced physicians), suggesting fetal distress and prompting unnecessary surgical intervention. In the United States, after EFM became a routine practice for all women in labor, there was a significant increase in cesarean sections.

Artificial rupture of the amniotic membranes (AROM) is a medical intervention practiced routinely for decades. Intact membranes (bag of waters) cushion the fetus and protect against infection and serve to equally distribute uterine pressure on the fetus and act as a wedge to help dilate the cervix during labor. Physicians artificially ruptured membranes before labor to induce it or during labor to shorten it, using a device similar to a long crochet hook, called an amniohook. AROM is also necessary to allow for the application of an internal monitor. Unfortunately, according to hospital protocols, AROM commits the doctor to delivering the mother within twenty-four hours, since the risk of infection rises dramatically after that time period. This kind of "routine" or "standard" interference in normal childbirth is totally unnecessary and can be harmful, often leading to infection, operative delivery, and other complications.

Labor induction and augmentation of labor (stimulation after normal labor has started) have been used for years even when there are no medical indications. Induction of labor is sometimes indicated if delivery should occur without delay when there are no signs of labor. Reasons for induction include high blood pressure, pre-eclampsia (formally known as toxemia of pregnancy) resistant to treatment, placenta aging, diabetes, a small-for-dates baby (failing to thrive), and an overdue baby that is literally "out-growing" its placenta. It is also indicated if the fetus has died. Like planned cesarean births, inductions can be planned ahead. This is not only convenient for the woman, but also for her doctor, who doesn't have to be called in the middle of the night. Inductions, therefore, can be timed for the convenience of the nursing and medical staff, as well as for "social" reasons (the mother's schedule).

Oxytocin (more commonly known as Pitocin or Syntocin), the drug most commonly used to stimulate labor for induction or augmentation, is a powerful drug that mimics the natural hormone, secreted by the posterior pituitary gland, that stimulates and controls uterine contractions. In the body, endogenous (natural) oxytocin is released in small amounts during normal labor to synchronize labor contractions. Given exogenously, the drug is mixed in an intravenous solution, and administered to the mother slowly in incremental amounts to simulate its natural secretion. However, oxytocin infusion may have dangerous side effects and should not be used unless medical complications exist or the baby is considerably overdue. It can over-stimulate the uterus, causing it to tire and work less efficiently and lead to more painful uterine contractions than would occur without interference with the natural physiologic state. Continuous fetal monitoring is required.

The routine use of Pitocin to speed up all labors became a widespread practice, and the philosophy "if labor is indicated, 'pit' is indicated" prevailed in many institutions. It is dubious that women have been sufficiently informed about the possible risks associated with artificial stimulation of labor, including over-stimulating the uterus, fetal distress, more painful contractions, and the cascade of procedures that may follow.

The use of epidural anesthetic for labor and delivery escalated during the 1980s and, in some hospitals, soared to ninety-plus percent of deliveries.[7] Epidural analgesia and anesthesia can give dramatic pain relief in labor and provide effective anesthesia for a complicated labor and delivery, including cesarean delivery. It has the advantage of allowing the mother to avoid heavy sedation and remain conscious and involved with her labor and birth. The biggest advantage of an epidural is that it is effective (for the most part) in blocking the pain sensations of uterine contractions.

Epidurals became very popular with physicians, who saw them as the "Cadillac of anesthesias," and have now become routine, even for healthy women in normal labor. Even when women have planned to have a natural birth, in many hospital settings they are approached by physicians and nurses during labor who ask, "Why have pain when you can have an epidural?" Their inherent ability to give birth is questioned, and many midwives have had the experience of seeing women who were working well with their contractions, unrestrained by fetal monitors and intravenous devices, being seduced into believing they could not go on and that an epidural was in their best interests. It is often the support person who wants immediate relief for his partner, encouraging her to give up.

The epidural must be given by a skilled anesthesiologist (who remains in attendance). Prior to starting the epidural, intravenous fluids must be infusing and continuous fetal monitoring must be initiated. The procedure begins with the mother curled up in a ball, or sitting on one side of the bed, presenting her back to the anesthesiologist. The epidural needle is inserted into her back between two lower vertebrae (numbed first with local anesthetic), into the epidural space between the spinal cord and spine. Then an epidural catheter is threaded through the needle to the epidural space and the needle is removed. The anesthetic agent is injected through the catheter, anesthetizing the nerves in the area, and relieving pain within about twenty minutes. "Top-ups" during labor can be given every hour or two, or there may be a small continuous dose infusion.

Epidurals in normal labor are controversial and do pose certain risks. Women lose the sensation to push effectively unless the epidural wears off, thereby prolonging labor. The normal reflex responses in the body that cause the baby's head to turn to the optimal delivery position may be absent. Ultimately, it may be necessary to assist delivery using forceps or vacuum extraction. If the dura (thick protective covering for the spinal cord) is punctured, the woman may develop a very painful headache persistent for several days. Temporary urinary problems and backache are also fairly common complaints. Only about fifty percent of all women find that pain is entirely relieved. The catheter sometimes bends and therefore works on only one side of the body or not at all. Sometimes the medicine is given too late. Labor that has been progressing normally may slow or stop. The bottom line is that epidurals do pose unnecessary risks for women experiencing normal childbirth who are adequately prepared to cope with labor contractions.

Rare but serious complications following epidural include a dangerous drop in the woman's blood pressure, an allergic reaction, or paralysis. A severe allergic reaction or overdose can be fatal. Although these risks are rare, they are usually downplayed by physicians. Furthermore, anesthesia use adds greatly to the overall cost of maternity care and childbirth. "The total national health care cost of using epidural analgesia for normal labor and delivery can be great, especially if it results in associated complications, cesarean section, and/or long-term health problems."[8] A reduction in the use of epidural anesthesia would mean significant savings to parents and also to hospitals, in terms of staffing and resources.

Operative deliveries—including forceps or vacuum extraction, episiotomy, and cesarean birth—became popular since men began to manipulate childbirth and the advent of anesthesia. Back in the 1920s, DeLee advocated routine forceps delivery and episiotomy, mainly to protect the woman's pelvic floor and prevent perineal injury. But often the opposite outcome occurs: these interventions cause injury as explained in previous chapters.

Forceps, which look like a pair of long-handled spoons, are passed up through the vagina and applied to the sides of the baby's head to draw the baby down. An episiotomy must be performed and the bladder emptied with a catheter before forceps are used. A safe forceps delivery depends on the degree of difficulty and on the skill of the obstetrician. Many physicians routinely used forceps for all first-time mothers. It was customary to use forceps routinely to rotate the baby's head if it didn't rotate naturally. Rotation would ordinarily occur naturally when a woman squats during birth. In teaching hospitals, forceps were often applied just for the sake of giving interns and residents experience.

Vacuum extraction, first introduced in 1954, involves applying a small suction cup to the baby's head during the second stage of labor to guide the head through the vagina while the mother pushes. It can be used instead of forceps to assist with delivery when the baby is in distress or the mother is too exhausted to push. A lack of progress during the second stage of labor accounts for about half of vacuum-assisted births.

The procedure requires skill (midwives have been trained in this procedure) and should not be attempted for more than twenty minutes. It is less traumatic than forceps and safer than a cesarean, although the baby's head may have some swelling for a few hours after birth. The baby's appearance may be disturbing to the family, but the swelling is usually not serious and will subside eventually. A bloody bruise beneath the baby's scalp (cephalhematoma) results between one and eighteen percent of the time, and very rarely (in about 0.35 percent of cases), intracerebral hemorrhage (bleeding into the brain) occurs.[9]

The cesarean section rate increased dramatically during the second half of the twentieth century. In 1970, five in one hundred women gave birth by cesarean; by the end of the century, about thirty in one hundred did so.[10] Medical or obstetric indications include prolonged labor, failure to progress in labor, failed induction when the membranes have been ruptured, placenta abruptio (the placenta separates before the birth, cutting off the baby's oxygen supply), placenta previa (the placenta is lying across the cervix with risk of severe bleeding if labor continues), and abnormal fetal positions (baby is not coming head first). These are classic, undisputed indications for operative birth. Cesarean section is also indicated when it is clear that the fetus cannot tolerate labor, or when labor would be injurious to the woman. In many instances, it is a judgment call.

Cesarean section poses the same risks as other major operations and greater risk than normal delivery, including infection, injury to the bladder and uterine blood vessels, hemorrhage, anesthesia accidents, clots, embolism, bowel complications, increase in postpartum pain and recovery time, and increased cost.[11] Over several years, improvements in surgery have made cesarean birth safer. The "classic" long scar has been replaced by a low transverse "bikini cut" below the pubic hairline; and general anesthesia has been replaced by epidural or spinal anesthesia, resulting in fewer complications to mothers and babies.

The World Health Organization recommends no more than a fifteen percent cesarean section rate. Yet in 1991 the C-section rate in the United States was 23.5 per one hundred births and, according to the Centers for Disease Control and Prevention, "doctors in the United States performed 349,000 unnecessary caesarean sections, which cost the nation more than $1 billion."[12] Liability and financial issues contributed to the increase in C-sections. In the litigious culture in the United States, many obstetricians and hospital administrators favored cesarean deliveries if there was any possibility of an adverse outcome, rather than risk a complication and subsequent lawsuit. There is also a considerable difference in the physician's payment for a cesarean birth compared with an uncomplicated delivery.

In contrast to the standard practice in western Europe of allowing women to attempt a vaginal birth after cesarean (VBAC), the philosophy of "once a cesarean section, always a cesarean section" prevailed in the United States. This policy, based on a number of factors, including fears of a torn uterus and brain damage in the newborn, as well as convenience, and the risk of litigation, accounted for one-third of all cesareans in the United States. In 1980, a National Institutes of Health committee encouraged a relaxation of the policy and encouraged natural birth attempts after cesarean section in selected women.[13] In 1988, an ACOG bulletin encouraged a vaginal birth trial after cesarean birth (VBAC), a change applauded by advocates for normal childbirth.[14] Natural births after cesarean peaked at twenty-eight percent in the United States in 1996.[15]

A major problem most critics had, and still have, with technology related to childbirth was the doctors' lack of commitment to giving their patients sufficient, accurate, and current information for them to make informed decisions. The "doctor knows best" attitude often resulted in failure to provide such information. Parents need time to process information, reflect, and weigh the risks and benefits of a given technology and routine procedures, when making decisions of serious import. Many care providers were threatened and even angered by questions that educated and empowered parents posed, and assumed that any question was a challenge to trust in the doctor-patient relationship. Over time, this would change with the changing climate in health care and the economic realities created by health-care consumers who demanded a greater share in decision-making and were willing to shop around for doctors willing to listen to their concerns.

In addition to technological advances, profound social and political changes in the second half of the twentieth century had a dramatic impact on childbirth practices and the delivery of maternity care. These included the civil rights, the anti-war, and the women's liberation movements. A backlash against activism also changed the picture of women's reproductive care.

The 1960s were turbulent and anxious years, as the restless baby boomers came of age and expressed their disillusionment with American government and society. Politically active blacks and supportive whites, led by the Rev. Martin Luther King, struggled to end racial discrimination. Milestones included the decision to desegregate Little Rock, Arkansas in 1957, the passage of the Civil Rights Act in 1964, and the Watts riots in 1965. Martin Luther King, Jr., and Robert Kennedy were assassinated in 1968. Over time, the protesters prevailed. There was an end to segregation in all public areas, including many hitherto segregated clinics and hospitals. In addition to the civil rights movement, a growing frustration with the Vietnam War in the '60s resulted in anti-war protests and violence on college campuses.

The questioning of authority that dominated both the civil rights movement and the anti-war movement extended from the political arena to every aspect of society, including medical care. In response to this public unrest, President Johnson implemented his "Great Society" program. It included Medicaid, which reduced financial barriers to health care by providing coverage to low-income pregnant women and their families.

Activists demanded more control over their own health care and the recognition of patients' rights. Between 1965 and 1968, the National Institutes of Health ushered in a new era in health care delivery and ethics when it called for informed consent for surgery, tests, and procedures. *The Cultural Warping of Childbirth*, by Doris Haire, published in 1972, outlined the negative aspects of medical intervention during childbirth and contrasted birth in the United States unfavorably with other developed countries where labor was managed by midwives.[16] Haire demanded that the rights of pregnant women be respected.

The "Pregnant Patient's Bill of Rights," developed by the Maternity Center Association, revised and expanded in 1999, included, among other rights: the right to be informed of potential risks of drugs and procedures to herself or her unborn baby; the right to learn the benefits and risks of proposed therapies and alternative therapies; the right to refuse a drug or procedure without any pressure from the care-provider; the right to know the name and qualifications of her care-providers; the right to have a companion with her during labor and birth; the right to choose her own position for labor and birth; the right to keep her baby at her bed-side and feed on demand if the baby was normal; the right to be informed in writing of the name and qualifications of the person who actually delivered her baby; the right to know of any aspect of her baby's care or condition that might cause later difficulties; and the right to have access to her complete medical records.[17] The fact that these "rights" had to be asserted, and in many cases, fought for, says volumes about the arrogance and paternalism that characterized the system at the time. In 1990, the federal Patient Self-Determination Act required that every patient in a medical facility be informed of his or her medical rights, including the right to refuse unwanted interventions.[18]

Social and political unrest also gave rise to an influential countercul-ture movement into experimentation with drugs and all things new. As part of the general counterculture movement, and in response to the medicalization of birth, more and more women opted to give birth at home. By the 1960s, some women were choosing home births, even though obstetricians insisted that the hospital was the only safe place to give birth. Obstetricians denied prenatal care to women planning home birth and even threatened them with arrest for child abuse. Women were often treated with contempt if they showed up at the hospital late in labor, due to a complication during home birth. Those women who gave birth in their own homes attended by midwives, often reflected the cultural diversity of the United States. While some women presented a direct challenge to the system, others were simply trying to go back to their roots.[19]

In the sixties, Stephen Gaskin, an instructor at San Francisco State College who taught classes on zen, mysticism, and other spiritual sub-jects, attracted a following on the Haight-Ashbury hippy scene. Gaskin and his wife, Ina May, left San Francisco in 1970 with hundreds of pot-smoking hippie faithfuls. Seven months later, in May 1971, they founded a commune, "The Farm," with about 250 followers on 1,700 acres of land near Summerville, Tennessee. While traveling, three babies were born and Ina May Gaskin began her career as a lay midwife. She learned her craft from midwifery manuals, standard obstetrical texts, and sympathetic doctors.[20] High-risk women were sent to the doctor. The essentially healthy women who delivered at home, supported in labor by a circle of other caring women in the commune, had very good outcomes compared to physician-attended births, as shown in a survey of 1,707 women who gave birth at the Farm between January 1971 and

June 1989. Conclusions from the Natality/National Fetal Mortality Survey stated:

> Elective interventions, which are used more frequently in-hospital, may increase the risk of various adverse outcomes in low-risk women. In addition, it is possible that the unfamiliar setting and the presence of unfamiliar personnel, the limited presence and role of family members, and the restricted freedom of movement of the laboring woman may all create an atmosphere at a hospital birth that undermines self-confidence and encourages passivity on the part of the laboring woman, diminishing her ability to deliver spontaneously. [21]

Gaskin's book, *Spiritual Midwifery*, published in 1977, became an immediate best seller. It sold more than half a million copies and was translated into several languages. By 1989, Ina May reported that of 1,700 births; only 4.8 percent of the women were hospitalized; only 1.5 percent had cesarean sections; and only 0.5 percent had forceps deliveries. By this time, the commune had abandoned farming for business enterprises, and Ina May's midwifery service was serving both the Farm and the nearby Amish community.[22]

The home-birth movement was woman-centered. It affirmed that women's bodies were meant to bear children, and, in contrast to prevailing medical opinion, accepted birth as a holistic and natural event, denying that pregnancy was a "stress." Women who chose the home-birth option were not convinced that the hospital was the safest place for birth. Hospitals posed unique dangers for birthing women and babies; including the overuse of medication, a higher risk of infection, and interference in the natural birth process. It was still socially acceptable for a woman to ask "that she be knocked out when she got to the hospital and not brought to until she had a clean, preferably diapered, baby to be brought to her."[23] Most obstetricians were happy to oblige.

Home birth statistics, reported by the American College of Obstetricians and Gynecologists (ACOG), made home births appear unsafe; but the data, which made no distinction between planned home births and unplanned rapid labors in which birth at home was by accident or premature, were skewed. No research study has proven that hospital births are safer than home births.[24] Lewis Mehl and associates conducted a study comparing 1,046 planned home births with planned hospital births. Women were matched for age, parity, socioeconomic status and risk factors. The research found home births were safer. Infant death rates were the same, but there were three times more cesarean sections in planned hospital deliveries, nine times more episiotomies, and nine times more perineal or vaginal tears. Less than five percent of women who gave birth at home received drugs, compared with seventy-five percent of the hospital patients. Almost all women in both groups attended childbirth classes.[25]

The choices confronting care providers were to either bring personal autonomy and social support into the hospital, or to make home birth safer. Many American women resented the loss of personal autonomy and the absence of the loving and supportive atmosphere of home, but for the most part, they were convinced that the hospital was the safest place to give birth. In contrast to a small, vocal minority opting for home birth, they worked to change and reform the system. For doctors, the risks in doing home births outweighed the benefits. They were socialized into delivering in hospitals and they feared malpractice suits.

The women's movement of the 1960s and '70s also brought about changes in childbirth practices. Women had worked outside the home during World War II, but during the post-war years and throughout the 1950s, they returned to the traditional women's roles of housewife and homemaker. Men in corporate America were forced to relocate in places distant from the extended family, and in pursuit of the "American Dream," there was a mass move to the suburbs. The nuclear family became more and more isolated, as America became a nation of "nomadic house and job swappers," in Vance Packard's words.[26] Many women, failing to find fulfillment in domesticity, felt isolated and discontented with their roles. In 1963, *The Feminine Mystique,* a best seller written by Betty Friedan, gave voice to the feelings of frustration and emptiness experienced by many women, unable to find fulfillment other than from their husbands and children.

Taking its cue from the movement for racial equality, a vigorous feminist movement, led by Gloria Steinem, Betty Friedan, and Bella Abzug, pressed for equal rights for women in the 1960s and 1970s. Feminists criticized American society as patriarchal—male-dominated and male-oriented—and argued that women should have the same political, economic, and social rights as men. Discrimination against women in education and employment was blatant. There was no such thing as equal pay for women, and maternity leave was rarely granted. The central issue was always about choices for women that had long been available to men, but denied to women. Across America, women of all age groups met in small consciousness-raising sessions, questioning popular notions about feminine interests and abilities, traditional roles assigned to women, and social, educational, and political inequalities between men and women.

The social and political unrest that contributed to the development of the women's liberation movement and to change in the status of women in society had a dramatic impact on women's health care and maternity care. By 1968, younger women, experienced in political protest during the civil rights and anti-war demonstrations, joined the women's movement. They were assertive, educated and articulate and realized that reproductive rights were the key to equal rights in every area.

In the 1900s, abortion was illegal in every state, except when necessary to save the life of a woman or for other therapeutic reasons. By the 1950s, over a million abortions were performed annually and over a thousand women died from complications. During the 1960s civil rights, anti-war, and women's rights movements, women and their supporters rallied, demonstrated, and lobbied for abortion rights. Finally, on January 22, 1973, The U.S. Supreme Court voted to legalize abortion in the famous *Roe v. Wade* decision. There were still issues to be resolved, but the new law brought better and safer abortion services to women.[27]

A women's conference on health care in Boston in 1969 resulted in a book, *Our Bodies, Ourselves*, which included information on nutrition, exercise, sexually transmitted diseases, self-esteem, childbearing, and the health care system. By 1980, women's new freedom to regulate their fertility without fear or danger resulted in sexual behaviors and attitudes that closely mirrored men's. Women became more independent in decision-making about family size, when to have children, under what circumstances, and when to stop. Out-of-wedlock motherhood rose dramatically in the 1980s.[28]

Feminists also embraced struggles over basic power issues in childbirth and midwifery. In 1982, Rothman wrote, "For the feminists, childbirth tends to be one of many fronts on which the struggle for women's control of their lives is taking place."[29] According to feminists, the medical model, fostered by a male profession in a patriarchal society, reflected the technological orientation of modern, industrial society that views the body as a machine and the male body as the norm. In *Immaculate Deception: A New Look at Women and Childbirth in America* (1975), Arms noted, "Childbirth is one of the most profound, personal experiences a woman can have. Yet our present system of uniform care does not allow her the freedom to choose her own way of birth and reclaim the experience as her own."[30]

Feminists demanded the right to control their own bodies as they did long ago. They wanted freedom of choice during pregnancy and childbirth and the right to labor and give birth free from unnecessary intervention and technology. They also wanted women to take responsibility for themselves, to trust their bodies, and to educate themselves about birth. They championed the home-birth movement: "The midwives and mothers involved in the home-birth movement are part of the larger struggle of feminism to redefine women in women's terms.... They are coming to grips with a feminism that embraces rather than denies women's biological realities."[31]

By 1968, the upheaval in the country created by feminists, anti-war, and civil-rights protesters was met head on by main-stream conservatives. Labeling the activists communists, they reacted in a backlash against the student demonstrations and uprisings and responded with Nixon's law-and-order presidential campaign and Reagan's campaign for governor of California. Both conservatives were elected in 1968. By the 1980s the New Right ideology declared war on feminists, the National Organization for Women, and Planned Parenthood, sparking the anti-abortion movement in a war of semantics that used terms such as "pro-life" and "the unborn." Liberated women were denounced for disparaging the nuclear family, opting for open marriage, and choosing to have fewer children. Attacks on brighter married white women, who neglected their reproductive duties for careers and higher education, warned that America was committing cultural suicide and would become a nation of "paupers, fools and foreigners."[32] The attacks on *Roe v. Wade*, the abortion rights law passed in 1973, were vicious and are ongoing. The advances in women's health care set in motion by the feminists continue to be eroded in subtle and not so subtle ways.

Midwives began to revive in light of the women's movement. There were three categories of midwives—direct-entry, lay, and nurse-midwives. Direct-entry midwives provided family-centered home births and some opened freestanding birth centers. These midwives were usually well-educated women who want to avoid the male domination of the hospital. Direct-entry midwives have a long history in both Europe, where nursing and midwifery are separate and distinct professions, and also, in America.

In Europe, midwives were absorbed into the system and educated, but in the United States they received no formal training, instead being taught by more experienced midwives. Diversity in their backgrounds and training, and wide variations in state law regarding the training and licensing of midwives, makes it difficult to generalize about their practice. Today there are education programs for midwives and a certification program administered by the North American Registry of Midwives (NARM). Trained midwives have their own professional organizations, such as NARM and the Midwives Alliance of North America (MANA), but the practice of direct-entry midwives without certification is illegal in some states.[33]

In 1974, the Board of Medical Examiners, State Department of Consumer affairs (SDCA) in California, using an undercover agent, arrested two birth center midwives for practicing medicine without a license.[34] They stormed the birth center, confiscating notebooks and other materials as evidence. In the 1980s, midwives continued to be harassed by the medical establishment and government agents.

The second half of the century saw the reemergence of another kind of midwife—this time, the nurse-midwife. Nurse-midwives were also known as Certified Nurse-Midwives (CNMs). Their professional organization, the American College of Nurse-Midwives (ACNM), was incorporated in 1955 to "evaluate and approve CNM services and education programs." In 1958, when hospital prenatal clinics and labor/delivery units in New York were overcrowded and inadequately staffed, Dr. Louis Hellman introduced CNMs into the system. He initiated hospital-based formal midwifery education when he invited the transfer of the Maternity Center School of Nurse-Midwifery into the hospital-medical center setting at King County Hospital, in affiliation with Downstate University of New York in Brooklyn.[35]

Over the next twenty years, the universities of Utah, Mississippi, Illinois, South Carolina, Kentucky, Minnesota, California, St. Louis, Loma Linda, CA, Emory, Meharry Medical College, Georgetown University in DC, and the New Jersey College of Medicine developed educational programs. The United States Air Force also started a nurse-midwifery program. There were variations in the educational programs, but typically, after a registered nurse (R.N.) with a B.S. or B.A. degree had a year of experience working in labor and delivery, she could complete a program of one and one-half to two years, leading to a master's degree in midwifery.

Wherever nurse-midwives worked, the statistical data has improved. There are many examples of the difference that midwives made in newborn outcomes. For example, in 1960, Madeira County (California) Hospital employed two CNMs to improve care to childbearing women. In 1959, before the midwives came, the preterm birth rate had been 11.0 percent. It was reduced dramatically to 6.4 percent in 1961. In 1964–1966, after the cessation of special grant funding terminated the program, the preterm rate again increased to 9.8 percent.[36]

Roosevelt Hospital in New York City was the first hospital to employ nurse-midwives in 1964. New York City's Maternal and Infant Care Project (MIC) pioneered in integrating nurse-midwives into the city hospitals and community-based obstetrical-perinatal care teams. CNMs were salaried employees, worked shifts, and worked in a variety of settings. Acceptance by consumers was overwhelmingly positive. A growing body of research indicated that maternal-child health programs that included midwifery care for normal births and obstetric care for complicated births resulted in more satisfied consumers and lower rates of complications for both mothers and infants.

Physicians officially welcomed the nurse-midwife into the hospital setting, explaining that she was different from granny midwives. Most doctors, however, provided backup only for CNMs who cared for indigent patients. They were not willing to let them practice independently or secure their own clients. Doctors resisted any move to take birth out of the hospital or return control to women. Fearing competition and loss of income, doctors denied hospital privileges to CNMs who wanted to practice independently or in partnership with a private physician. Later, the Federal Trade Commission (FTC) would support CNMs, charging the doctors with restraint of trade and competition. The FTC threatened doctors with anti-trust laws, and went after insurance companies that denied insurance to doctors who collaborated with CNMs. The whole second half of the twentieth century was marked by this struggle.

In 1972, at the International Congress of Midwives, Professor G. J. Kloosterman of Holland, the chief of obstetricians and gynecologists at the University of Amsterdam Hospital, summed up the problem when obstetricians cared for normal women:

> Spontaneous labor in a healthy woman is an event marked by a number of processes which are so complex and so perfectly attuned to each other that any interference with these processes will only detract from their optimum character. [The attendant] must show respect for this physiological birth and therefore comply with the first rule of medicine, that of 'nil nocered'; injure nothing.... The doctor always on the lookout for pathology, eager to interfere, will much too often change true physiological aspects of human reproduction into pathology. [Many western doctors think they can improve everything, even natural childbirth in a healthy woman.] This philosophy is the philosophy of people who think it deplorable that they were not consulted at the creation of Eve, because they would have done a better job.[37]

The American College of Obstetricians and Gynecologists (ACOG), their nurses' association (NAACOG), and the American College of Nurse-Midwives (ACNM) issued a "Joint Statement on Maternity Care" in 1971, establishing midwifery in the mainstream of American health care. Federal guidelines for Maternal and Infant Care Projects across the country recommended that CNMs be included in the health care teams. New educational programs were developed in response to the large numbers of nurses seeking nurse-midwifery education. That same year, ACNM standardized the basic competency level of the professional midwife with the National Certification Examination. Once midwifery moved into the hospital setting, some midwives were socialized into the patriarchal, medical culture, but overall, they brought about a positive change in the care of mothers and babies, incorporating family-centered support into their hospital practice.

In the 1960s CNMs were employed extensively in New York City to manage the prenatal and postpartum care of indigent women in community-based clinics; they also managed the complete care of mothers with normal labors in the hospital, consulting with the obstetrician if problems developed. A five-year report of one of New York City's midwifery services demonstrated that nurse-midwives could also manage certain complications as part of a medically directed obstetric-perinatal team.[38]

Laws governing midwifery practice were still confusing, according to a state-by-state investigation regarding the legal status of nurse-midwives, as reported by the ACNM in 1974. Many states gave nurse-midwives legal recognition, but not as independent practitioners; other states had permissive laws, but no legal recognition. Colorado and Nebraska prohibited nurse-midwifery and midwifery practice. Midwifery practice was restricted or narrowly defined in several other states.[39]

By 1975, 19,686 hospital births were attended by nurse-midwives. The number rose in 1987 to 98,425, and by 1989 to more than 120,000. In 1991, there were more than four thousand nurse-midwives working in hospitals, health-maintenance organizations (HMOs), public health clinics, and private practice settings with physicians or their own birthing centers. In an analysis of all births in the United States in 1991, 94.7 percent of babies born in the United States were delivered by physicians, 4.1 percent by nurse-midwives, and 0.4 percent by other midwives (0.8 percent by unknown or other attendants). By 1994, ninety-five percent of all nurse-midwife deliveries were in hospitals.[40]

Nurse-midwives were eventually covered by most insurance carriers, Medicaid, and managed-care programs. The use of nurse-midwives was seen as a solution to improving access to care while lowering costs. With more hospital privileges and better collaborative arrangements with doctors, nurse-midwives are delivering services to more high-risk women, especially those in poverty and from different ethnic backgrounds, than initially. Still, about six percent of CNMs report that they were not listed as the birth attendant on the birth certificates of babies they delivered.[41] They are still sometimes denied reimbursement by insurers.

According to numerous studies, mothers and babies have had distinctly better outcomes when midwives attended births, either in or out of hospitals. MacDorman and Singh found that "the risk of experiencing an infant death was nineteen percent lower for certified nurse-midwife attended births than for physician attended births, the risk of neonatal mortality was thirty-three percent lower, and the risk of delivering a low birthweight infant was thirty-two percent lower," even when cesarean births were excluded from the study.[42] Better outcomes may be related to the nurse-midwife's excellent emotional support and patient education—they are more likely to remain with women during labor, allow food and drink, encourage ambulation in labor, use alternative positions for delivery, and employ intermittent, rather than continuous fetal monitoring. Certified nurse-midwives are skilled in communication with patients and in preventive interventions.[43]

Nurse-midwives drew on their professional skills to give family-oriented, safe, and personalized health care. Focusing on wellness and consumer choice, helping women to make informed decisions, they taught women self-reliance and trust in their own bodies. They were also more cost-effective. A 1989 study at Kaiser Permanente Medical Centers in California reported a thirteen percent or $292,000 decrease in payroll costs at one center and a seven percent or $2 million reduction at another center where CNMs were employed.[44]

In 1997, the Public Citizen's Health Research Group wrote: "The training of CNMs and their orientation toward childbirth as a normal event makes them particularly well suited to play an increasingly important role in remedying two difficult problems in U.S. obstetric care—the excessive use of costly and often unnecessary medical interventions during births of normal, low-risk women in U.S. hospitals and our country's slow progress in improving the health status of newborns." They concluded that "the nurse-midwifery approach to maternity care allows for flexible, individualized care and the judicious use of medical technology."[45]

The development of birth centers for low-risk women presented an alternative to the hospital for those who wanted to avoid the sterile, impersonal atmosphere of the hospital. Birth centers were homey, low-tech places that allowed family and friends to provide support to the laboring woman. Candidates were carefully screened to rule out medical or obstetrical problems. Since normal labor and birth were anticipated, women were usually allowed to eat or drink during labor, or relax in a Jacuzzi or birth pool. Birth centers were supplied with oxygen, IV supplies, and Isolettes for the newborn, but were not equipped to give Pitocin to stimulate labor or perform instrumental deliveries or cesareans. Some centers were freestanding and others were on hospital grounds or attached to a hospital.

A report by the National Association of Childbearing Centers, appearing in the *New England Journal of Medicine* in 1989, on 11,814 women admitted to eighty-four birth centers staffed by CNM staffs with obstetrician backup between 1956 and 1986, concluded that birth centers offered a safe and acceptable option for selected pregnant women, particularly women who had previous children. The cost was half the cost of normal hospital births.[46] Despite numerous studies that prove birth centers are safe for low-risk healthy women, most American doctors remain skeptical.

The "natural childbirth" movement coincided with the social and political forces of the 1960s. Pioneered by Grantly Dick-Read in the 1940s, the natural childbirth movement developed in the United States to do away with excesses in medical management (as discussed in the previous chapter). Dick-Read's method seemed to be a noble, but unattainable, goal that led to a sense of failure in many women. Its chief tenet was continual comfort and emotional support throughout labor and it required an environment of peaceful, protective calm. These were impossible conditions in the hostile environment of the noisy, modern American hospital, with its paging system, bright lights, routines, and shift changes.

In her 1972 book, *The Experience of Childbirth*, Sheila Kitzinger, an influential British sociologist and prenatal educator, noted that most women embarked upon childbirth ignorant of their task in labor, without any thought or preparation on their part. Kitzinger stressed the need for prenatal education with a psychological and sociological approach, taking into account the differences in individual women.[47]

Natural childbirth gained a broader scope of acceptance in America in the 1960s after Dr. Ferdinand Lamaze of France had written a book, *Painless Childbirth* in 1956. In 1959, Marjorie Karmel, an American woman who had gone to France for her delivery by Dr. Lamaze, wrote *Thank You, Dr. Lamaze*, describing her ecstatic childbirth experience with him. In 1960, Karmel, Elisabeth Bing, a physiotherapist, and Benjamin Segal, MD founded the American Society for Psychoprophylaxis in Childbirth (ASPO) in New York City to promote Lamaze childbirth.

The intent of the Lamaze method was to alter a woman's natural experience from deep involvement inside her body to controlled distraction. Psychoprophylaxis consisted of education about labor, continuous labor support by the woman's companion and a repertoire of relaxation and breathing strategies practiced during pregnancy. Distraction techniques and detachment became the means of overriding the pain of contractions.[48] Its scientific approach was more acceptable to physicians than was Dick-Read's method. Lamaze's method was geared to the American hospital and the American way of birth, but challenged the use of anesthesia, substituting psychological preparation for pharmacological control of pain. Doctors were still in charge, and medication and anesthesia were not ruled out. Women were able to help in the birthing process and take part in decision-making.

Lamaze became popular with baby boomers (1946–1964) coming of age, especially with middle-class, educated women. Being awake and aware for childbirth became the goal. The term "natural childbirth" was replaced by "prepared childbirth," which gradually became widely accepted, even though there was widespread confusion regarding the term. Women presented birth plans to their physicians, outlining their expectations regarding labor, birth, and hospital practices.

Some physicians who saw their patients leaving for other doctors became more accepting of prepared childbirth, and learned to at least tolerate some involvement in decision-making by the couple. Nurses who ridiculed the young couples that arrived in the labor and delivery suite with their pillows and lollypops, confident of their ability to cope with the horrors of labor, gradually became more supportive. Hospitals that saw their patients opting to deliver at those institutions that advertised family-centered care soon began to welcome change and competed for patients. Preparation for childbirth became the expectation, rather than the exception.

By the end of the century, as epidurals became increasingly popular, Lamaze classes looked different from the way they looked forty years before. According to the chair of the Lamaze International Certification Council writing in the 1990s, Lamaze could not compete as a pain control technique with the epidural, but Lamaze teaching "prepares women to trust their inherent ability to give birth and to begin to understand that pain, while a fact of birth (and life), is meant neither to be eliminated nor endured; ... the goal is not pain reduction per se but using pain as a guide while women move through labor ... on a personal journey only they can take. Their pain guides them in their journey; it is about trusting one's inner wisdom, having the freedom to work with one's body as labor progresses, and being supported by health care providers, family, and friends who wait patiently for nature to do its incredible work."[49]

In 1965, Dr. Robert Bradley updated Grantly Dick-Read's theory with another popular natural-childbirth approach in his book, *Husband-Coached Childbirth*. His goal was to make pregnancy an event shared by the couple, to restore the ease and happiness of the experience of birth. His method advocated drug-free labor and protected the passivity of the woman through the constant support of the husband. Bradley encouraged couples to look for younger, more understanding physicians instead of trying to educate older, more resistant ones. Bradley was a pioneer, but critics would argue that his method made the husband a hero alongside the physician-hero, with the woman becoming dependent on both.[50]

Another trend surfaced in the United States in the 1970s. Frederick Leboyer, a French physician, advocated more respect for the newborn by facilitating a gentle transition to extra-uterine life—"Isn't it time to do for the child what we've been trying to do for the mother?" The "Leboyer delivery" in a darkened delivery room, with decreased noise, delayed cord-clamping, gentle massage and a warm-water bath for the baby became fashionable among well-read couples.[51]

Based on the pioneering birthing techniques of Igor Charkowsky, a swimming teacher and midwife in Russia, water births gained popularity with parents in the 1980s. Midwives, who helped laboring women relax in a tub of warm water, noted that labor seemed to progress faster and women could move freely into more comfortable positions. Midwives and some physicians allowed water baths if requested by their patients. Trust in the method increased as caregivers watched the baby emerge gently and serenely from the mother's body.[52]

Michel Odent in Pitiviers, France, promoted water births, which became popular and spread to other centers throughout the world. Many hospitals in the United States now provide pools in the labor and delivery suite. In 1995 at the First International Water Birth Conference in London, statistics from over nineteen thousand water births were presented. Research worldwide on thousands of water births presented evidence that water births result in shorter labors and births, fewer episiotomies, greater mobility during the second stage, and fewer drugs and medical interventions. However, at least two infant deaths during underwater birth have been reported; and five babies died and two were brain damaged in births in which water was used for relaxation.[53] Research on the safety of water birth is ongoing, and standards for safe practice have been established.

While the Lamaze method and other approaches in the prepared childbirth movement focused on childbirth, they did not deal with issues such as breastfeeding and separation of mother and baby. In the 1950s and '60s, babies were whisked off to the nursery immediately after delivery. In the 1970s, Klaus and Kennell advocated non-separation of the mother and baby after delivery and stressed the importance of skin-to-skin contact and eye contact in promoting mother-infant bonding. They cited numerous examples of animal behavior.[54] By this time, many hospitals were quick to implement change. Family-centered care became standard policy. Hospitals began offering tours of the labor and delivery unit before birth, non-separation of mother and baby during the critical hour after birth, rooming in and unrestricted visiting hours for husbands and grandparents. As birth came to be recognized as a normal life event (and as hospital costs rose and insurance companies sought to reduce costs), hospital stays were shortened and early discharge became the rule.

La Leche League was another grassroots movement, founded in

1956, advocating breastfeeding. This organization focused on woman-centered mothering, and challenged the routine separation of the mother and baby after birth and the scheduled infant feedings, rather than the more desirable feeding on demand. Although most preparation for child-bearing classes included content on breastfeeding, La Leche, in addition to offering classes, also provided support groups for women intending to breastfeed or who were already breastfeeding.

By the 1970s, the birth rate in the United States dropped to its low-est level, cooled off by the pill, relaxed abortion laws, and a slowed econ-omy that increased the number of working wives. Parents averaged 2.1 children per couple, as a presidential commission urged a national pol-icy goal of a stabilized population.[55] The fertility rate was 1.8 children per woman in the 1980s, unchanged since 1976.[56] Having fewer children, couples focused more on each birth as a very special event and expected each child to be perfect. Women became more involved with their births and more selective in choosing care providers and places to give birth. These events led hospitals to compete for maternity patients. Most hos-pitals began offering classes advocating their own version of natural child-birth, explaining why routine practices and interventions were necessary for safe care, subtly advocating conformity and compliance. Neverthe-less, by the 1960s, fathers were allowed in the labor room, and by the 1970s, they were allowed in the delivery room.[57]

In the 1980s and '90s, the use of "doulas"—experienced attendants who provide continuous labor support—became increasingly popular, largely due to Klaus and Kennell's research. A doula's sole responsibil-ity is to provide a constant presence, giving comfort to the laboring woman, and support to the labor partner. Research supports the benefits of doulas; they reduce the chances of unnecessary medical interventions and operative births and shorten the length of labor by reducing stress and pain. From their research, Klaus and Kennell have shown that the presence of a doula significantly reduces the overall cesarean rate, length of labor, oxytocin use, the need for pain medication, the need for for-ceps, and the need for epidurals.[58]

Hospitals responded to the challenge of the home-birth movement with innovative ways to attract women, such as decorating labor rooms with attractive wallpaper and furniture. Some rooms were designated as "birthing rooms," which allowed women to labor and give birth in the same room instead of being transferred by stretcher from a labor room to a delivery room. Despite these accommodations, doctors still held the power. Feminists attacked interior-decorated labor rooms. It was easy to change wallpaper, but was much harder to change attitudes. Skeptical physicians and many nurses were slow to lose their prejudices, resenting any changes or challenges to their authority and "the way it had always been done." Although childbirth was pronounced healthy and normal, medical dominance was so entrenched and so rigid that it was difficult to modify. Technology continued to become more complex and surgical intervention increased. In many institutions, natural childbirth became anything short of a cesarean section. Uneducated women, poor women, especially, and those who did not go to classes, were dominated by the system. It was easier for some women to let the doctor take charge, without questioning. These women were still powerless.

Educated and determined couples who persevered, supported by their childbirth educators, the growing presence of nurse-midwives, and women's advocacy groups, enjoyed shared decision-making, and often had a joyful childbirth experience. Against great odds, these resilient pioneers changed society and made the system more tolerant and woman-friendly. They won many options for women and childbearing families in America, options in danger of being taken for granted and lost. In every generation, women must be reminded of their responsibility to be educated consumers, making informed choices, if they wish to preserve the gains made by those who came before.

CHAPTER 11

The Twenty-First Century: Technological Childbirth Challenged

For her first two births in 1988 and 1990, Lisa labored the usual way, in a hospital hooked up to an electronic fetal monitor. She remained in bed throughout her labor with intravenous fluids infusing, and was not allowed to eat or drink, except for some ice chips. Having worked as a registered nurse in labor and delivery, and also having assisted birthing women as a doula, Lisa chose a home birth when she became pregnant with her third child in 1996. She wanted a natural birth, free of medical technology. There were no birth centers on the rural eastern shore where she lived and certified nurse-midwives could not risk their licenses by attending home births. Lisa did her research and was able to engage two lay midwives who agreed to attend her in her own home.

Lisa described her labor, which began at 2 P.M. on July 10, 1996, as "totally comfortable, unbelievable." She wanted to be alone through most of her labor, so she sent her midwives to roam around the nearby town with beeper in hand, while she and Dave walked around outside her home on that beautiful sunny day in July. She was able to eat lightly and drink to satisfy her thirst and hunger as desired. She went into the house to take a bath when her contractions became more intense. Before long, she felt the urge to "push" and called her midwives. While bearing down, she developed severe sciatic pain. Her midwives gave her a homeopathic herb, "black cohash." Lisa got on her hands and knees and rocked to relieve the pain. With one last "push," the midwives caught little Summer Day at 5:30 P.M. on the tenth day of July, only three-and-a-half hours after labor began.

Lisa gave birth to three more children, whom she had planned to have at home. However, Sophie was 14 days overdue and at the midwife's decision was born in the hospital. David was nine days late and because of a lack of faith and patience, he, too, was born in the hospital, by cesarean. Her last child, Jonathan, was born at home the 29th of June, 2004, attended only by her husband, Dave. Lisa told me, "It was an awesome birth."[1]

Most hospital births today take place in hospitals and are still managed by technology and routine obstetric procedures practiced for over a century. Although childbirth is unique to each woman, a typical hospital birth might be managed in the following way. The woman enters the labor unit, greeted by a nurse who will connect her to the electronic fetal monitor (EFM), take her pregnancy and labor history, and then report her status to her physician. If she is in very early labor, she probably will be sent home. If she stays and her fetus is doing well (assessed by the monitor recording), she probably will be allowed to walk around for awhile. If her contractions are strong and frequent, she will be examined by the nurse or her physician to determine her cervical dilation and station (how far the fetus has descended in her pelvis) to estimate labor progression. If the physician determines that her labor is progressing too slowly, he or she will likely order an oxytocin infusion to speed up her labor. Her doctor will probably rupture her membranes artificially. As her pain intensifies, the woman will request and receive an epidural anesthesia or analgesia. With these interventions, it is unlikely she will have further opportunity to walk around, take a bath or shower, urinate as often as she should, or participate in other comfort measures that would naturally help her labor progress and ease her pain.

Labor management does vary from hospital to hospital and among providers of care. Some hospitals are now leaning toward evidence-based care—those practices that are indicated, based on scientific evidence. However, the use of technology and other obstetric interventions still prevail, even when labor and birth are normal. The medicalized way of childbirth was not designed to facilitate and support natural childbirth. Nature never intended machines, procedures, or artificial uterine stimulants to replace normal physiology of labor and birth. Women have been given more choices in childbirth since the second half of the twentieth century, but the question of how well they have been informed about the consequences of obstetric procedures remains obscure.

Back in 1947, Dr. Grantly Dick-Read, speaking at a meeting of the Academy of Medicine at the Maternity Center Association in New York City, stated, "When parturition is neither inhibited nor disturbed by mechanical, chemical or psychological factors it may be termed physiological labor. All interference when there is no inhibitory or disturbing factor superimposes a pathological state upon physiologic function."[2] He explained how neurohormones are released by our nervous system during times of stress, causing muscles to tense and blood pressure to rise, thereby diverting blood from the uterus. Then, less oxygen is delivered to the uterus, placenta, and fetus, causing more painful uterine contractions and fetal distress. Dick-Read coined this cascade the "fear-tension-pain cycle."

The response to stress has also been known as the "fight or flight" response. Women in labor aren't likely to fight or take flight. Research has shown that the female animal's response to stress or danger is to protect the young. Women are more likely to "tend and befriend"; that is, to tend to their young and befriend (affiliate with) a social group, which reduces the risk of danger and the accompanying stress.[3] The social birth, before childbirth became medicalized, served this need. If women are not completely informed about the pros and cons of obstetric procedures and technology, they will trust that their provider is taking the best action, and some women will not even question the decisions made for them. The process of labor is not predictable and complications can arise at any time. However, anxiety and interference with the natural process play a large role in the way labor progresses.

Dr. Loel Fenwick, an advocate of non-interference in the natural state of childbirth, stated, "Whereas common obstetric practice manages the parturient's physical functions to conform to a medically determined ideal (the medical pathway), the more conservative 'physiologic pathway' gains maximum benefit from her inherent physical and psychosocial resources to make childbirth more natural, more satisfying, and safer."[4] Not only has medicalized childbirth prevailed all these years, but ever-advancing technology in the management of women in childbirth has continued into the twenty-first century.

Technology has created wonders in medical diagnosis and treatment. It has helped infertile women conceive, sustained the life of premature and sick infants, allowed us to see the fetus developing, diagnosed a myriad of fetal disorders, and even enabled surgeons to perform fetal surgery. It has created medical miracles. However, it has created controversy over its extensive use when labor is progressing normally, without complications. In childbirth, technology interferes with personalized and effective care. Doctors and nurses tend to focus more on the technology than on the parturient woman. I remember when a male nursing student related to me that, while with his wife during her childbirth, he was intently watching the fetal monitor strip (which also records a woman's contractions) and told her that her contractions were getting stronger and closer together. His wife responded, "I'm in labor, not that machine."

I have personally witnessed busy nurses entering their patients' rooms briefly to study the monitor strip and make notes, but spend only a few minutes conversing with and comforting their patients. Nurses and doctors tend to get caught up in evaluating the enormous amount of data, trouble-shooting malfunctioning equipment, sacrificing precious time spent with their patients, and "may overlook the subtle, human cues that something is amiss."[5]

In her 1997 book, *Sisters on a Journey: Portraits of American Midwives*, Penfield Chester interviewed Jo-Anna Rorie, an African American midwife and health care administrator in a residential treatment program for pregnant and drug-addicted women. In discussing her views, Rorie indicated that today midwives coming on staff don't have to struggle for the right to practice, can write prescriptions, and are welcomed by hospitals. However, there just aren't enough of them. She stated, "I learned first-rate technology at Yale and at Georgetown. But I learned to be a midwife on my own. And that part of my learning is inside me and connects me to other women." She continued, "Technology is losing its flair so to speak and that it's time to give up health care practices dictated by the medical model, because it just doesn't work anymore."[6]

In recent years, health care providers have been conducting and reviewing clinical trials to test the effectiveness of routine interventions and technology used in normal labor and birth. One common technological intervention, the use of routine, continuous electronic fetal monitoring during the course of normal labor, has been unchallenged for decades. The original intent of continuous fetal monitoring was based on the supposition that fetal problems would be recognized early so appropriate action could be taken in a timely fashion and that the rate of fetal mortality and neurological damage in the newborn would be reduced. This didn't happen. The results of systematic reviews of randomized clinical trials evaluating a total of 17,510 women who carried their pregnancies to term demonstrated that there was no relationship between continuous EFM and the expected outcomes.[7] Moreover, after EFM became a routine practice in obstetrics, the rate of cesarean births has increased dramatically to an all-time high of 26.1 percent of all live births in the U.S. in 2002. According to the CDC Report, "Births: Final Data for 2002," "...it has been suggested that increasing use of medical technology, such as continuous EFM and induction of labor, has contributed to the increased rate of cesarean births...."[8]

Other clinical trials have been conducted in recent years to test the reliability and need for routine obstetric procedures employed since the beginning of obstetric practice in hospitals. Obstetric procedures still routinely used for normal as well as high-risk births include, in addition to continuous EFM, intravenous infusions, artificial rupture of fetal membranes, labor induction or augmentation with oxytocin or other drugs, epidural anesthesia or analgesia, the use of instruments to assist birth, and episiotomy (surgical incision of the pelvic floor). Other technological equipment includes machines that automatically measure women's blood pressure, pulse, temperature, and blood oxygenation. There is also an enormous amount of technology used to evaluate fetal status, which is necessary in many cases.

Most of the time, medical interventions are employed without considering the woman's choice or obtaining informed consent. Women do sign general permission for care forms on admission to the labor unit, but these forms generally do not list all procedures and potential risks. In many instances, women are still discouraged from getting out of bed, walking around as desired, or taking a bath or shower, all of which are comforting and help move labor along. Also, in most hospitals the "rule" of nothing to eat or drink, "in case" the parturient woman needs an emergency cesarean section, still prevails. Many rules and procedures, laid down since the 1920s, are still followed. It is not infrequent that the cascade of events that follow any obstetric procedure lead to other interventions and, possibly, operative deliveries.

As stated previously, the rate of cesarean births has been rising steadily for the last several decades, reaching a new high of 29.1 percent in 2004. The goal of Healthy People 2010 is fifteen percent of cesarean births. The main reasons for the high rates are still fear of liability, and possibly the higher fees received for surgical procedures. Thus far, no data have shown that the increased rate of cesareans has decreased the number of lawsuits. A female obstetrician, on the staff of a southern hospital, was actually chastised for having a record of cesarean deliveries less than ten percent. She was told by the hospital administration to increase this rate. She subsequently resigned.[9]

It is not just technology and liability issues that have driven this occurrence, but also women who are choosing this option even when there are no medical indications. Many professional women wait until their thirties to have their first babies and choose to have a cesarean because it is convenient for them or they are afraid to go through the pain of labor. "The evolving social acceptability of cesarean on demand may be driven by a new consumerism.... Structured, elective cesarean section is easier for the surgeon."[10] Proponents of elective cesarean births claim that having a cesarean protects women against pelvic floor damage. This is the same argument DeLee gave to promote his "prophylactic forceps operation" in 1920. Normal vaginal births do not damage a woman's pelvic floor muscles. Instruments, manual manipulations, and perineal incisions (episiotomies) do cause pelvic floor injuries!

The United States is not the only country with escalating cesarean birth rates. Sheila Kitzinger declared that Britain has a higher rate of cesareans than the rest of Europe. She exclaimed, "I am skeptical about how widespread the 'too-posh-to-push' syndrome is, but certainly some career women seem to have concluded that it is better to get the whole messy business over rapidly by opting for cesarean, and the system conspires to encourage this."[11]

In the United States, the trend toward "elective" cesarean birth has increased by thirty-six percent from 2001 to 2003. As stated above, the overall rate of cesarean births in 2004 was 29.1 percent. Women who have chosen this option likely have not been given all the facts. At least ninety percent of the time, childbirth is a natural process that proceeds without complications. Women having normal vaginal births are more likely to have fewer long-term complications, easier breastfeeding, and fewer complications than women having cesarean births. Elective cesarean deliveries "pose serious and life-threatening complications for mothers and babies."[12] Women who have elective cesarean sections have a three times greater risk of death than women who opt for normal birth.[13]

Cesarean sections are major surgical operations that pose the same risks as other major operations; these risks include hemorrhage, infection, urinary bladder injury, plus the risks associated with anesthesia. It takes a longer time to heal and recover following a cesarean operation than it does following a normal, spontaneous vaginal birth. There is generally more pain following a cesarean than following a vaginal birth, unless the woman has sustained severe perineal lacerations. Cesarean births also lead to potential serious complications in succeeding pregnancies and births.

Results of a large research study have shown that one or more cesarean births increase the risk of placental complications in future pregnancies. There is a fifty percent risk of placenta previa (placenta lies over the cervix) in a second birth and a two-fold increase in a third birth after two previous cesareans. There is a thirty percent chance of placental abruption (separation of placenta before birth), which has a high fetal mortality rate.[14]

Women's health care organizations stress that the policy—"cesarean on demand"—downplays the risks of operative delivery and could deny women access to fully informed consent. Lamaze International President Barbara Hotelling states, "No evidence supports the idea that cesareans are as safe as vaginal births for mother or baby, and pregnant women should be given all of the facts they need to make an educated decision." Prominent obstetricians Ingrid Nygaard and Dwight Cruikshank commented, "It is currently ill-advised to routinely give all prenatal patients the choice of their desired mode of delivery." They meant in the context of this statement to express concern about the risks of complications after cesarean operations, such as placenta previa and uterine rupture in subsequent pregnancies, when uninformed women opt for cesarean birth.[15]

Today there is still subtle propaganda to convince women that technology is necessary for a safe birth. It is certainly more convenient for the busy obstetrician. As women became more informed in the '60s and '70s, many rebelled against total obstetric control and won some of their battles. They gained more of a say, such as less or no pain medication and family-centered care, but the use of technology in the birthing rooms never ceased. It just kept on advancing. In 2002, out of every one thousand live births in the United States, 852 women were hooked to continuous fetal monitors, 206 had their labors induced, 173 had their labors augmented, and twenty had their membranes artificially ruptured.[16]

In 2002, The Maternity Center Association, in partnership with the Johnson and Johnson Pediatric Institute, surveyed 1,583 women who had given birth over the past twenty-four months. The results of this "Listening to Mothers Survey," showed that the use of technology has continued to increase since the 1960s. It was found, as reported by the women, that seventy percent of the mothers attended childbirth education classes, indicating that they had some knowledge of the birth process and what could be expected. Ninety-three percent reported they had continuous electronic fetal monitoring; eighty-five percent had intravenous infusions; sixty-seven percent had their membranes artificially ruptured; sixty-three percent had oxytocin used to start or stimulate their labors; and sixty-three percent had epidural analgesia or anesthesia for pain relief. Seventy-one percent of the mothers reported that they didn't walk around during labor, mainly because they were hooked up to the monitor or had pain medication. Only twelve percent were allowed to eat and thirty-one percent were allowed oral fluids. Eleven percent of the women reported their births were assisted with forceps or vacuum extraction, thirty-five percent had an episiotomy, and twenty-four percent had a cesarean birth.[17]

A second National U.S. "Listening to Mothers" survey was conducted in January and February 2006. This report did not clarify how decisions were made in the first survey, but this was addressed in the second one. In the new survey, participants were asked if they had experienced pressure from a health provider to have a cesarean even when there were no medical indications. Nine percent said they experienced pressure. Survey results also indicated that participants were poorly informed about the potential complications of cesarean births.[18] Mothers were also asked if they were pressured to have other procedures. Eleven percent reported pressure for labor induction and seven percent reported being pressured to have an epidural. Asked if given a choice to have an episiotomy, eighteen percent of the mothers said yes, nineteen percent weren't sure, and seventy-three percent said they weren't given a choice.[19]

National statistics and reports from the mothers' surveys show that medical technology is applied far too frequently when not medically indicated. Natural childbirth is the act of letting labor and birth proceed naturally without interference unless it is absolutely necessary. As noted previously, Dr. Grantly Dick-Read challenged the medicalization of childbirth in the early twentieth century. Today, health care researchers are challenging the "technicalization" of childbirth. Randomized clinical trials (RCT) have been conducted in recent years to determine the efficacy of routine obstetric procedures and technologies in normal labor. There is now a body of research evidence demonstrating that many of these interventions and technologies used routinely for so many years have not been necessary in normal births and have not proven to be efficacious.

"Evidence-based practice" is a new concept in health care today. "Evidence-based maternity care" is defined as "using the best research about safety and effectiveness of specific tests, treatments, and other interventions to help guide maternity care decisions."[20]

Extensive research has been conducted in recent times to determine the need for continuous electronic fetal monitoring (EFM). It has long been established that the normal fetal heart rate (FHR) is between 100 and 180 beats per minute. As long as this range was maintained, it was believed that the fetus was doing well. However, the fetoscope (that preceded the EFM) cannot pick up possible variations in the fetal heart rate. These variations during or immediately following contractions can possibly indicate a "fetal distress" signal. Since the early 1960s, when the early electronic monitors arrived on the scene, it was speculated that such variations were related to a decrease in the amount of oxygen delivered to the fetus. There is lack of scientific evidence that this is so. It was further determined that continuous EFM would decrease the rate of neonatal pathology and mortality. Research has shown that this is also a false assumption.[21]

Based on a systematic review of nine clinical trials, including a total of 18,561 women, there is clear evidence that continuous EFM is of no benefit to women in normal labor. Results indicated there were no differences in fetal and newborn death rates or development of cerebral palsy between those women who had continuous EFM and those who had intermittent auscultation of the FHR (listening to the FHR with a handheld Doppler).[22] Even with this new evidence, continuous EFM is still routinely used most of the time because of fear of liability and also because it is difficult to change how it has always been done. Because of the diversity in interpretation of any deviance of the "normal" fetal heart rate pattern, lawyers may misinterpret the cause of the birth outcome.[23] In court the premise has been that alterations in fetal heart rate are related to oxygen deprivation, which was believed to cause cerebral palsy or other neurological damage. However, current research evidence suggests that infection and preterm birth are the causes of these outcomes.[24]

Intermittent auscultation, with a handheld Doppler, is just as effective as continuous EFM and is recommended by the Association of the College of Obstetrics and Gynecology for low-risk women. Without being strapped to a continuous monitor, women are free to be out of bed and move around as desired.

Another obstetric practice that has been used far too frequently is labor induction. In 2002, the rate of inductions was 20.6 percent.[25] As stated earlier, oxytocin, the drug most commonly used to stimulate labor, has dangerous side effects and is not indicated unless medical complications exist or the baby is considerably overdue. It is also indicated if the fetus has died.

Today, two-thirds of labor inductions are medically indicated. A new rationale for induction is "psychological indication."[26] Like planned cesarean births, any birth can be planned ahead by scheduling an induction. This is not only convenient for the woman, but also for her doctor, who doesn't have to be called in the middle of the night. However, if not medically indicated, artificial stimulation of labor with oxytocin or other drugs, in addition to risks, inhibit mobility, increase labor pain, and often lead to a cascade of other procedures and a good chance of cesarean delivery.

Labor augmentation (giving oxytocin after labor has begun spontaneously) is also common practice. The rationale for augmenting labor is to achieve normal labor progress. One out of every two women is given oxytocin so their labor will progress more rapidly.[27] Can it be possible that half of all women giving birth don't have normally progressing labors? Midwives never put a time limit on the length of labor. There is great variability in the way labor progresses for each woman. From the time men entered the picture they performed maneuvers to rush the process of labor and birth. It was more profitable for them and they didn't have the patience to wait it out. Augmentation of labor with oxytocin has the same risks and consequences as labor induction.

In earlier times there was no such thing as an "average" length of labor. Without such definitions, midwives recognized when the baby was about to be born. It is so obvious. Women naturally start grunting and bearing down if they are not sedated or have not had an epidural. However, since Friedman plotted the average length of normal labor, physicians used "failure to progress" as the basis for augmenting labor. As discussed in the previous chapter, Friedman published the "Friedman Curve" in 1954, suggesting time lines for the different stages of labor.

A recent study was conducted to reevaluate Friedman's curve. Results indicated that the average length of labor was similar to what Friedman had described, except there was a wider range of normal. In this study, some of the women having their first births were in first stage of labor up to twenty-six hours and up to eight hours in their second stage without any adverse effects.[28]

Oxytocin is used far too frequently to start or augment labor when it is not indicated. In most instances, women are not given the choice, nor are they given sufficient information about the potential risks. When labor lasts much longer than expected, it becomes more difficult for parturient women to cope and deal with the pain. They may also become exhausted. At this point, if offered pain medication or an epidural, they will gratefully accept it. If the nurse, midwife, or other caretaker would encourage women to get out of bed, walk around, or take a shower, it is more likely their labors would progress more effectively. There are other ways to relieve pain, such as massage, soft music, dim lights, and someone constantly present to provide support.

Fear, anxiety, immobility, and withholding food and beverages all contribute to dysfunctional labor. Dr. Loel Fenwick, an advocate of the "physiologic pathway" of managing labor and birth, stated, "Women throughout the world use body positioning to make labor more comfortable and efficient." Fenwick claimed that the woman "gains maximum benefit from her inherent physical and psychosocial resources." The opposite of the "physiologic pathway" is the "medical pathway" of care, which involves "placing a woman in a labor bed, taking away her clothing and personal belongings, interdicting food and drink, and starting an intravenous infusion," all of which are likely to slow labor down.[29] The medical model imposes a vicious cycle by interfering with the natural physiological progress of labor. One intervention leads to others until labor and birth become pathological.

Other routine obstetric interventions that have been practiced for decades have not stood the tests of scientific reasoning. For example, the rationale given for performing an amniotomy (artificial rupture of membranes) is to augment labor. Research has shown that early amniotomy is associated with reducing the duration of labor by about one to one-and-a-half hours, but it also increases the risk of cesarean birth.[30] When membranes remain intact, the bag of water cushions and protects the fetus and umbilical cord against pressure and infection. Also, if membranes are ruptured early in labor and the fetal head lies above the mother's pelvis, there is a potential risk of the cord prolapsing down the birth canal, which greatly decreases the fetus's oxygen supply. An emergency cesarean is then necessary.

Epidural anesthesia or analgesia continues to be a frequent and popular method of pain relief during labor. Pain is unique to each individual, greatly influenced by past experiences, culture, degree of fear and anxiety, and coping mechanisms. Expression of pain also varies widely across cultures. Some women may cry out, seeming to have intense pain, yet feel less pain than women who express more stoicism. Some women simply do not experience great pain while in labor.

In recent years, clinical trials have been conducted to examine the efficacy and consequences of epidural analgesia and anesthesia. The recent findings from a 2003 review of a large number of randomized controlled trials (RCTs) were: incomplete pain relief in up to twenty-five percent of women; seventy-four percent of women had hypotension (drop in blood pressure); sixty-eight percent had difficulty urinating during their labors; and sixty-eight percent experienced itching from the analgesic (morphine) used in the epidurals.[31]

Results of another systematic review of RCTs, including a total of 3,157 women, revealed that "epidural analgesia was associated with greater pain relief than non-epidural methods," but also was associated with longer labors, increase in faulty fetal position, increased use of oxytocin to stimulate labor, and increased use of instruments during birth.[32]

Other trials have revealed longer labors, increased maternal hypotension, increased use of oxytocin, higher rates of instrument-assisted births, and higher rates of newborn infections.[33] Are women made aware of all these possible consequences of epidurals? It is doubtful. Regardless of these potential outcomes, the majority of women choose epidural. It is indeed their choice, but they should be made aware of these facts and alternative methods of pain relief. Women do not need to suffer in childbirth as they once did.

Nature "has not failed U.S. childbearing women to the extent that one out of four women requires abdominal surgery to give birth, one out of four requires artificial rupture of their membranes to initiate or stimulate labor, one out of two requires exogenous oxytocin to achieve normal labor progress, and one out of three requires an episiotomy, forceps, and/or vacuum to give birth."[34] Interventions during the second stage of labor are also still prevalent today. The medical premise has been that the shorter the second stage of labor, the better for the mother and her baby, as advocated by Joseph DeLee in the 1920s. Friedman placed a time limit on the stages of labor. Sometimes women don't yet feel the urge to bear down even though they are told they have reached the second stage of labor, or they may feel the urge before complete dilation. For decades doctors and nurses have urged women in second-stage labor to hold their breath for a count of ten and push as hard as they could. This maneuver decreases the amount of oxygen perfusing the baby, who isn't very happy about it.

I remember an incident while observing a birth at a hospital where I worked as a childbirth educator. Naomi was in the labor bed in a semi-reclined position trying to bear down as hard as she could, being urged by her doctor to "push harder" while his hand was in her vagina. She had been pushing as instructed for quite awhile and was just too exhausted to do better. Her doctor, losing his patience, threatened to pull the baby out with vacuum suction or do a cesarean section. I asked Naomi's nurse why she didn't suggest giving it a rest for awhile and getting Naomi out of bed and walking. The nurse just looked at me, indicating it was the doctor's call. He did end up performing a cesarean operation. Given other options, Naomi could have had a normal birth.

Women who push on demand before they have the urge to do so become easily fatigued. There is now research evidence showing that there are actually two phases of the second stage of labor—an "early" phase, in which the fetus descends the birth canal, and an "active" phase, in which the fetus is pressing on nerves in the pelvic floor muscles that cause a strong urge to bear down. This urge may precede complete cervical dilation or not occur for a period of time after complete dilation.[35]

The onset of these phases requires careful interpretation of the signs of the active phase by listening and paying close attention to the mother's cues. Intensive pushing prior to the urge to bear down can result in injury to the mother's perineum and lead to fatigue. Pushing then becomes ineffective, and then may need obstetric assistance with forceps or vacuum extraction. Women who squat during second-stage labor rarely need such additional assistance to birth their babies. Bearing down just occurs naturally. "Upright positions in birth have been used throughout history and across cultures because they use gravity to help the baby descend and tend to be less painful than supine positions. Studies of upright positions report lower rates of obstetric interventions, especially instrumental delivery."[36]

Another common operative procedure, performed extensively since DeLee's time, is the episiotomy. There has been a downward trend in performing this surgical procedure in the last twenty years or so. Out of every one hundred women giving birth in 1980, sixty-four had episiotomies, compared to 32.7 out of one hundred women in 2000.[37] In most instances, episiotomies are unnecessary and can be harmful, causing possible local bleeding, infection, tearing into the anus, and postpartum pain. The pain can last weeks or months, particularly during sexual intercourse. The rationale given by DeLee back in the 1920s for performing episiotomy was to avoid spontaneous perineal tears that are more difficult to suture, take longer to heal, prevent damage to the perineal floor and prevent fetal head injury. None of these reasons are valid. Women's bodies are designed for childbearing.

There is no clinical evidence that a straight surgical cut heals any faster than a spontaneous tear. Episiotomies have been performed so frequently for so long that the so-called benefits are "deeply rooted in the practice of obstetrics in America."[38] There are other ways to prevent perineal tears, such as applying warm compresses to the perineal area, and lubricating and gently stretching the vagina as the baby emerges. Tears are more likely to occur when women are on their backs with their legs up on stirrups. Squatting, kneeling, and side-lying positions do not stretch the perineal tissue as much as the back reclining position.

Obstetrics has been proclaimed to be founded on scientific theories, but many of them have not been validated by research. The American system of childbirth was based on pathology and control rather than on the assumption that childbirth is a normal event. The management of childbirth follows the industrial model of production in the United States as "a series of controls, measures, monitors, and interventions."[39] Putting greater emphasis on production than on protection engenders risk of adverse outcomes.

Childbirth should be celebrated with pride and dignity, not with control and interference. In the words of Sheila Kitzinger, "We are in danger of forgetting that birth is a wonderful process which should be celebrated, and there is an art in enabling it to unfold—except where there is the genuine prospect of complications—at nature's pace."[40] Change is long overdue. Rules that have been followed since obstetrics took control need to be tested and re-evaluated.

The medical model of care has been associated with interventions and technology, whereas the midwifery model has been associated with non-interference. Midwives trust women to be capable of making their own decisions. In a recent study conducted to explore the values of midwifery, researchers listened to narrative reports from fourteen experienced midwives. Consistent themes in these midwives' reports were: (1) the belief in the normalcy of birth, that women's bodies were physically prepared for childbirth; (2) the midwives' willingness to "wait and see" (not to rush the birth process); (3) trust in the woman's knowledge and instincts; and (4) "presence," that is, remaining physically present with the woman throughout her labor and birth.[41]

Results of another qualitative study, looking at "exemplary" midwifery practices, showed that the essential characteristics were not rushing the process of birth, not intervening unless necessary, providing personalized care, using a wide array of options, and respecting and empowering women. The critical characteristic of "exemplary" midwifery care was the art of "doing nothing well—insuring that normalcy continued through vigilant and attentive care."[42] In essence, midwives empower women, provide resources they need to make their own decisions, and support those decisions. In addition to all the above qualities, midwives are safe birth attendants, having a long history of good birth outcomes. Yet, only ten percent of pregnant women choose midwives as their primary caregiver in the United States, whereas in other countries, such as the Netherlands, United Kingdom, Sweden, and Japan, midwives are the primary birth attendants in a much larger percentage of births.[43]

Another unique quality of midwifery care is that of maintaining a "constant presence" throughout labor. The concept of midwifery care can be summed up as "the provision of emotional, physical, spiritual, and psychological presence and support by the caregiver as desired by the parturient woman."[44] A close friend, relative, or doula can provide constant presence and support. A doula is someone who is trained in labor support or has had much experience in this role.

There is now clinical evidence that continuous support during labor is physically and psychologically beneficial to parturient women. The results of a systematic review of fifteen randomized clinical trials, involving 12,791 women who had continuous intrapartum support, have shown that women were less likely to need analgesic medication, epidural, or operative/assisted births than the women who did not have continuous support. It was also found that the benefits were greater when the support person was not a member of the hospital staff.[45] It is rare that nurses, burdened with responsibility of more than one patient at a time and enormous amounts of paperwork, have the opportunity to provide continuous support. A woman's husband or male partner can also fill this role. Some men do well, but others are not comfortable or have difficulty dealing with their own emotions.

Dr. Robert Bradley, mentioned in the preceding chapter, was a strong advocate of the father as the support person. If the father has difficulty fulfilling this role, it would be helpful to also have a female support person present. Achterberg commented, "Women have always found solace and joy in each other's kitchens, and arms, and words. Sisterhood has been the bond that has held women healers together in the dimmest days of Western civilization."[46]

Doulas, as discussed earlier, provide continuous physical and emotional support to women during labor and birth. Doulas are trained birth assistants and generally are paid fees by the women. Unfortunately, doulas aren't always welcome in some hospital birth settings. Their acceptance depends largely on the attitudes of the medical and nursing staff and administration. There is now scientific evidence that continuous labor support helps reduce the need for pain medications, epidurals, and obstetric interventions.

When labor doesn't progress as well as expected, it is often due to fear, anxiety, and loss of control. The more women know about labor and birth, the less anxious they generally are. According to Dr. Loel Fenwick, childbirth education should begin early, even before pregnancy, because "attitudes toward childbirth are influenced by her experiences since childhood."[47] Women should have a good understanding about the process of normal labor and birth, indications for all medical interventions, the effects of fear and anxiety on labor progress, alternative ways to relieve pain and anxiety, and options available to them.

Women would do well by not rushing to the hospital during the early phase of labor, but instead relaxing in the comfort and familiarity of their own homes, free of rules, equipment, and procedures. When I taught childbirth classes, I urged the women to stay home as long as possible, until they were fairly sure they were in active labor. When I spoke to some of the women after their births, they related to me that my advice worked, that once they got to the hospital, their labors only lasted a short time. There is now research evidence that early admissions to hospital labor units are associated with increased length of labor, increased incidence of complications, and increased use of obstetric interventions.

A study conducted to determine the effects of when in the course of their labors women arrived on the labor unit, compared the obstetric model of care with the midwifery model of care. In this study, 1,414 women received care from a collaborative group (midwives with physician backup) and 783 women were under the care of obstetricians. The results showed that almost half the women in the obstetric care group were admitted to the hospital in early labor (cervix less than four centimeters dilated), compared to only a fourth, in the same stage of early labor, under the care of the collaborative group. Also, there were up to thirty percent more assisted or operative births in the obstetric group than in the collaborative group.[48] This study showed that early admission to a hospital labor unit is more likely to be associated with greater anxiety, longer labors, and medical interference.

In this present day and age, there are still some women who choose to give birth at home, but they are frowned upon by the obstetric community. Actual home births are not necessarily relics of the past. There are women who prefer to give birth in the comforts and familiarity of their own homes without unnecessary medical interference. Lisa's story, told at the beginning of this chapter, is a true one. After two conventional hospital births and experience as a nurse in labor and delivery, she did not want any interference nor have decisions made for her during her next birth.

The story of another home birth appeared in a local newspaper in northern New Jersey in 2003. Sandra was giving birth to her third baby in her own bedroom "where dim rainy-day light leaks through drawn shades and vanilla-scented candles flicker." Midwife Valerie spread out a tablecloth with her supplies while waiting for the birth. Maya, "pink as bubble gum, loud as a teakettle, 8 pounds, 6 ounces, 21 inches long," was born, while Sandra sat on a cushion on the floor with her back against her bed, clutching her belly while husband Chris massaged her shoulders. "Maya is one of just 24,000 babies born at home this year in the United States, out of approximately 4 million newborns. That percentage—about 6 in every 1,000 births—has held steady the last few years."[49]

A large prospective study was conducted in 2000 to determine the outcomes of 5,418 home births, attended by 409 certified professional midwives. Results showed that fetal and newborn mortality rates were 1.7 deaths per one thousand births, consistent with national rates of all births inside or outside hospitals. The study results confirmed "that infrequent use of interventions can be associated with excellent perinatal outcomes" and showed that home births are as safe as planned hospital births for low-risk childbearing women.[50] A home-like birth environment may be the next best choice. Home-like settings are freestanding birth centers or areas (birthing rooms) sectioned off from regular hospital labor units. The unfamiliar hospital environment, with its machines, unfamiliar personnel, and rules, are likely to increase anxiety. A review of six clinical trials was conducted to determine the effects of a home-like birth environment. A total of nine thousand women participated in these trials. Research results showed that home-like birth settings were associated with lower rates of analgesia or anesthesia use, less use of oxytocin to augment labor, and less operative birth procedures, than were births in conventional hospital settings. Research findings also showed greater satisfaction with care among women who birthed in these alternative birth settings.[51]

In the 2002 National Vital Statistics Report, 9,679 lay midwives attended birthing women in their homes and 12,705 lay midwives attended women in freestanding birthing centers that year. Certified Nurse Midwives (CNMs) attended 3,475 home births, 5,689 births in freestanding birthing centers, and 298,073 hospital births. There were a total of 22,980 live babies born at home, compared with a total of 3,986,190 (ninety-nine percent of all live babies) born in hospitals.[52] Today, CNMs mainly practice independently or in collaboration with obstetricians, depending on the state and jurisdiction where they practice. In most cases, their insurance coverage does not include home births and a rare medical doctor will condone home births.

From the time of recorded history, women were afraid of childbirth because of anticipated pain and of the possibility of death. Maternal death is so rare today that it is no longer feared, but the fear of pain prevails. In the early twentieth century, Grantly Dick-Read challenged the belief that pain in childbirth is inevitable and also challenged the medicalization of childbirth. It was again challenged in the 1960s and '70s by women wanting more control in their own childbirth experience. The general picture has not greatly changed. Medical intervention and technology still play a major role in the management of women in childbirth. Technology has its place in medicine and abnormal childbirth, but its application to normal childbirth is now being challenged through scientific research. The results of many clinical trials have shown that medical interventions and technologies used routinely for most of the twentieth century until the present time are not indicated when childbirth is uncomplicated.

Today, women need more than a choice of alternatives. They need more accurate and complete information, including the indications and potential risks of all medical interventions, in order to make more informed choices. Midwifery care is safe, cost-effective, supportive, and uniquely sensitive to the needs of childbearing women. Home births have also been shown to be safe for low-risk women. Evidence-based maternity care should lead the way in returning to more natural ways of managing childbirth. There are safe options for today's childbearing women who elect to choose.

CHAPTER 12

Conclusion:
Women in Power

Lisa planned another home birth for her seventh child. Her contractions began at 5:00 A.M. on December 14, 2006. She waited an hour, to be certain she was in true labor. Monica, her eighteen-year-old daughter, who was resting on the couch, then took the other children to their grandmother's house, and returned home to help her mother. Lisa walked around as her contractions intensified. To help her relax, she went outside and got into the hot tub. (It was winter!) However, Lisa was able to calm down and cool down. She told me, "It was so nice to be in different places and in different positions." "Dave [husband] was with me every step of the way ... got in the shower with me and did whatever I wanted or did not want." When Lisa felt the urge to push, she got into a squatting position and on all fours. But then her contractions stopped. The baby was crowning, but seemed to stay that way forever. Finally, there was another contraction and "the baby's head came out up to her eyes. Two to four minutes passed before the next contraction; then finally the baby was out." Ruby Faith Patience Lilley was born 9:15 in the morning. Dave was the only birth attendant; Monica waited in the other room, but "was wonderful after the birth."[1]

Lisa told me that she believes the "process of birth never fails" and that a "good physical birth is also a spiritual birth." I definitely agree that childbirth is a spiritual experience and the greatest joy. Unfortunately, problems do exist from time to time, and they may require medical intervention. However, women's physiology works well in the process of birth most of the time. Most important, a successful outcome of a healthy baby and mother is certainly an ecstatic and spiritual experience.

Women should be given the opportunity to let nature perform its miracles, the way they choose to do so, unimpeded by unnecessary interference and technological intervention.

In the nineteenth century, physicians promised women that they would have a safer birth under their care than under the care of midwives. In the early decades of the twentieth century, when hospital births began replacing home births, women lost their autonomy and all the other advantages they had in their own homes. Then, when childbirth became firmly entrenched in hospitals, medical intervention and technology became routine practice throughout the twentieth century. Women were unaware of what they sacrificed when they traded in their midwives for doctors, their homes for hospitals, and their social networks for isolation. It wasn't until the second half of the twentieth century when women did begin to question this regime. Family-centered care and the concept of choice of alternatives in childbirth became new themes. However, medicalized childbirth persists.

In this day and age, the majority of women still accept medical interventions, hospital rules, and ever-expanding technology without question. We haven't progressed as much as it may seem. Many women are still unaware of the various choices they have and all the ramifications of medical interventions. Also, some women make choices that are not in their best interests, such as cesarean deliveries on demand. Attitudes within the walls of hospitals continue to prevail in a culture that still views childbirth as pathological.

Obstetrics was founded on the principles of pathology and a determination to control. Obstetric interventions and technology were originally fashioned by men and became routine protocols without sound scientific basis. In America, obstetrics is "troubled by the shadows of litigation, rising costs, fragmentation of care, and a cavalier attitude to intervention in normal processes."[2] As shown in the preceding chapter, many of the medical interventions and technologies used routinely for decades are not indicated in normal labor and childbirth. Technology has its place in medicine and surgery and in obstetrics when there are complications in pregnancy, labor, or birth.

The history of childbirth as told in this book was presented to demonstrate how and why childbirth became a medical event and was treated as such. In so doing, it is hoped that women will gain a better understanding of what was lost in the process and what can be gained with a better understanding of the pros and cons of current practices, established long ago.

In telling the history of childbirth, I focused on men, because initially it was men who sought power and changed the ways in which childbirth had been conducted for centuries past. Of course, women physicians have risen in status equal to male physicians. Obstetrics is a necessary medical and surgical specialty that performs wonders in today's scientific and technological age. But unnecessary routine protocols in normal births continue for various reasons, as previously described, and it is difficult to change the way of things as they have been done for over a century. Obstetricians do consider women's wishes in most instances. This book focused on power. The power now needs to shift back to childbearing women, the consumers of health care. Women need to be part of the team and be able to make well-informed, educated decisions about how, where, and by whom their care is managed.

What lies ahead? Evidence-based practice is catching on. A blending of past traditions with today's advanced scientific knowledge can produce safe and rewarding birth experiences and empower women during one of the most crucial experiences of their lives. Childbirth is a normal event that should be conducted with dignity in safe and satisfying ways. American standards and attitudes should copy those of other countries where educated and certified midwives provide care to low-risk, healthy childbearing women, and where obstetricians mainly provide care to women with medical problems and obstetric complications. Midwives are increasing their numbers in America and many are in collaborative practices with obstetricians, but America has a long way to go to equal the system as practiced in most of Europe.

It would be so logical to advance the practice of midwifery in this country. In the words of Sheila Kitzinger, "Women then need midwives, the guardians of normal childbirth, rarely obstetricians."[3] Midwives are safe practitioners as is evidenced by the lowest maternal and infant mortality rates among many European countries, particularly the Scandinavian countries, where midwives are plentiful. Midwives provide safe, cost-effective, continuous, sensitive, and satisfying care.

There is now a crisis in health care in the United States, particularly in the field of obstetrics. Insurance premiums and liability costs have escalated to higher rates than ever before, a factor that has driven the increased use of technology and surgical procedures in obstetrics. In fact, the rapid rise in medical liability premiums threatens access to obstetric care as obstetricians are foregoing their obstetric practices and medical students are deterred from entering the field. More obstetricians are focusing on gynecology and other related fields, such as infertility.

According to a 2004 survey by the American College of Obstetricians and Gynecologists (ACOG), one in seven obstetricians gave up their obstetric practices, nine percent limited their practices, and twenty-two percent decreased the number of their high-risk patients. Consequently, women travel longer distances, have longer waits during their visits, and have shorter visits. Legislation has been proposed by ACOG to place a cap on litigation. Such reforms were effective in Texas. They have been passed in the House of Representatives and are being pushed in the Senate.[4]

More women are expressing concerns about the way childbirth is managed in hospitals. An article appearing in the *Silver Spring Voice*, a community publication, reported comments from several women about their home births and the reasons they chose their homes instead of hospitals, and midwives instead of doctors. The author of the article, Tamara Tomlinson, stated that it is "little wonder that when talking to women about the experience of labor and delivery, words like 'exciting,' 'liberating,' 'amazing,' and 'comfortable' don't often make their way into the conversation."[5] However, those women who choose home births do use such expressions in describing their birth experiences.

The women who chose home births after giving birth to previous children in hospitals wanted more control and fewer interventions in their more recent births. In describing her home birth, one woman related that, in addition to her midwife attending her, her mother, older sons, four friends, and a midwife assistant were also present. Another woman wanted her second child born at home "in familiar surroundings, where the labor and delivery would be treated as a natural event and not as a medical procedure."[6] The other women who chose home births expressed similar reasons—more control, familiar surroundings, and wanting birth to be treated as a natural event. What these women experienced goes back to how it was in the beginning, but now with present scientific knowledge to prevent many past complications of birth.

The experiences of these women just described are not unique, particularly when natural childbirth proceeds unimpeded. Unfortunately, all births don't progress so smoothly. However, when childbearing women and their fetuses are carefully evaluated, labor and birth can proceed without unnecessary interference and technological intervention, even in certain "high-risk" cases. Women should certainly be given the opportunity to let nature perform its own miracles.

It has never been my intention to suggest that the ways of childbirth should regress back in time as it was conducted in past centuries, but to borrow from the past those comforting and supportive measures that were effective and to evaluate the present ways in which childbirth is conducted. More women need to trust their bodies to perform well in childbirth and let nature's way unfold.

Technology and routine obstetric procedures in normal childbirth are still driven by persistent fear of poor outcomes and litigation. Birth outcomes have been defined in terms of fetal, neonatal, or maternal morbidity or mortality. However, the increasing rates of technology and interventions used in obstetrics have not generally improved perinatal outcomes. In fact, a risk-based approach to care may constitute a self-fulfilling prophecy. A different approach is the new concept of "optimality." This approach strives for the "best possible outcome with minimal number of interventions rather than searching for what can go wrong."[7] A research tool, the Optimality Index–U.S., has recently been developed to measure outcomes in a framework of normalcy. This index shifts the focus to evidence-based, "best possible" events.[8] With this concept in mind, childbirth should be perceived as a natural event and treated as such, unless there is reason to intervene.

What does the future hold? Evidence-based practice will replace traditional routine practices. Midwifery will continue to expand and be accepted practice in normal childbirth, but will be employed in collaboration with obstetrics if complications do arise. Ideally, there will be more freestanding birth centers in proximity to hospitals across the country or as a part of a large hospital complex. Home births will become more acceptable by health care providers, if women choose this option. When couples attend childbirth education classes, it would be a good idea for the woman to bring another woman, such as mother, sister, or close friend, along with her husband or partner, for additional (female) support. Foremost, women will be told all indications, contraindications, and all possible consequences of obstetric interventions and be made aware of the various alternatives they have in childbirth. Knowledge empowers. When this power is given back to women, they will be better equipped to take control of their own bodies, do it their way, and embrace and celebrate the wonder and beauty of childbirth.

Notes

1. Childbirth in Primitive and Ancient Times

1. R.P. Finney, *The Story of Motherhood*. New York: Liveright (1937): 10.

2. G.J. Engelmann, "Pregnancy, Parturition, and Childbed among Primitive People," *American Journal of Obstetrics and Diseases of Women and Children*, Vol. 14 (1881): 602–618, 828–847.

3. H. Graham, *Eternal Eve: The History of Gynaecology and Obstetrics*. New York: Doubleday (1951): 4.

4. Ibid., 17.

5. Ibid., 7–10.

6. N. Newton, "Some Aspects of Primitive Childbirth," *Midwife and Health Visitor*, Vol. 2, (August 1996): 324–329.

7. E.C. Whitmont, *Return of the Goddess*. New York: Crossroad Publishing (1984): 42.

8. J. Achterberg, *Woman as Healer*. Boston and London: Shambhala (1991): 2.

9. Ibid., 10.

10. H.G. Wells, *The Outline of History: Being a Plain History of Life and Mankind*. New York: Macmillan (1921): 131–135.

11. Achterberg, *Woman as Healer*, 15–17.

12. Ibid., 20–24.

13. M. Chamberlain, *Old Wives' Tales: Their History, Remedies and Spells*. London: Virago Press (1981): 8–11.

14. S. Lock, J.M. Last, and G. Dunea (eds.), *Oxford Illustrated Companion to Medicine*. Oxford: Oxford University Press (2001): 866.

15. Chamberlain, *Old Wives' Tales*, 12.

16. Graham, *Eternal Eve*, 14–16.

17. A. Diamont, *The Red Tent*. New York: Picador USA (1997): 40. This passage was Dinah's description of her mother's first birth as told to her by her Aunt Rachel. It demonstrates the beauty of childbirth and love the attendants bestowed on women giving birth.

18. Whitmont, *Return of the Goddess*, 42.

19. Chamberlain, *Old Wives' Tales*, 13.

20. Achterberg, *Woman as Healer*, 25–29.

21. Chamberlain, *Old Wives' Tales*, 16.

22. Graham, *Eternal Eve*, 37.

23. Finney, *The Story of Motherhood*, 36.

24. P.M. Dunn, "Hippocrates (460–356 B.C.) and the Founding of Perinatal Medicine," *Archives of Diseases in Childhood*, Vol. 69 (1993): 540–541.

25. Ibid.

26. Graham, *Eternal Eve*, 49.

27. Dunn, "Hippocrates."

28. Finney, *The Story of Motherhood*, 38.

29. L. Townsend, "Obstetrics through the Ages," *The Medical Journal of Australia*, Vol. 1 (April 1952): 557–565.

30. Graham, *Eternal Eve*, 57.

31. W.M. Goodell, "Some Ancient Methods of Delivery," *American Journal of Obstetrics and Diseases of Women and Children*, Vol. 4 (1871): 663–676.

32. D.P. Stille, *Extraordinary Women of Medicine*. New York: Grolier (1997): 9–10.

33. Achterberg, *Woman as Healer*, 31–32.

34. Goodell, "Some Ancient Methods of Delivery."

35. Graham, *Eternal Eve*, 61–63.

36. Achterberg, *Woman as Healer*, 35–36.

37. Finney, *The Story of Motherhood*, 141.

38. Townsend, "Obstetrics through the Ages."

39. R. York, "The History of Induction," *Midwife Health Visitor and Community Nurse*, Vol. 20 (1984): 1–6.

40. Findley, *The Story of Childbirth*, 107.

41. Graham, *Eternal Eve*, 81.

42. *The Holy Scriptures, Exodus*, I, 16, (1917): 65.

43. Goodell, "Some Ancient Methods of Delivery."

44. Ibid.

45. Chamberlain, *Old Wives' Tales*, 26–27.

46. Ibid.

47. P. Donahue, *Nursing, the Finest Art: An Illustrated History*, St. Louis: C.V. Mosby (1985): 109–110.

48. *The Holy Scriptures, Exodus*, I, 16: 65.

49. J. Murphy-Lawless, *Reading Birth and Death: A History of Obstetric Thinking*. Bloomington, IN: Indiana University Press (1998): 9.

50. R. Wertz and D.C. Wertz, *Lying-In: A History of Childbirth in America*. New York: Schoekin Books (1977): 1.

2. The Middle Ages: An Era of Despair and Persecution

1. Passage taken from birth scene described in a novel by Sigrid Undset, *Kristin Lavransdotter II: The Mistress of Husaby*. Translated by C. Archer. New York: Alfred A. Knopf (1925). Bantam Edition (1978): 69–70. Original title: *Husfriel*. Oslo: H. Aschebauy, 1921.

2. J.A. Butler, "Mediaeval Midwifery," *Nursing Times*, Vol. 77 (Oct. 7, 1981): 1762–1763.

3. Finney, *The Story of Motherhood*, 51.

4. H.G. Wells, *The Outline of History: Being a Plain History of Life and Mankind*. New York: Macmillan (1921): 524.

5. S.B. Burns, "A Pictorial History of Healing," *Clinical Reviews*, Vol. 13 (May 2003): 24–25.

6. Achterberg, *Woman as Healer*, 41.

7. Wells, *The Outline of History*, 607.

8. J. Michelet, *Satanism and Witchcraft: A Classic Study of Medieval Superstition*. New York: Harper and Row (1992): 21.

9. Ibid., x.

10. Chamberlain, *Old Wives' Tales: Their History, Remedies and Spells*. London: Virago Press (1981): 30–31.

11. J.H. Aveling, *English Midwives—Their History and Prospects*. London: Hugh K. Elliott (1962 reprint of 1872 edition): 5–10.

12. Butler, "Mediaeval Midwifery," 1762–1763.

13. Chamberlain, *Old Wives' Tales*, 40–41.

14. Michelet, *Satanism and Witchcraft*, 22.

15. P. Donahue, *Nursing, the Finest Art: An Illustrated History*, St. Louis: C.V. Mosby (1985): 143.

16. Wells, *The Outline of History*, 655.

17. T.S. Szasz, *The Manufacture of Madness: A Comparative Study of the Inquisition and the Mental Health Movement*. New York: Harper & Row (1970): 5.

18. Michelet, *Satanism and Witchcraft*, 16.

19. M.A. Murray, *The Witchcult of Western Europe*. Oxford: Clarendon Press (1921; reprinted 1963): 9.

20. J. O'Faolain and J. Martines (eds.), *Not in God's Image. Women in History from the Greeks to the Victorians*. New York: Harper Torchbook (1973): 207.

21. Murray, *The Witchcult of Western Europe*, 5.

22. Ibid., 28.

23. Szasz, *The Manufacture of Madness*, 6.

24. Ibid., 5–6.

25. O'Faolain and Martines, *Not in God's Image*, 20.

26. B. Ehrenreich and D. English, *Witches, Midwives, and Nurses: A History of Women Healers*. New York: Doubleday (1973): 10–15.

27. Achterberg, *Woman as Healer*, 66.

28. Szasz, *The Manufacture of Madness*, 6.

29. Chamberlain, *Old Wives' Tales*, 54. Quoted from J. Sprenger and H. Kramer in *Malleus Maleficarum*.

30. J.N. Hayes, *The Burdens of Disease*. New Brunswick, NJ and London: Rutgers University Press (2003): 33–43.

31. Chamberlain, *Old Wives' Tales*, 45.

32. Townsend, "Obstetrics through the Ages."

33. Michelet, *Satanism and Witchcraft*, xix.

34. Achterberg, *Woman as Healer*, 57.

35. B. Ehrenreich and D. English, *For Her Own Good*. New York: Doubleday (1978): 34.

36. Szasz, *The Manufacture of Madness*, 86.

37. Murray, *The Witchcult of Western Europe*, 40.

38. Ibid., 19.

39. Szasz, *The Manufacture of Madness*, 7.

40. Michelet, *Satanism and Witchcraft*, 132.

41. O'Faolain and Martines, *Not in God's Image*, 208.

42. Michelet, *Satanism and Witchcraft*, 129.

43. O'Faolain and Martines, *Not in God's Image*, 208. Quotes taken from H. Kramer and J. Sprenger, *Malleus Maleficarum*, trans. by Montague Summers (Arrow Books, 1971): 112, 116–17, 119, 122.

44. Ibid., 209.

45. Ehrenreich and English, *For Her Own Good*, 31.

46. Szasz, *The Manufacture of Madness*, 9–10.

47. Ibid., 30–33.

48. Ibid., 43.

49. Murray, *The Witchcult of Western Europe*, 16.

50. Wells, *The Outline of History*, 709–711.

51. Townsend, "Obstetrics through the Ages."

3. The Sixteenth Century: A Renaissance

1. H. Graham, *Eternal Eve: The History of Gynaecology and Obstetrics*. New York: Doubleday (1951): 144.

2. T. Denman, *An Introduction to the Practice of Midwifery*, Vol. I. New York: James Oram (1802): xiv.

3. R.H. Shryock. *Medicine in America: Historical Essays*. Baltimore: Johns Hopkins Press (1966): 4.

4. S. Lock, J.M. Last, and G. Dunea, *Oxford Illustrated Companion to Medicine*. Oxford: Oxford University Press (2001): 88.

5. H. Graham, *Eternal Eve*, 156–157.

6. Ibid., 157–158.

7. Lock et al., *Oxford Illustrated Companion to Medicine*, 88.

8. J. Achterberg, *Woman as Healer*. Boston and London: Shambhala (1991): 103.

9. B.M. Willmott Dobbie, "An Attempt to Estimate the True Rate of Maternal Morbidity, Sixteenth to Eighteenth Centuries," *Medical History*, Vol. 26 (1982): 79–90.

10. R.L. Petrelli, "The Regulation of French Midwifery during the Ancient Regime," *Journal of History of Medicine and Allied Science*, Vol. 26 (1971): 276–292.

11. J. Gelis, *History of Childbirth: Fertility, Pregnancy and Birth in Early Modern Europe*. Translated by Rosemary Morris. Boston: Northeastern University Press (1991): 99.

12. Ibid., 96.

13. Ibid., 97.

14. J.H. Aveling, *English Midwives: Their History and Prospects*. London: Hugh K. Elliot (1962, reprint of 1872 edition): 10.

15. Graham, *Eternal Eve*, 144.

16. L. Townsend, "Obstetrics through the Ages," *The Medical Journal of Australia*. Vol. 1 (17) (1952): 557–565.

17. Aveling, *English Midwives*, 10.

18. Ibid., 13.

19. Graham, *Eternal Eve*, 149–151.

20. P. Rhodes, "Obstetrics in Seventeenth Century England," *Nursing RSA Verpleging*. Vol. 5 (10) (1990): 28–31.

21. L. Dundees, "The Evolution of Maternal Birthing Position," *American Journal of Public Health*. Vol. 77 (5) (1987): 636–640.

22. Ibid.

23. Rhodes, "Obstetrics in Seventeenth Century England."

24. J. Jarco, *Postures and Practices during Labor among Primitive Peoples*. New York: Paul B. Holler (1934): 23.

25. D.N. Burns and L.D. Calache, "An Evaluation of Some Early Obstetrical Instruments," *Caduceus*. Vol. 3 (1987): 33–41.

26. Rhodes, "Obstetrics in Seventeenth Century England."

27. Burns and Calache, "An Evaluation of Some Early Obstetrical Instruments."

28. Denman, *An Introduction to the Practice of Midwifery*, 85.

29. Lock et al., *Oxford Illustrated Companion to Medicine*, 158.

30. Graham, *Eternal Eve*, 165.

31. N.H. Naqvi, "James Barlow (1767–1839): Operator of the First Caesarean Section in England," *British Journal of Obstetrics and Gynaecology*. Vol. 92 (May 1985): 468–472.

32. Townsend, "Obstetrics through the Ages."

33. Naqvi, "James Barlow."

34. R.W. Wertz and D.C. Wertz, *Lying-In: A History of Childbirth in America*. New York: Schocken Books (1977): 6.

35. Petrelli, "The Regulation of French Midwifery."

4. The Seventeenth Century: Men and Their Instruments

1. J. Gelis, *History of Childbirth: Fertility, Pregnancy, and Birth in Early Modern Europe.* Translated by Rosemary Morris. Boston: Northeastern University Press (1991): 99.

2. Ibid., 97–101.

3. Ibid., 109.

4. R.P. Finney, *The Story of Motherhood.* New York: Liveright (1937): 102.

5. Gelis, *History of Childbirth*, 91.

6. P. Rhodes, "Obstetrics in Seventeenth Century England," *Nursing RSA Verpleging*, Vol. 5 (10) (1990): 28–31.

7. I.S. Cutter and H.R. Viets, *A Short History of Midwifery.* Philadelphia and London: W.B. Saunders (1964): 74.

8. R.E. Roush, "The Development of Midwifery—Male and Female, Yesterday and Today," *Journal of Nurse-Midwifery*, Vol. 24 (5) (May/June 1979): 27–37.

9. Housholder, "A Historical Perspective of the Obstetric Chair" (1994). *Surgery, Gynecology, and Obstetrics.* Vol. 139 (1974): 423–430.

10. H. Graham, *Eternal Eve: The History of Gynaecology and Obstetrics.* New York: Doubleday (1951): 242.

11. R.W. Wertz and D.C. Wertz, *Lying-In: A History of Childbirth in America.* New York: Schocken Books (1977): 31.

12. Graham, *Eternal Eve*, 242.

13. Cutter and Viets, *A Short History of Midwifery*, 9.

14. J.H. Aveling, *English Midwives—Their History and Prospects.* London: Hugh K. Elliot (1962; reprint of 1872 edition): 35.

15. Rhodes, "Obstetrics in Seventeenth Century England."

16. Graham, *Eternal Eve*, 257.

17. H. Arthure, "The Midwife—In Simpson's Time and Ours," *The Journal of Obstetrics and Gynaecology of the British Commonwealth,* Vol. 80 (1973): 1–9.

18. L. Dundes, "The Evolution of Maternal Birthing Position," *American Journal of Public Health,* Vol. 5 (10) (1987): 636–640.

19. C.B. Ingraham, "The Chamberlens and the Obstetric Forceps," *American Journal of Obstetrics and Diseases of Women and Children,* Vol. 63 (1911): 827–848.

20. L. Townsend, "Obstetrics through the Ages," *The Medical Journal of Australia,* Vol. 1 (17) (1952): 557–565.

21. Ingraham, "The Chamberlens and the Obstetric Forceps."

22. Rhodes, "Obstetrics in Seventeenth Century England."

23. Townsend, "Obstetrics through the Ages."

24. Rhodes, "Obstetrics in Seventeenth Century England."

25. J. Mitford, *The American Way of Birth.* New York: Dutton (1992): 27.

26. Cutter and Viets, *A Short History of Midwifery*, 49.

27. Ibid., 50.

28. Townsend, "Obstetrics through the Ages."

29. Graham, *Eternal Eve*, 196.

30. Cutter and Viets, *A Short History of Midwifery*, 51.

31. Townsend, "Obstetrics through the Ages."

32. Ibid.

33. P.M. Dunn, "Francois Mauriceau (1637–1709) and Maternal Posture for Parturition," *Archives of Diseases in Childhood,* Vol. 66 (1991): 78–79.

34. Dundes, "The Evolution of Maternal Birthing Position," *American Journal of Public Health,* Vol. 5 (10) (1987): 636–640.

35. W.M. Goodell, "Some Ancient Methods of Delivery," *American Journal of Obstetrics and Diseases of Women and Children,* Vol. 4 (1871): 663–676.

36. Dunn, "Francois Mauriceau."

37. Ibid.

38. Dundes, "The Evolution of Maternal Birthing Position."

39. Goodell, "Some Ancient Methods of Delivery."

40. Ibid.

41. Housholder, "A Historical Perspective of the Obstetric Chair."

42. Dunn, "Francois Mauriceau," Taken from Mauriceau's *Treatise.*

43. Aveling, *English Midwives*, 50. Quoted from J. Sharp, *The Midwives' Book.*

44. Graham, *Eternal Eve*, 230.

45. Aveling, *English Midwives*, 50. Quoted from J. Sharp, *The Midwives' Book.*

46. Ibid., 53.

47. Ibid., 198. Quoted in Sharp. Apparently the "eagle-stone" was of vegetable origin and was supposed to possess miraculous powers.

48. Cutter and Viets, *A Short History of Midwifery*, 95 and 201.

49. Graham, *Eternal Eve*, 238–240.

50. Ibid., 231.

5. The Eighteenth Century: Men and Science

1. E. Nihell, *A Treatise on the Art of Midwifery—Setting Forth Various Abuses Therein, Especially as to the Practice with Instruments.* London: A. Morley (1760): 92.

2. J.H. Aveling, *English Midwives—Their History and Prospects.* London: Hugh K. Elliot (1962; reprint of 1872 edition): 132.

3. J. Murphy-Lawless, *Reading Birth and Death—A History of Obstetric Thinking.* Bloomington, IN: Indiana University Press (1998): 17.

4. B.K. Rothman, *Giving Birth.* New York: Penguin Books (1982): 53.

5. H. Graham, *Eternal Eve: The History of Gynaecology and Obstetrics.* New York: Doubleday (1951): 269–270.

6. T. Denman, *An Introduction to the Practice of Midwifery,* Vol. I. New York: James Oram (1802): 52–53.

7. L. Townsend, "Obstetrics through the Ages," *The Medical Journal of Australia,* Vol. 1 (17) (1952): 557–565.

8. Graham, *Eternal Eve,* 272.

9. E. Nihell, *A Treatise on the Art of Midwifery,* 50.

10. Graham, *Eternal Eve,* 274.

11. T. Denman, *An Introduction to the Practice of Midwifery,* Vol. II. New York: James Oram (1802): 53.

12. Graham, *Eternal Eve,* 275.

13. Nihell, *A Treatise on the Art of Midwifery,* 111.

14. Graham, *Eternal Eve,* 292.

15. Nihell, *A Treatise on the Art of Midwifery,* 111.

16. Townsend, "Obstetrics through the Ages."

17. Nihell, *A Treatise on the Art of Midwifery,* 50.

18. Ibid., 71.

19. Ibid., viii.

20. Ibid., 54.

21. Ibid., 90.

22. Ibid., 454.

23. Denman, *An Introduction to the Practice of Midwifery,* Vol. II, 54.

24. Ibid., Vol. I, 171.

25. Ibid., 170–171.

26. Nihell, *A Treatise on the Art of Midwifery,* 257.

27. Murphy-Lawless, *Reading Birth and Death,* 79.

28. S. Lock, J.M. Last, and G. Dunea (eds.), *Oxford Illustrated Companion to Medicine.* Oxford: Oxford University Press (2001): 577.

29. N.H. Naqvi, "James Barlow (1767–1839): Operator of the First Caesarean Section in England," *British Journal of Obstetrics and Gynaecology,* Vol. 92 (May 1985): 468–472.

30. J.I. Ashford, "A History of Accouchement Force: 1550–1985," *Birth,* Vol. 13 (4) (Dec. 1986): 240–248.

31. L.D. Longo, "A Treatise of Midwifery in Three Parts. Gielding Ould," *American Journal of Obstetrics and Gynecology,* Vol. 172 (4) (April 1995): 1317–1319.

32. Ibid. Quotes taken from Ould's *Treatise.*

33. Ibid.

34. I. Cutter and H.R. Viets, *A Short History of Midwifery.* Philadelphia and London: W.B. Saunders (1964): 36.

35. Graham, *Eternal Eve,* 313.

36. Ibid.

37. Ibid., 309–313.

38. Cutter and Viets, *A Short History of Midwifery,* 43.

39. J. Gelis, *History of Childbirth: Fertility, Pregnancy and Birth in Early Modern Europe.* Translated by Rosemary Morris. Boston: Northeastern University Press (1991): 247.

40. Z. Loudon, "Deaths in Childbed from the Eighteenth Century to 1935," *Medical History,* Vol. 30 (1986): 1–41.

41. Ibid.

42. Ibid.

43. A, Eccles, "Obstetrics in the Seventeenth and Eighteenth Centuries and Its Implications for Maternal and Infant Mortality," *Society for the History of Medicine Bulletin,* No. 20–21 (1977): 8–15.

44. W. Dobbie, "An Attempt to Estimate the True Rate of Maternal Mortality, Sixteenth to Eighteenth Centuries," *Medical History,* Vol. 26 (1982): 79–90.

45. Loudon, "Deaths in Childbed."

46. Eccles, "Obstetrics in the Seventeenth and Eighteenth Centuries."

47. Graham, *Eternal Eve,* 376.

48. J.G. Adami, *Charles White of Manchester (1728–1813) and the Arrest of Puerperal Fever.* Reprinted from Charles White's published writing on puerperal fever. London: University Press of Liverpool (1922): 52.

49. Cutter and Viets, *A Short History of Midwifery,* 105.

50. Adami, *Charles White of Manchester,* 55.

51. Cutter and Viets, *A Short History of Midwifery*, 106–107.

52. Adami, *Charles White of Manchester*, 67.

53. Ibid., 82–83.

54. Cutter and Viets, *A Short History of Midwifery*, 111.

6. The Nineteenth Century: Men and Disease

1. T. M. Madden, "On Sudden Death Soon after Parturition," *The American Journal of Obstetrics and Diseases of Women and Children*, Vol. IV (2) (August 1871): 193–198+. Story taken from a case study presented in this article.

2. Z. Loudon, "Deaths in Childbed from the Eighteenth Century to 1935," *Medical History*, Vol. 30 (1986): 1–41.

3. Madden, "On Sudden Death Soon after Parturition."

4. J. Murphy-Lawless, *Reading Birth and Death: A History of Obstetric Thinking*. Bloomington, IN: Indiana University Press (1998): 109.

5. Ibid., 137.

6. Cutter and H. R. Viets, *A Short History of Midwifery*. Philadelphia and London: W.B. Saunders (1964): 36. Quoted by Robert Collins in his 1835 *Treatise*.

7. Ibid., 114, 124.

8. H. Graham, *Eternal Eve: The History of Gynaecology and Obstetrics*. Garden City, New York: Doubleday (1951): 403.

9. Ibid., 402.

10. J. Mitford, *The American Way of Birth*. New York: Dutton (1992): 30.

11. Graham, *Eternal Eve*, 403.

12. Excerpts taken from P. Semmelweis, *The Etiology, the Concept, and the Prophylaxis of Childbed Fever* (1861). Translated by Frank P. Murphy in the series, *Medical Classics*, Vol. 5 (5) (January 1941). Reprinted in *Reviews of Infectious Diseases*, Vol. 3 (4) (July-August 1981), (Edited): 808–811.

13. Ibid., 809.

14. Ibid., 810.

15. Ibid., 811.

16. Ibid.

17. Graham, *Eternal Eve*, 408.

18. K.C. Carter, "Ignaz Semmelweis, Carl Mayrhofer and the Rise of Germ Theory," *Medical History*, Vol. 29 (1985): 33–53.

19. Graham, *Eternal Eve*, 418.

20. C.N.B. Camac, *Classics of Medicine and Surgery*. New York: Dover (1909): 393.

21. T. DiBacco, "Childbed Fever and Handwashing," *The Washington Post* (March 23, 1993.)

22. L. Townsend, "Obstetrics through the Ages," *The Medical Journal of Australia*, Vol. 1 (April 26, 1952): 557–565.

23. Graham, *Eternal Eve*, 401.

24. Camac, *Classics of Medicine and Surgery*, 394.

25. M.P. Donahue, *Nursing, the Finest Art: An Illustrated History*. St. Louis: C.V. Mosby (1985): 198.

26. Carter, "Ignaz Semmelweis, Carl Mayrhofer,"

27. Ibid.

28. R.P. Finney, *The Story of Motherhood*. New York: Liveright (1937): 231.

29. Ibid., 236–237.

30. Ibid., 238–239.

31. Ibid., 239–240.

32. Graham, *Eternal Eve*, 418.

33. Ibid., 556–560.

34. Finney, *The Story of Motherhood*, 248.

35. Ibid., 248–250.

36. Finney, *The Story of Motherhood*, 158.

37. G. Collins, *America's Women: 400 Years of Dolls, Drudges, Helpmates, and Heroines*. New York: HarperCollins (2003): 253.

38. Finney, *The Story of Motherhood*, 160.

39. D. Stampone, "The History of Obstetric Anesthesia," *Journal of Perinatal and Neonatal Nursing*, Vol. 4 (1990): 1–13.

40. Finney, *The Story of Motherhood*, 163.

41. C.N.B. Camac, *Classics of Medicine and Surgery*. New York: Dover (1909): 393.

42. Ibid., 304.

43. Finney, *The Story of Motherhood*, 169.

44. Camac, *Classics of Medicine and Surgery*, 362.

45. Graham, *Eternal Eve*, 476.

46. C.D. Pitcock and R. Clark, "From Fanny to Fernand: The Development of Consumerism in Pain Control during the Birth Process," *American Journal of Obstetrics and Gynecology*, Vol. 167 (3) (1992): 277–862.

47. Graham, *Eternal Eve*, 475–479.

48. Pitcock and Clark, "From Fanny to Fernand," Quote taken from N.C. Keep, "The Letheon Administration in a Case of Labor," *Boston Medical Journal*, Vol. 36 (1847).

49. Graham, *Eternal Eve*, 483–484.

50. Camac, *Classics of Medicine and Surgery*, 380.

51. Graham, *Eternal Eve*, 485.

52. Pitcock and Clark, "From Fanny to Fernand."

53. Ibid.

54. P.M. Dunn, "Dr. John Snow (1813–1858) of London: Pioneer of Obstetric Anaesthesia," *Archives of Diseases in Childhood*, Vol. 75 (1996): F141–F142.

55. R. Mander, "A Reappraisal of Simpson's Introduction to Chloroform," *Midwifery*, Vol. 14 (3) (September 1998): 181–189.

56. Graham, *Eternal Eve*, 483.

57. Mander, "A Reappraisal of Simpson's Introduction to Chloroform."

58. Ibid. Quote taken from paper presented by J.Y. Simpson to the Medico-Chirurgical Society of Edinburgh, 10th November 1847.

59. Louden, "Deaths in Childbed from the Eighteenth Century to 1935."

60. Murphy-Lawless, *Reading Birth and Death*, 82.

61. R. York, "History of Induction," *Midwife Health Visitor and Community Nurse*, Vol. 20 (April 1984): 109.

62. R.L. Dickinson, "Accouchement Force," *American Journal of Obstetrics and Diseases of Women and Children*, Vol. 48 (1903): 10–15.

63. J.B. DeLee, "The Bossi Dilator, Its Place in Accouchement Force," *American Journal of Obstetrics and Diseases of Women and Children*, Vol. 48 (1903): 27–30.

64. A.J.P. Hardin, "Discussion of Dr. Dill's Paper on, 'The Use of the Midwifery Forceps,'" *Dublin Journal of Medical Science*, Vol. 68 (1879): 170–173.

65. C.C.P. Clark, "Management of the Obstetrical Forceps," *American Journal of Obstetrics and Diseases of Women and Children*, Vol. 4 (1871): 138–141.

66. P.M. Dunn, "Dr. Thomas Radford (1793–1881) of Manchester and Obstructed Labor," in the series, *Perinatal Lessons from the Past, Archives of Diseases of Childhood*, Vol. 69 (1993): 327–329.

67. Ibid.

68. Graham, *Eternal Eve*, 572.

69. H. Arthure, "The Midwife—In Simpson's Time and Ours," *The Journal of Obstetrics and Gynaecology of the British Commonwealth*, Vol. 80 (1973): 1–8.

70. J. Aveling, *English Midwives: Their History and Prospects*. London: Hugh K. Elliot (1962 reprint of the 1872 edition): 163–165.

71. Ibid., 165–167.

72. Arthure, "The Midwife—In Simpson's Time and Ours."

73. Aveling, *English Midwives*, 171.

74. Ibid., 172–173.

7. Childbirth in Early America

1. C.K. Drinker, *Not so Long Ago: A Chronicle of Medicine and Doctors in Colonial Philadelphia*. New York: Oxford University Press (1937): 58.

2. H. Speert, *Obstetrics and Gynecology in America: A History*. Baltimore: Waverly Press (ACOG) (1980):7.

3. R.P. Finney, *The Story of Motherhood*. New York: Liveright (1937): 144.

4. S.R. Williams, *Demeter's Daughters*. New York: Atheneum Press (1976): 174.

5. Finney, *The Story of Motherhood*, 140–141.

6. G. Collins, *America's Women: 400 Years of Dolls, Drudges, Helpmates, and Heroines*. New York: HarperCollins (2003): 48.

7. H. Thoms, *Chapters in American History*. Springfield, IL: Charles C. Thomas (1933 and 1961): 5.

8. Collins, *America's Women*, 30.

9. Speert, *Obstetrics and Gynecology in America*, 11.

10. R.W. Wertz and D.C. Wertz, *Lying-In: A History of Childbirth in America*. New York: Schocken Books (1977): 23.

11. F. Hill, *A Delusion of Satan: The Full Story of the Salem Witch Trials*. New York: Doubleday (1943 and 1995): 15.

12. Ibid., 2.

13. Ibid., 16.

14. Ibid., 1.

15. Collins, *America's Women*, 45.

16. A.D. Gordon and M.J. Buhle, "Sex and Class in Colonial and Nineteenth-Century America," in B.A. Carroll (ed.), *Liberating Women's History: Theoretical and Critical Essays*. Chicago: University of Illinois Press (1976): 278–281.

17. Thoms, *Chapters in American History*, 3.

18. D. Weatherford, *Milestones—A Chronology of American Women's History*. New York: Fitzhenry and Whiteside (2002): 7.

19. Thoms, *Chapters in American History*, 3.

20. Ibid., 9.

21. Wertz and Wertz, *Lying-In*, 13.

22. Speert, *Obstetrics and Gynecology in America*, 11.

23. Collins, *America's Women*, 57.

24. J.A. Chaney, "Birthing in Early America," *Journal of Nurse-Midwifery*, Vol. 25 (2) (1980): 5–13.

25. Speert, *Obstetrics and Gynecology in America*, 3.

26. R.H. Shryock, *Medical Licensing in America, 1650–1965*. Baltimore: Johns Hopkins Press (1967): 23.

27. P.M. Donahue, *Nursing, the Finest Art: An Illustrated History*. St. Louis, C. V. Mosby (1967): 270.

28. R.H. Shryock, *Medicine in America: Historical Essays*. Baltimore: Johns Hopkins Press (1966): 6–7.

29. J.W. Leavitt, *Brought to Bed: Childbearing in America, 1750–1950*. New York and Oxford: Oxford University Press (1986): 4.

30. Collins, *America's Women*, 56.

31. H. Graham, *Eternal Eve: The History of Gynaecology and Obstetrics*. Garden City, New York: Doubleday (1951): 303.

32. Speert, *Obstetrics and Gynecology in America*, 7.

33. Thoms, *Chapters in American History*, 11.

34. Graham, *Eternal Eve*, 303.

35. Speert, *Obstetrics and Gynecology in America*, 3.

36. Ibid., 12.

37. Shryock, *Medical Licensing in America*, 9.

38. Ibid., 4. Taken from *A Summary of…. The Present State of the British Settlements in North America*. Boston (1753): 351.

39. Speert, *Obstetrics and Gynecology in America*, 5.

40. F.C. Irving, *Safe Deliverance*. Boston: Houghton Mifflin (1942): 74.

41. Ibid., 77.

42. C. Binger, *Revolutionary Doctor, Benjamin Rush, 1746–1830*. New York: W.W. Norton (1966): 12.

43. Shryock, *Medicine in America*, 18.

44. Binger, *Revolutionary Doctor*, 84.

45. Thoms, *Chapters in American History*, 20.

46. L.D. Longo, "Obstetrics and Gynecology," in R.P. Numbers (ed.), *The Education of American Physicians*. Berkeley: University of California Press (1980): 206.

47. Thoms, *Chapters in American History*, 20.

48. Longo, "Obstetrics and Gynecology," 205.

49. Quoted in Thoms, *Chapters in American History*, 21 and in Longo, "Obstetrics and Gynecology," 206.

50. J.P. Rooks, *Midwifery and Childbirth in America*. Philadelphia: Temple University Press (1997): 19.

51. Shryock, *Medical Licensing in America*, 17.

52. Thoms, *Chapters in American History*, 22.

53. Speert, *Obstetrics and Gynecology in America*, 73.

54. Thoms, *Chapters in American History*, 32.

55. Rooks, *Midwifery and Childbirth in America*, 19.

56. Leavitt, *Brought to Bed*, 36.

57. Ibid., 9.

58. J.W. Leavitt, "'Science' Enters the Birthing Room: Obstetrics in America since the Eighteenth Century," *The Journal of American History*, Vol. 70 (1983): 282–304.

59. C.K. Drinker, *Not so Long Ago: A Chronicle of Medicine and Doctors in Colonial Philadelphia*. New York: Oxford University Press (1937): 58.

60. Ibid.

8. Nineteenth-Century America: The Birth of Obstetrics and Gynecology

1. F.C. Irving, *Safe Deliverance*. Boston: Houghton Mifflin (1942): 141–143.

2. M.P. Donahue, *Nursing, the Finest Art: An Illustrated History*. St. Louis: C. V. Mosby (1985): 273.

3. H. Thoms, *Chapters in American History*. Springfield, IL: Charles C. Thomas (1933 and 1961): 27.

4. Ibid., 26. Quoted by Bard in *A Compendium of the Theory and Practice of Midwifery*, 1812.

5. Ibid., 30.

6. Author unknown, "Complete Dilatation of the Cervix Uteri, an Essential Condition to the Typical Forceps Operation," *Journal of the American Medical Association*, Vol. 5 (August 29, 1885): 238–240.

7. Thoms, *Chapters in American History*, 38.

8. C.E. Rosenberg, *The Care of Strangers*. New York: Basic Books (1987): 31.

9. Irving, *Safe Deliverance*, 62–70.

10. Donahue. *Nursing, the Finest Art,* 272.

11. I.S. Cutter and H.R. Viets, *A Short History of Midwifery.* Philadelphia: W.B. Saunders (1964): 156.

12. G. Collins, *America's Women: 400 Years of Dolls, Drudges, Helpmates, and Heroines.* New York: HarperCollins (2003): 125.

13. Thoms, *Chapters in American History,* 57.

14. Ibid., 87.

15. Cutter and Viets, *A Short History of Midwifery,* 213.

16. S.M. Stowe, "Obstetrics and the Work of Doctoring in the Mid-Nineteenth-Century American South," *Bulletin of the History of Medicine,* Vol. 64 (Winter 1990): 540–566.

17. Collins, *America's Women,* 153.

18. D.G. White, *Aren't I a Woman? Female Slaves in the Plantation South.* New York and London: W.W. Norton (1985): 84.

19. Stowe, "Obstetrics and the Work of Doctoring."

20. J. Mitford, *The American Way of Birth.* New York: Dutton (1992): 56.

21. J.W. Leavitt, "'Science' Enters the Birthing Room: Obstetrics in America since the Eighteenth century." *The Journal of American History,* Vol. 70 (1983): 282–304.

22. G.J. Barker-Benfield, *The Horrors of the Half-Known Life: Male Attitudes toward Women and Sexuality in Nineteenth Century America.* New York: Harper and Row (1976): 61.

23. J.P. Rooks, *Midwifery and Childbirth in America.* Philadelphia: Temple University Press (1997): 19.

24. J. Achterberg, *Woman as Healer,* Boston: Shambhala (1990): 131.

25. D.R. Stille, *Extraordinary Women of Medicine.* New York and London: Grolier (1997): 77–79.

26. J.B. Litcoff, *American Midwives, 1860 to the Present.* Westport, CT: Greenwood Press (1978): 11. Quote taken from "An appeal to the Medical Society of Rhode Island in behalf of women to be restored to her natural rights as 'Midwife' and elevated by education to the physicians of her own sex," 1851, 4.

27. L.D. Longo, "Obstetrics and Gynecology," in R.P. Numbers (ed.), *The Education of American Physicians.* Berkeley: University of California Press (1980): 211.

28. Ibid., 212.

29. Irving, *Safe Deliverance,* 133.

30. Litcoff, *American Midwives,* 13.

31. Barker-Benfield, *Horrors of the Half-Known Life,* 63.

32. Irving, *Safe Deliverance,* 81–85.

33. Ibid., 143.

34. R.H. Shryock, *Medical Licensing in America, 1650–1965.* Baltimore: Johns Hopkins Press (1967): 26.

35. H. Speert, *Obstetrics and Gynecology in America: A History.* Baltimore: Waverly Press (ACOG) (1980): 76.

36. Barker-Benfield, *Horrors of the Half-Known Life,* 77–78.

37. J.N. Hayes, *The Burdens of Disease.* New Brunswick, NJ and London: Rutgers University Press (2003): 227.

38. Ibid., 225–226.

39. Shryock, *Medical Licensing in America,* 26.

40. Ibid., 34.

41. Ibid.

42. Speert, *Obstetrics and Gynecology in America: A History,* 77.

43. R.H. Shryock, *Medicine in America: Historical Essays.* Baltimore: Johns Hopkins Press (1966): 128–130.

44. Speert, *Obstetrics and Gynecology in America,* 76.

45. Barker-Benfield, *Horrors of the Half-Known Life,* 62.

46. Rooks, *Midwifery and Childbirth in America,* 18.

47. Barker-Benfield, *Horrors of the Half-Known Life,* 61.

48. Litcoff, *American Midwives,* 21. Quote from R.B. Morris (ed.), *Encyclopedia of American History.* New York (1965): 574.

49. Ibid., 34–35.

50. Ibid., 36–40.

51. Ibid., 21–22. Quote from H.J. Garreques in "Midwives," *Medical News,* Vol. 72 (1899): 233–235.

52. A.D. Gordon and M.J. Buhle, "Sex and Class in Colonial and Nineteenth Century America," in B.A. Carroll (ed.), *Liberating Women's History.* Chicago: University of Illinois Press (1976): 278–281.

53. Ibid., 285.

54. Achterberg, *Woman as Healer,* 134–135.

55. Collins, *America's Women,* 55.

56. Gordon and Buhle, "Sex and Class in Colonial and Nineteenth Century America," 286.

57. Barker-Benfield, *Horrors of the Half-Known Life,* 112.

58. Ibid., 106.

59. Achterberg, *Woman as Healer*, 136.
60. C. Smith Rosenberg and C.C. Rosenberg, "The Female Animal: Medical and Biological Views of Woman and Her Role in Nineteenth Century America," *The Journal of American History*. Vol. 60 (1973): 332–560.
61. R.M. Morantz-Sanchez, *Sympathy and Science*. New York and Oxford: Oxford University Press (1985): 118.
62. Collins, *America's Women*, 127–128.
63. Gordon and Buhle, "Sex and Class in Colonial and Nineteenth Century America," 286–287.
64. E.C. DuBois, *Elizabeth Cady Stanton–Susan B. Anthony Reader—Correspondence, Writings, Speeches*. Boston: Northeastern University Press (1992): 2–9.
65. Ibid., x.
66. Ibid., 137. Taken from E. Stanton, "Home Life," *Elizabeth Cady Stanton Papers*. C (1875): Library of Congress.
67. Smith-Rosenberg and Rosenberg, "The Female Animal."
68. Ibid.
69. Barker-Benfield, *Horrors of the Half-Known Life*, 83. Quote from Meigs, *Women*, 54.
70. Smith-Rosenberg and Rosenberg, "The Female Animal."
71. Ibid.
72. Barker-Benfield, *Horrors of the Half-Known Life*, 85. Quote from M. Fishbein, *History of AMA*, Saunders (1947): 82–83.
73. Ibid., 88. Quote from J. Todd, *Conjugal Sins*, 1870.
74. Collins, *America's Women*, 118.
75. H. Graham, *Eternal Eve: The History of Gynaecology and Obstetrics*. Garden City, NY: Doubleday (1951): 446–447.
76. H.P. Newman, "Prolapse of the Female Pelvic Organs," *Journal of the American Medical Association*, Vol. 21 (September 2, 1893): 334–338.
77. S.D. Gross, "Lacerations of the Female Sexual Organs Consequent upon Parturition: Their Causes and Their Prevention," *Journal of the American Medical Association*, Vol. 3 (September 27, 1884): 337–345.
78. Collins, *America's Women*, 120.
79. Ibid., 252.
80. D.K. McGregor, *From Midwives to Medicine: The Birth of American Gynecology*. New Brunswick, NJ and London: Rutgers University Press (1998): 15–24.
81. Ibid., 39, 45 (in Sims, *Story of My Life*).
82. Ibid., 46–47.

83. Ibid., 47.
84. Graham, *Eternal Eve*, 449–452.
85. Barker-Benfield, *Horrors of the Half-Known Life*, 95.
86. Graham, *Eternal Eve*, 446–447.
87. McGregor, *From Midwives to Medicine*, 50–51.
88. Graham, *Eternal Eve*, 449–452.
89. Barker-Benfield, *Horrors of the Half-Known Life*, xii–4. Analysis based on Alexis de Tocqueville's view of the effects of democracy on American men in the nineteenth century.
90. Ibid., 21.

9. Early Twentieth-Century America: The "Midwife Problem" and Medicalized Childbirth

1. Personal interview of Joan Thompson; story of her own birth as related to her by her mother.
2. J.P. McEvoy, "Our Streamlined Baby," *Reader's Digest*. Vol. 32 (May 1938): 15–18.
3. R.H. Shryock, *Medical Licensing in America, 1650–1965*. Baltimore: Johns Hopkins Press (1967): 50.
4. J.B. Litoff, *American Midwives—1860 to the Present*. Westport, CT: Greenwood Press (1978): 50.
5. Shryock, *Medical Licensing in America*, 64.
6. Litoff, *American Midwives*, 50. Quote taken from A.B. Flexnor, *Medical Education in the U.S. and Canada: A Report to the Carnegie Foundation of the Advancement of Teaching*. Boston (1910): viii, x, 26, 57, 143, 154.
7. R.M. Morantz-Sanchez, *Sympathy and Science*. Oxford and New York: Oxford University Press (1985): 242.
8. J.S. Baker, *Fighting for Life*. New York: Macmillan (1939): 54–57.
9. Ibid., 86–87.
10. Ibid., 111.
11. Ibid., 112.
12. Morantz-Sanchez, *Sympathy and Science*, 207.
13. Baker, *Fighting for Life*, 113–114.
14. G.L. Meigs (United States Children's Bureau), *Maternal Mortality from All Conditions Connected with Childbirth*. Washington, DC: Government Printing Office, No. 19 (1917): 7.

15. Ibid., 14–17.

16. J.P. Rooks, *Midwifery and Child-birth in America*. Philadelphia: Temple University Press (1997): 16.

17. H. Arthure, "The Midwife—In Simpson's Time and Ours," *Journal of Obstetrics and Gynaecology of the British Commonwealth*, Vol. 80 (1973): 1–9.

18. C.D. Noyes, "Training of Midwives in Relation to the Prevention of Infant Mortality," *American Journal of Obstetrics and Diseases of Women and Children*. Vol. 66 (1912): 1051–1059.

19. Meigs, *Maternal Mortality*, 22–23.

20. L. Valanne, "The Finnish Midwife and Her Renewed Challenges," in S. Kitzinger (ed.), *The Midwife Challenge*. London: Pandora Press (1988): 215–221.

21. H. Farida, "The Midwife in France," in Kitzinger, *The Midwife Challenge*, 197–199.

22. B. Smulders and A. Limbury, "Obstetrics in the Netherlands," in Kitzinger, *The Midwife Challenge*, 235–238.

23. F. Kobrin, "The American Midwife Controversy: A Crises of Professionalization," *Bulletin of the History of Medicine* (1966): 350–360.

24. Noyes, "Training of Midwives."

25. Ibid.

26. Kobrin, "The American Midwife Controversy."

27. D. Weatherford, *Milestones—A Chronology of American Women's History*. New York: Fitzhenry and Whiteside (1997): 209.

28. Noyes, "Training of Midwives."

29. T. Darlington, "The Present Status of the Midwife," *The American Journal of Obstetrics and Diseases of Women*, Vol. 63 (1911): 870–876. This paper was read before the New York Academy of Medicine, February 23, 1911.

30. J.W. Williams, "Medical Education and the Midwife Problem in the United States," *The Journal of the American Medical Association*, Vol. 58 (1) (1912): 1–6.

31. Ibid.

32. Ibid.

33. I.M. Gaskin, "Midwifery Re-Invented," in Kitzinger (ed.), *The Midwife Challenge*, 48.

34. Weatherford, *Milestones—A Chronology of American Women's History*, 210.

35. Charles E. Ziegler, "The Elimination of the Midwife," *American Association for the Study and Prevention of Infant Mortality. Transactions of the Annual Meeting*, Vol. 3 (1912): 222–223, and 258.

36. Ibid.

37. Ibid.

38. Ibid.

39. Williams, "Medical Education and the Midwife Problem in the United States."

40. Noyes, "Training of Midwives."

41. M.P. Donahue, *Nursing, the Finest Art: An Illustrated History*. St. Louis: C. V. Mosby (1985): 343.

42. Ibid., 339.

43. Baker, *Fighting for Life*, 138.

44. Hogan, "A Tribute to the Pioneers," *Journal of Nurse-Midwifery*, Vol. 20 (1975): 6–11.

45. Donahue, *Nursing, the Finest Art*, 339.

46. Hogan, "A Tribute to the Pioneers," R.W. Holmes, R.D. Mussey, and F.I. Adair, "Factors and Causes of Maternal Mortality," *Journal of the American Medical Association*, Vol. 93 (November 1929): 1440–47.

47. R.W. Holmes, R.D. Mussey, and F.I. Adair, "Factors and Causes of Maternal Mortality," Journal of the *American Medical Association*, Vol. 93, (November 1929): 1447–1447.

48. Donahue, *Nursing, the Finest Art*, 350.

49. Rooks, *Midwifery and Childbirth in America*, 36.

50. C.A. Stern, "Midwives, Male-Midwives, and Nurse-Midwives," *Obstetrics and Gynecology*, Vol. 39 (2), (February 1972): 308–311.

51. Donahue, *Nursing, the Finest Art*, 350–352.

52. Rooks, *Midwifery and Childbirth in America*, 29. Taken from the Report of the White House Conference on Child Health and Protection, 1932.

53. Hogan, "A Tribute to the Pioneers."

54. Litoff, *American Midwives*, 67. Quote taken from J.B. DeLee, "Report of Sub-Committee for Illinois," *Transactions of the American Association of the Study and Prevention of Infant Mortality*, Vol. 5 (1914): 231.

55. J.B. DeLee, "The Prophylactic Forceps Operation," *The American Journal of Obstetrics and Gynecology*, Vol. 1 (1), (1920): 34–44. Paper read at the 45th Annual Meeting of the American Gynecological Society in Chicago, May 24–26, 1920.

56. Ibid.

57. A.E. Feldhusen, "The History of Midwifery and Childbirth in America: A Time-Line," *Midwifery Today* (2000): 1–22. http://www.midwiferytoday.com/articles/timeline.asp.

58. DeLee, "The Prophylactic Forceps Operation."

59. M. Nicoll, "Maternity as a Public Health Problem," *American Journal of Public Health*, Vol. 19 (9), (September 1929): 961–968.

60. Ibid.

61. J.W. Leavitt, "'Science' Enters the Birthing Room: Obstetrics in America since the Eighteenth Century," *Journal of American History,* Vol. 70 (1983): 282–302.

62. Feldhusen, "The History of Midwifery and Childbirth in America."

63. H. Speert, *Obstetrics and Gynecology in America: A History.* Boston: Waverly Press (1980): 147.

64. S. Rinker, "To Cultivate a Feeling of Confidence," *Nursing History Review*, Vol. 8 (2000): 117–135.

65. H. Hemschemeyer, "Midwifery in the United States: How Shall We Care for the Million Mothers Whose Babies Are Born at Home?" *The American Journal of Nursing*, Vol. 39 (11) (1939): 1181–1187.

66. Hogan, "A Tribute to the Pioneers."

67. Ibid.

68. Hemschemeyer, "Midwifery in the United States."

69. Ibid.

70. Ibid.

71. P. Chester, *Sisters on a Journey: Portraits of American Midwives.* New Brunswick, NJ: Rutgers University Press (1955): 11.

72. G. Dick-Read, *Childbirth Without Fear*, 5th ed. Revised and edited by Helen Wessel and Harlan F. Ellis, MD. New York and London: Harper and Row (1987): 249–250. Excerpts were taken from this book with permission from Pollinger, Limited Publishers, London, England.

73. Ibid., 253–255.

74. Ibid., 262.

75. Ibid., 268–270.

76. Ibid., 673.

77. Ibid., 274.

10. The Second Half of the Twentieth Century: Technology-Managed Childbirth

1. Personal interview.

2. LiuYuen Chou, "The Effects of the Upright Position during Childbirth," *Image: Journal of Nursing Scholarship*, Vol. 21 (1) (1989):14–18.

3. E.A. Friedman. "The Graphic Analysis of Labor," *American Journal of Obstetrics and Gynecology*, Vol. 68 (6) (December 1954): 1568–1575.

4. A. Charlish and L.H. Holt, *Birth-Tech: Tests and Technology in Pregnancy and Birth.* New York: Facts on File (1991): 57.

5. J. Mitford, *The American Way of Birth.* New York: Dutton (1992): 111.

6. L.L. Albers et al., "The Relationship of Ambulation in Labor to Operative Delivery," *Journal of Nurse-Midwifery*, Vol. 42 (1) (Jan/Feb 1997): 4–8.

7. L.K. Capik, "Health Beliefs of Childbearing Women: The Choice of Epidurals for Pain Management," *The Journal of Perinatal Education*, Vol. 7 (3) (1998): 7–17.

8. Ibid.

9. C. Winkelman, *The Complete Guide to Pregnancy after 30.* Avon, MA: Adams Media Corporation (2002): 526–527.

10. Maternity Center Association, What Every Pregnant Woman Needs to Know About Cesarean Section. New York: MCA (July 2004): 2.

11. Mitford, *The American Way of Birth,* 138.

12. S. Napierala, *Water Birth: A Midwife's Perspective.* Westport, CT: Bergin & Garvey (1994): 41.

13. "Study Reviews Natural Birth after C-Section." Portland Press Herald (Dec. 12, 2004).

14. Mitford, *The American Way of Birth*, 129.

15. "Study Reviews Natural Birth after C-Section."

16. D. Haire, *The Cultural Warping of Childbirth.* International Childbirth Association—Special Report. Hillside, NJ: International Childbirth Association (1972).

17. Napierala, *Water Birth*, 43–45.

18. "Fifty Years of Change," USA TODAY (Oct. 5, 2005): 6D.

19. H. Butler and B.J. Kay, "State Laws and the Practice of Lay Midwifery," *American Journal of Public Health*, Vol. 78 (1988): 1161–1169.

20. Mitford, *The American Way of Birth*, 198–202.

21. M.A. Durand, "The Safety of Home Birth: The Farm Study," *American Journal of Public Health*, Vol. 82 (3) (1992): 450–453.

22. Mitford, *The American Way of Birth*, 206.

23. B.K. Rothman, *Giving Birth: Alter-*

natives in Childbirth. New York: Penguin Books (1982): 17.

24. Napierala, *Water Birth,* 50.

25. Rothman, *Giving Birth,* 43.

26. V. Packard, "The Year in Books: A Time for Thinking Back and Waxing Roth," *A Nation of Strangers* (Dec. 29, 1972): 42.

27. The Boston Women's Health Book Collective, *Our Bodies, Ourselves: For the New Century.* New York: Simon & Schuster (1998): 408–410.

28. S. Faludi, *Backlash: The Undeclared War against American Women.* New York: Crown (1991): 404.

29. Rothman, *Giving Birth,* 94–95.

30. S. Arms, *Immaculate Deception: A New Look at Women and Childbirth in America.* (1975): xiii.

31. Rothman, *Giving Birth,* 49.

32. Faludi, *Backlash,* 32.

33. Winkelman, *The Complete Guide to Pregnancy after 30,* 378.

34. Rothman, *Giving Birth,* 217–218.

35. D.M. Lang, "The American College of Nurse-Midwives: What Is the Future for Certified Nurse-Midwives? In Hospitals? Childbearing Centers? Homebirths?" Chap. 11 in *21st Century Obstetrics Now!* Vol.1, L. Stewart and D. Stewart (eds.), a NAPSAC Publication (1977): 89–103.

36. Ibid.

37. Arms, *Immaculate Deception,* 160–161.

38. D.M. Lang, "Modern Midwifery," Chap. 8 in *Maternal and Infant Care,* E.J. Dickason and M.O. Schult (eds.), New York: McGraw Hill (1979): 145–157.

39. Rothman, *Giving Birth.*

40. M.F. MacDorman and G.K. Singh, "Midwifery Care: Social and Risk Factors and Birth Outcomes in the United States," *Journal of Epidemiology and Community Health,* Vol. 52 (1998): 310–317.

41. Ibid.

42. Ibid.

43. U.S. Congress, Office of Technology Assessment. *Nurse Practitioners, Physician Assistants, and Certified Nurse-Midwives: A Policy Analysis.* Health Technology Case Study 37, OTA-HCS-37. Washington, DC: U.S. Government Printing Office (1986): 25.

44. K. Bell and J.I. Mills, "Certified Nurse-Midwife Effectiveness in the Health Maintenance Organization Obstetric Team," *Obstetrics and Gynecology,* Vol. 74 (1) (July 1989): 112–116.

45. M. Gabay and S. Wolfe, "The Beneficial Alternative: Nurse-Midwifery," from Public Citizen's Health Research Group in *Public Health Reports,* Vol. 112 (5), U.S. Public Health Service (1997): 386–394.

46. J.P. Rooks, N.L. Weatherby, E.K. Ernst, S. Stapleton, and A. Rosenfield, "Outcomes of Care in Birth Centers. The National Birth Center Study," *The New England Journal of Medicine,* Vol. 26 (Dec. 28, 1989): 321.

47. S. Kitzinger, *The Experience of Childbirth,* 5th ed. Harmondsworth, England: Penguin Books (1972): 10.

48. Arms, *Immaculate Deception,* 146.

49. J.A. Lothian, "Questions from our Readers: Does Lamaze 'Work'?" *Journal of Perinatal Education,* Vol. 8 (3) (1999): 25.

50. Arms, *Immaculate Deception,* 146.

51. F. Leboyer, *Birth Without Violence.* New York: Alfred A. Knopf (1975).

52. Napierala, *Water Birth,* 1–2.

53. J.E. Halek, "Report on the First International Water Birth Conference," *The Journal of Perinatal Education,* Vol. 4 (3) (1995): 7–8.

54. M.H. Klaus and J. Kennell, *Maternal Infant Bonding.* St. Louis: Mosby (1976).

55. "Population Control: The Bottom Drops Out of the Baby Boom," *Life* (Dec. 29, 1972): 53.

56. Faludi, *Backlash,* 34.

57. Rothman, *Giving Birth,* 86–87.

58. J. Kennell, M. Klaus, S. McGrath, S. Robertson, and C. Hinkley, "Continuous Emotional Support during Labor in a U.S. Hospital: A Randomized, Controlled Trial." *JAMA,* Vol. 265 (1991): 2197–2201.

11. The Twenty-First Century: Technological Childbirth Challenged

1. Lisa Lilly, personal interview.

2. G. Dick-Read, "An Outline of the Conduct of Physiological Labor," *American Journal of Obstetrics & Gynecology,* Vol. 54 (4) (October 1947): 702–710.

3. S.E. Taylor, L.C. Klein, B.P. Lewis, T.L. Gruenewald, R.A.R. Gurung, and J.A. Updegraff, "Biobehavioral Responses to Stress in Females: Tend-and-Befriend, Not Fight-or-Flight," *Psychological Review,* Vol. 107 (3), (2000): 411–429.

4. L. Fenwick, "Birthing Techniques for Managing the Physiologic and Psychosocial Aspects of Childbirth," *P-N* (May/June 1984): 51–62.

5. P. Gordin and B.H. Johnson, "Tech-

nology and Family-Centered Perinatal Care: Conflict or Synergy?" *Journal of Obstetric, Gynecological, & Neonatal Nursing,* Vol. 28 (4) (July/August 1999): 401–408.

6. P. Chester, *Sisters on a Journey: Portraits of American Midwives.* New Brunswick, NJ and London: Rutgers University Press (1997): 213–214.

7. R. Freeman, "Intrapartum Fetal Monitoring—A Disappointing Story," *New England Journal of Medicine,* Vol. 322 (9) (1990): 624–626.

8. J.A. Martin, B.E. Hamilton, P.D. Sutton, S.J. Ventura, F. Menacher, and M. Munson (Division of Vital Statistics), "Birth: Final Data for 2002," *National Vital Statistics Reports,* Vol. 52 (10) (December 2003).

9. M.L. Moore, "Increasing Cesarean Birth Rates: A Clash of Culture?" *Journal of Perinatal Education,* Vol. 4 (4) (2005): 5–8.

10. M.C. Klein, "Quick Fix Culture: The Cesarean-Section-on-Demand Debate," *Birth,* Vol. 31 (3) (September 2004): 161–164.

11. Sheila Kitzinger, "The Great Childbirth Blackmail," *International Journal of Childbirth Education,* Vol. 16 (4) (December 2001): 37. Reprinted with permission; published in Britain's *Daily Mail,* Thursday, June 14, 2001.

12. Lamaze International, "Elective Cesarean Sections Create Significant Risks for Maternal and Infant Health," New Lamaze White Paper. Washington, DC: *Lamaze International* (February 22, 2006).

13. Kitzinger, "The Great Childbirth Blackmail."

14. D. Getahun, Y. Oyelese, H. Salihu, and C.V. Ananth, "Previous Cesarean Delivery and Risk of Placenta Previa and Placental Abruption," *Obstetrics and Gynecology,* Vol.107 (4) (2006): 771–778.

15. Lamaze International Press Release, Washington, DC: November 19, 2003.

16. Martin et al., *National Vital Statistics Report.*

17. E.D. Declercq, S. Sakala, M.P. Corry, S. Applebaum, and P. Rishe, "*Results of Listening to Mothers Survey: The First National U.S. Survey of Women's Childbearing Experiences.*" New York: Maternity Center Association, 2002. *http://www.maternitywise.org/listeningtomothers/results_body.html.*

18. "Mothers Report Cesarean Views and Experiences: New National Listening to Mothers Survey," *Childbirth Connection*

(2006): 1–5. *http://childbirthconnection.com/article.asp?ck=10372.*

19. Ibid.

20. E. Hodnett, "Evidence-Based Maternity Care," *International Journal of Childbirth Education,* Vol. 19 (2) (June 2004): 4–6.

21. J.V. Schmidt and P.R. McCartney, "History and Development of Fetal Heart Assessment: A Composite," *Journal of Obstetric, Gynecologic, and Neonatal Nursing,* Vol. 29 (3) (May/June 2000): 295–305.

22. S.B. Thacker, D. Stroup, and M. Chang, "Continuous Electronic Rate Monitoring for Fetal Assessment during Labor," (Cochrane Review) in *The Cochrane Library,* Issue 4, Chichester, UK: John Wiley, 2004.

23. Schmidt and McCartney, "History and Development of Fetal Heart Assessment, 295–305.

24. K.D. Priddy, "Is There Logic behind Fetal Monitoring?" *Journal of Obstetric, Gynecologic, and Neonatal Nursing,* Vol. 33 (5) (September/October 2004): 550–553.

25. Martin et al., *National Vital Statistics Report.*

26. K.L Simpson and J. Atterbury, "Trends and Issues in Labor Induction in the United States: Implications for Clinical Practice," *Journal of Obstetric, Gynecologic, and Neonatal Nursing,* Vol. 32 (6) (2003): 767–777.

27. Ibid.

28. S.K. Cesario, "Reevaluation of Friedman's Labor Curve: A Pilot Study," *Journal of Obstetric, Gynecologic, and Neonatal Nursing,* Vol. 33 (6) (November/December 2004): 713–721.

29. Fenwick, "Birthing Techniques,"

30. W.D. Fraser, L. Turcot, I. Krauss, and G. Brisson-Carrol, "Amniotomy for Shortening Spontaneous Labor," (Cochrane Review) in *The Cochrane Library,* Issue 4, Chichester, UK: John Wiley, 2004.

31. J. Durhan, "Side Effects of Epidurals: A Summary of Recent Research Data," *International Journal of Childbirth Education,* Vol. 18 (30) (September 2003): 11–17.

32. C.J. Howell. "Epidural versus Non-Epidural Analgesia for Pain Relief in Labour," *The Cochrane Database of Systematic Reviews,* Issue 3 (1999). http://www.cochrane.us/library.htm.

33. E. Lieberman and C. O'Donoghue, "Unintended Effect of Epidural Analgesia during Labor: A Systematic Review," *American Journal of Obstetrics & Gynecology,*

Vol. 186 (5) (2002): S39–S64; and B.L. Leighton and S.H. Halpern, "The Effects of Epidural Analgesia on Labor, Maternal, and Neonatal Outcomes: A Systematic Review," *American Journal of Obstetrics & Gynecology*, Vol. 186 (5) (2002): S69–S77.

34. Simpson and Atterbury, "Trends and Issues in Labor Induction."

35. J.E. Roberts, "The 'Push' for Evidence: Management of Second Stage," *Journal of Midwifery & Women's Health*, Vol. 47 (1) (2002): 2–15.

36. C.L. Roberts, C.S. Algert, C.A. Cameron, and S. Torvaldsen, "A Meta-Analysis of Upright Positions in the Second Stage to Reduce Instrumental Deliveries in Women with Epidural analgesia," *Acta Obstetric et Gynecologia Scandinavica*, Vol. 84 (8) (2005): 794–798.

37. Simpson and Atterbury, "Trends and Issues in Labor Induction."

38. D.A. Webb and J. Culhane, "Hospital Variation in Episiotomy Use and the Risk of Perineal Trauma during childbirth," *Birth*, Vol. 29 (2) (2002): 132–136.

39. N.K. Lowe, "Amazed or Appalled, Apathy or Action?" (Editorial) *Journal of Obstetric, Gynecologic, & Neonatal Nursing*, Vol. 32 (3) (May/June 2003): 281–282.

40. Sheila Kitzinger, "The Great Childbirth Blackmail."

41. H.P. Kennedy and M.T. Shannon, "Keeping Birth Normal: Research Findings on Midwifery Care during Childbirth," *Journal of Obstetric, Gynecologic, & Neonatal Nursing*, Vol. 33 (5) (September/October 2004): 555–560.

42. H.P. Kennedy, "A Model of Exemplary Midwifery Practice: Results of a Delphi Study," *Journal of Midwifery & Women's Health*, Vol. 45 (1) (2000): 4–19.

43. L.P. Hunter, "Being with Woman: A Guiding Concept for the Care of Laboring Women," *Journal of Obstetric, Gynecologic, & Neonatal Nursing*, Vol. 31 (6) (November/December 2002): 650–657.

44. Ibid.

45. E.D. Hodnett, S. Gates, G.J. Hofmeyr, and C. Sakala, "Continuous Support for Women during Childbirth," (Cochrane Review) in *The Cochrane Library*, Issue 4. Chichester, UK: John Wiley, 2004.

46. J. Achterberg, *Woman as Healer*, Boston and London: Shambhala (1991): 201.

47. L. Fenwick, "Birthing Techniques."

48. D.J. Jackson, J.M. Lang, J. Echer, W.H. Swartz, and T. Heeren, "Impact of Collaborative Management and Early Admission in Labor of Method of Delivery," *Journal of Obstetric, Gynecologic, & Neonatal Nursing*, Vol. 32 (2) (March/April 2003): 147–157.

49. B. Ivy, "Non-Hospital Births Gaining Acceptance," *Bergen Record* (Bergen County, NJ, September 28, 2003).

50. K.C. Johnson and B.A. Davis, "Outcomes of Planned Home Births with Certified Professional Midwives: Large Prospective Study in North America," *British Medical Journal*, Vol. 330 (7505) (2005): 1416–1422.

51. E.D. Hodnett, "Home-Like versus Conventional Institutional Settings for Birth," (Cochrane Review) in *The Cochrane Library*, Issue 4, Chichester, UK: John Wiley, 2004.

52. Martin et al., *National Vital Statistics Report*.

12. Conclusion: Women in Power

1. Personal interview, Lisa Lilley.

2. N.K. Lowe, "Amazed or Appalled, Apathy or Action?" (Editorial) *Journal of Obstetric, Gynecologic, & Neonatal Nursing*, Vol. 32 (3) (May/June 2003): 281–282.

3. S. Kitzinger (ed.), *The Midwife Challenge*. London: Pandora Press (1988), 7.

4. *The Washington Post* (May 9, 2006): F5.

5. T. Tomlinson, "Home Delivery: Not Just for Pizza," *Silver Spring Voice* (October 2006): 29.

6. Ibid.

7. H.P. Kennedy, "A Concept Analysis of Optimality in Perinatal Health," *Journal of Obstetric, Gynecologic, & Neonatal Nursing*, Vol. 35 (6) (November/December 2006): 763–769.

8. P.A. Murphy and J.T. Fullerton, "Development of the Optimality Index as a New Approach to Evaluating Outcomes of Maternity Care." *Journal of Obstetric, Gynecologic, & Neonatal Nursing*, Vol. 35 (6) (November/December 2006): 770–778.

Bibliography

Achterberg, J. *Woman as Healer*. Boston & London: Shambhala, 1991.

Adami, J.G. *Charles White of Manchester (1728–1813) and the Arrest of Puerperal Fever*. (Reprinted from Charles White's published writing on Puerperal Fever). London: University Press of Liverpool, 1922.

Albers, L.L., D. Anderson, L. Cragin, S.M. Daniels, C. Hunter, K.D. Sedler, and D. Teaf. "The Relationship of Ambulation in Labor to Operative Delivery." *Journal of Nurse Midwifery* 42 (1997): 4–8.

Arms, S. *Immaculate Deception: A New Look at Women and Childbirth in America*. 1975.

Arthure, J.H. "The Midwife—In Simpson's Time and Ours." *The Journal of Obstetrics and Gynaecology of the British Commonwealth* 80 (1973): 1–9.

Ashford, J.I. "A History of Accouchement Force: 1550–1985." *Birth* 13 (1986): 240–248.

Aveling, J.H. *English Midwives—Their History and Prospects*. London: Hugh K. Elliot, 1872, 1962.

Baker, S.J. *Fighting for Life*. New York: Macmillan, 1939.

Barker-Benfield, G.J. *The Horrors of the Half-Known Life: Male Attitudes Toward Women and Sexuality in Nineteenth Century America*. New York: Harper and Row, 1976.

Bell, K. and J.I. Mills. "Certified Nurse-Midwife Effectiveness in the Health Maintenance Organization Obstetric Team." *Obstetrics and Gynecology* 74 (1989): 112–116.

Binger, C. *Revolutionary Doctor, Benjamin Rush, 1746–1830*. New York: W.W. Norton, 1966.

Bradley, R.A. *Husband-Coached Childbirth*. New York: Harper and Row, 1974.

Burns, S.B. "A Pictorial History of Healing." *Clinical Reviews* 13 (2003): 24–25.

Burns, D.N. and L.D. Calache. "An Evaluation of Some Early Obstetrical Instruments." *Caduceus* 3 (1987): 33–41.

Butler, H. and B.J. Kay. "State Laws and the Practice of Lay Midwifery." *American Journal of Public Health* 78 (1988): 1161–1169.

Camac, C.N.B. *Classics of Medicine and Surgery*. New York: Dover, 1909.

Carroll, B.A., ed. *Liberating Women's History: Theoretical and Critical Essays*. Chicago: University of Illinois Press, 1976.

Carter, K.C. "Ignaz Semmelweis, Carl Mayrhofer and the Rise of Germ Theory." *Medical History* 29 (1985): 33–53.

Cesario, S.K. "Reevaluation of Friedman's Labor Curve: A Pilot Study." *Journal of Obstetric, Gynecologic, and Neonatal Nursing* 33 (2004): 713–721.

Chamberlain, M. *Old Wives' Tales: Their History, Remedies and Spells*. London: Virago Press, 1981.

Chaney, J.A. "Birthing in Early America." *Journal of Nurse Midwifery* 25 (1980): 5–13.

Charlish, A. and L.H. Holt. *Birth-Tech: Tests and Technology in Pregnancy and Birth*. New York: Facts on File, 1991.

Chester, P. *Sisters on a Journey: Portraits of American Midwives*. New Brunswick, NJ: Rutgers University Press, 1955.

Clark, C.C.P. "Management of the Obstetrical Forceps." *American Journal of Obstetrics and Diseases of Women and Children* 4 (1871): 138–141.

Collins, G. *America's Women: 400 Years of Dolls, Drudges, Helpmates, and Heroines*. New York: HarperCollins, 2003.

Cutter, I.S. and H.R. Viets. *A Short History of Midwifery*. Philadelphia and London: W.B. Saunders, 1964.

Darlington, T. "The Present Status of the Midwife." *The American Journal of Obstetrics and Diseases of Women* 63 (1911): 870–876.

Declercq, E.D., S. Sakala, M.P. Corry, S. Applebaum, and P. Rishe. *Results of Listening to Mothers Survey: The First National U.S. Survey of Women's Childbearing Experiences.* (New York: Maternity Center Association, 2002). *http://www.maternitywise.org/ listeningtomothers/results_body.html*

DeLee, J.B. "The Bossi Dilator, It's Place in Accouchement Force." *American Journal of Obstetrics and Diseases of Women and Children* 48 (1903): 27–30.

_____. "The Prophylactic Forceps Operation." *The American Journal of Obstetrics & Gynecology* 1 (1920): 34–44.

Denman, T. *An Introduction to the Practice of Midwifery*. New York: James Oram, 1802.

Diamant, A. *The Red Tent*. New York: Picador USA, 1997.

DiBacco, T. "Childbed Fever and Handwashing." *The Washington Post*, March 23, 1993.

Dickinson, R.L. "Accouchement Force." *American Journal of Obstetrics and Diseases of Women and Children* 48 (1903): 10–15.

Dick-Read, G. *Childbirth Without Fear*. 5th ed. Revised and edited by Helen Wessel and Harlan F. Ellis, MD. New York and London: Harper and Row, 1987.

Dobbie, W.B.M. "An Attempt to Estimate the True Rate of Maternal Morbidity, Sixteenth to Eighteenth Centuries." *Medical History* 26 (1982): 79–90.

Donahue, P. *Nursing, the Finest Art: An Illustrated History*. St. Louis and Princeton: C.V. Mosby, 1985.

Drinker, C.K. *Not So Long Ago: A Chronicle of Medicine and Doctors in Colonial Philadelphia*. New York: Oxford University Press, 1937.

DuBois, E.C. *Elizabeth Cady Stanton—Susan B. Anthony Reader—Correspondence, Writings, Speeches*. Boston: Northeastern University Press, 1992.

Dundees, L. "The Evolution of Maternal Birthing Position." *American Journal of Public Health* 77 (1987): 636–640.

Dunn, P.M. "Francois Mauriceau (1637–1709) and Maternal Posture for Parturition." *Archives of Diseases in Childhood* 66 (1991): 78–79.

_____. "Dr. Thomas Radford (1793–1881) of Manchester and Obstructed Labor" in the series, Perinatal Lessons from the Past. *Archives of Diseases of Childhood* 69 (1993): 327–329.

_____. "Dr. John Snow (1813–1858) of London: Pioneer of Obstetric Anaesthesia." *Archives of Diseases in Childhood* 75 (1996): F141–F142.

Durand, A.M. "The Safety of Home Birth: The Farm Study." *American Journal of Public Health* 82 (1992): 450–453.

Durhan, J. "Side Effects of Epidurals: A Summary of Recent Research Data." *International Journal of Childbirth Education* 18 (2003): 11–17.

Eccles, A. "Obstetrics in the Seventeenth and Eighteenth Centuries and Its Implications for Maternal and Infant Mortality." *Society for the History of Medicine Bulletin*. No. 20–21 (1977): 8–15.

Ehrenreich, B. and D. English. *Witches, Midwives, and Nurses: A History of Women Healers*. New York: Doubleday, 1973.

_____. *For Her Own Good*. New York: Doubleday, 1978.

Engelmann, G.J. "Pregnancy, Parturition, and Childbed among Primitive People." *American Journal of Obstetrics and Diseases of Women and Children* 14 (1881): 602–618, 828–847.

Faludi, S. *Backlash: The Undeclared War against American Women*. New York: Crown, 1991.

Feldhusen, A.E. "The History of Midwifery and Childbirth in America: A Time-Line." *Midwifery Today* (2000): 1–22. *http://www.midwiferytoday.com/articles/timeline.asp*.

Fenwick, L. "Birthing Techniques for Managing the Physiologic and Psychosocial Aspects of Childbirth." *P–N* May/June (1984): 51–62.

Findley, P. *The Story of Childbirth*. New York: Doubleday, 1933.

Finney, R.P. *The Story of Motherhood*. New York: Liveright, 1937.

Fraser, W.D., L. Turcot, I. Krauss, and G. Brisson-Carrol. "Amniotomy for Shortening Spontaneous Labor." *Cochrane Review*. In *The Cochrane Library*, Issue 4. Chichester, UK: John Wiley, 2004.

Friedman, E.A. "The Graphic Analysis of Labor." *American Journal of Obstetrics and Gynecology* 68 (1954): 1568–1575.

Freeman, R. "Intrapartum Fetal Monitoring—A Disappointing Story." *New England Journal of Medicine* 322 (1990): 624–626.

Gabay, M. and S. Wolfe. "The Beneficial Alternative: Nurse-Midwifery." *Public Health Reports.* U.S Public Health Service, 1997.

Gaskin, I.M. *Spiritual Midwifery.* Summertown, TN: The Publishing Company, 1977.

_____. *Ina May's Guide to Childbirth.* New York: Bantam Books, 2003.

Gelis, J. *History of Childbirth: Fertility, Pregnancy and Birth in Early Modern Europe.* Translated by Rosemary Morris. Boston: Northeastern University Press, 1991.

Getahun, D., Y. Oyelese, H. Salihu, and C.V. Ananth. "Previous Cesarean Delivery and Risk of Placenta Previa and Placental Abruption." *Obstetrics and Gynecology* 107 (2006): 771–778.

Goodell, W.M. "Some Ancient Methods of Delivery." *American Journal of Obstetrics and Diseases of Women and Children* 4 (1871): 663–676.

Gordon, P. and B.H. Johnson. "Technology and Family-Centered Perinatal Care: Conflict or Synergy?" *Journal of Obstetric, Gynecological, & Neonatal Nursing* 28 (1999): 401–408.

Graham, H. *Eternal Eve: The History of Gynaecology and Obstetrics.* New York: Doubleday, 1951.

Gross, S.D. "Lacerations of the Female Sexual Organs Consequent upon Parturition: Their Causes and Their Prevention." *Journal of the American Medical Association* 3 (1884): 337–345.

Haire, D. *The Cultural Warping of Childbirth.* International Childbirth Association—Special Report. Hillside, NJ: International Childbirth Association, 1972.

Halek, J.E. "Report on the First International Water birth Conference." *The Journal of Perinatal Education* 4 (1995): 7–8.

Hardin, A.J.P. "Discussion of Dr. Dill's Paper on, 'The Use of the Midwifery Forceps.'" *Dublin Journal of Medical Science* 68 (1879): 170–173.

Hayes, J.N. *The Burdens of Disease.* New Brunswick, NJ and London: Rutgers University Press, 2003.

Hemschemeyer, H. "Midwifery in the United States: How Shall We Care for the Million Mothers Whose Babies Are Born at Home?" *The American Journal of Nursing* 39 (1939): 1181–1187.

Hill, F. *A Delusion of Satan: The Full Story of the Salem Witch Trials.* New York: Doubleday, 1943 and 1995.

Hodnett, E.D. "Evidence-Based Maternity Care." *International Journal of Childbirth Education* 19 (2004): 4–6.

_____. "Home-Like versus Conventional Institutional Settings for Birth." Cochrane Review. In *The Cochrane Library,* Issue 4. Chichester, UK: John Wiley, 2004.

_____, S. Gates, G.J. Hofmeyr, and C. Sakala. "Continuous Support for Women during Childbirth." Cochrane Review. In *The Cochrane Library,* Issue 4. Chichester, UK: John Wiley, 2004.

Hogan, A. "A Tribute to the Pioneers." *Journal of Nurse-Midwifery* 20 (1975): 6–11.

Holmes, R.W., R.D. Mussey, and F.I. Adair. "Factors and Causes of Maternal Mortality." *Journal of the American Medical Association* 93 (1929): 1440–47.

Holy Scriptures, Exodus, I, 16, 1917.

Housholder, M.S. "A Historical Perspective on the Obstetric Chair." *Surgery, Gynecology and Obstetrics* 139 (1974): 423–430.

Howell, C.J. "Epidural versus Non-Epidural Analgesia for Pain Relief in Labour." *The Cochrane Database of Systematic Reviews.* Issue 3 (1999). http://www.cochrane.us/library.htm

Hunter, L.P. "Being with Woman: A Guiding Concept for the Care of Laboring Women." *Journal of Obstetric, Gynecologic, & Neonatal Nursing* 31 (2002): 650–657.

Ingraham, C.B. "The Chamberlens and the Obstetric Forceps." *American Journal of Obstetrics and Diseases of Women and Children* 63 (1911).

Irving, F.C. *Safe Deliverance.* Boston: Houghton Mifflin, 1942.

Jackson, D.J., J.M. Lang, J. Echer, W.H. Swartz, and T. Heeren. "Impact of Collaborative Management and Early Admission in Labor of Method of Delivery." *Journal of Obstetric, Gynecologic, & Neonatal Nursing* 32 (2003): 147–157.

Jarco, J. *Postures and Practices during Labor among Primitive Peoples.* New York: Paul B. Holler, 1934.

Johanson, R., M. Newburn, and A. Macfarlane. "Has the Medicalisation of Childbirth Gone Too Far?" *British Medical Journal* 324 (2002): 892–895.

Johnson, K.C. and B.A. Davis. "Outcomes of Planned Home Births with Certified Professional Midwives: Large Prospective Study in North America." *British Medical Journal* 330 (2005): 1416–1422.

Kennedy, H.P. "A Model of Exemplary Midwifery Practice: Results of a Delphi Study." *Journal of Midwifery & Women's Health* 45 (2000): 4–19.

Kennedy, H.P. and M.T. Shannon. "Keeping Birth Normal: Research Findings on Midwifery Care during Childbirth." *Journal of Obstetric, Gynecologic, & Neonatal Nursing* 33 (2004): 555–560.

Kitzinger, S. *The Experience of Childbirth.* 3rd ed. Harmondsworth, England: Penguin, 1972.

_____, ed. *The Midwife Challenge.* London: Pandora Press, 1988.

_____. "The Great Childbirth Blackmail." *International Journal of Childbirth Education* 16 (2001): 37.

Klaus, M.H. and J. Kennell. *Maternal Infant Bonding.* St. Louis: Mosby, 1976.

_____, J.H. Kennell, and P.H. Klaus. *The Doula Book: How a Trained Labor Companion Can Help You Have a Shorter, Easier, and Healthier Birth.* Cambridge, MA: Perseus, 1993.

Klein, M.C. "Quick Fix Culture: The Cesarean-Section-on-Demand Debate." *Birth* 31 (2004): 161–164.

Kobrin, F. "The American Midwife Controversy: A Crisis of Professionalization." *Bulletin of the History of Medicine* (1966): 350–360.

Lamaze International. "Elective Cesarean Sections Create Significant Risks for Maternal and Infant Health." New Lamaze White Paper. Washington, DC: Lamaze International, 2006.

Lang, D.M. "The American College of Nurse-Midwives: What Is the Future for Certified Nurse-Midwives: In Hospitals? Childbearing Centers: Homebirths?" In *21st Century Obstetrics Now!* edited by L. Stewart, and D. Stewart, 89–103. a NAPSAC Publication (1977).

_____. "Modern Midwifery." Chap. 8 in *Maternal and Infant Care,* edited by E.J. Dickason and M.O. Schult, 145–157. New York: McGraw Hill, 1979.

Leavitt, J.W. "'Science' Enters the Birthing Room: Obstetrics in America since the Eighteenth Century." *The Journal of American History* 70 (1983): 282–304.

_____. *Brought to Bed: Childbearing in America, 1750–1950.* New York and Oxford: Oxford University Press, 1986.

Leboyer, F. *Birth Without Violence.* New York: Alfred A. Knopf, 1975.

Leighton, B.L. and S.H. Halpern. "The Effects of Epidural Analgesia on Labor, Maternal, and Neonatal Outcomes: A Systematic Review." *American Journal of Obstetrics & Gynecology* 186 (2002): S69–S77.

Lieberman, E. and C. O'Donoghue. "Unintended Effect of Epidural Analgesia During Labor: A Systematic Review." *American Journal of Obstetrics & Gynecology* 186 (2002): S39–S64.

Litcoff, J.B. *American Midwives, 1860 to the Present.* West Port, CT: Greenwood Press, 1978.

Lock, S., J.M. Last, and G. Dunea, eds. *Oxford Illustrated Companion to Medicine.* New York and Oxford: Oxford University Press, 2001.

Longo, L.D. "Obstetrics and Gynecology." In *The Education of American Physicians,* edited by R.P. Numbers. Berkeley: University of California Press, 1980.

_____. "A Treatise of Midwifery in Three Parts. Gielding Ould." *American Journal of Obstetrics and Gynecology* 172 (1995): 1317–1319.

Lothian, J.A. "Questions from our Readers: Does Lamaze 'Work'?" *Journal of Perinatal Education* 8 (1999): 25.

Loudon, Z. "Deaths in Childbed from the Eighteenth Century to 1935." *Medical History* 30 (1986): 1–41.

Lowe, N.K. "Amazed or Appalled, Apathy or Action?" *Journal of Obstetric, Gynecologic, & Neonatal Nursing* 32 (2003): 281–282.

MacDorman, M.F. and G.K. Singh. "Midwifery Care: Social and Risk Factors and Birth Outcomes in the United States." *Journal of Epidemiology and Community Health* 52 (1998): 310–317.

Madden, T.M. "On Sudden Death Soon after Parturition." *The American Journal of Obstetrics and Diseases of Women and Children* IV (1871): 193–198+.

Mander, R. "A Reappraisal of Simpson's Introduction to Chloroform." *Midwifery* 14 (1998): 181–189.

Martin, J.A., B.E. Hamilton, P.D. Sutton, S.J. Ventura, F. Menacher, and M. Munson (Division of Vital Statistics). "Birth: Final Data for 2002." *National Vital Statistics Reports* 52 (2003).

McEvoy, J.P. "Our Streamlined Baby," *Reader's Digest* 32 (1938): 15–18.

McGregor, D.K. *From Midwives to Medicine—The Birth of American Gynecology.* New Brunswick, NJ and London: Rutgers University Press, 1998.

Meigs, G.L. (United States Children's Bureau). *Maternal Mortality from All Conditions Connected with Childbirth.* Washington, DC: Government Printing Office, 19 (1917): 7.

Mitford, J. *The American Way of Birth.* New York: Dutton, 1992.

Moore, M.L. "Increasing Cesarean Birth Rates: A Clash of Culture?" *Journal of Perinatal Education* 4 (2005): 5–8.

Morantz-Sanchez, R.M. *Sympathy and Science.* New York and Oxford: Oxford University Press, 1985.

"Mothers Report Cesarean Views and Experiences: New National Listening to Mothers Survey." *Childbirth Connection* (2006): 1–5. http://childbirthconnection.com/article.asp?ck=10372

Murphy-Lawless, J. *Reading Birth and Death—A History of Obstetric Thinking.* Bloomington, IN: Indiana University Press, 1998.

Murray, M.A. *The Witchcult of Western Europe.* Oxford: Clarendon Press, 1921. Reprinted 1963.

Napierala, S. *Water Birth: A Midwife's Perspective.* Westport, CT: Bergin & Garvey, 1994.

Naqvi, N.H. "James Barlow (1767–1839): Operator of the First Caesarean Section in England." *British Journal of Obstetrics and Gynaecology* 92 (1985): 468–472.

Newman, H.P. "Prolapse of the Female Pelvic Organs." *Journal of the American Medical Association* 21 (1893): 334–338.

Newton, N. "Some Aspects of Primitive Childbirth." *Midwife and Health Visitor* 2 (1966): 324–329.

Nicoll, M. "Maternity as a Public Health Problem." *American Journal of Public Health* 19 (1929): 961–968.

Nihell, E. *A Treatise on the Art of Midwifery—Setting Forth Various Abuses Therein, Especially as to the Practice with Instruments.* London: A. Morley, 1760.

Noyes, C.D. "Training of Midwives in Relation to the Prevention of Infant Mortality." *American Journal of Obstetrics and Diseases of Women and Children* 66 (1912): 1051–1059.

O'Faolain, J. and J. Martines, eds. *Not in God's Image: Women in History from the Greeks to the Victorians.* New York: Harper Torchbook, 1973.

Petrelli, R.L. "The Regulation of French Midwifery during the Ancient Regime." *Journal of History of Medicine and Allied Science* 26 (1971): 276–292.

Pitcock, C.D. and R. Clark. "From Fanny to Fernand: The Development of Consumerism in Pain Control during the Birth Process." *American Journal of Obstetrics and Gynecology* 167 (1992): 277–862.

Priddy, K.D. "Is There Logic Behind Fetal Monitoring?" *Journal of Obstetric, Gynecologic, and Neonatal Nursing* 33 (2004): 550–553.

Rhodes, P. "Obstetrics in Seventeenth Century England." *Nursing RSA Verpleging* 5 (1990): 28–31.

Rinker, S. "To Cultivate a Feeling of Confidence." *Nursing History Review* 8 (2000): 117–135.

Roberts, C.L., C.S. Algert, C.A. Cameron, and S. Torvaldsen. "A Meta-Analysis of Upright Positions in the Second Stage to Reduce Instrumental Deliveries in Women with Epidural analgesia." *Acta Obstetric et Gynecologia Scandinavica* 84 (2005): 794–798.

Roberts, J.E. "The 'Push' for Evidence: Management of Second Stage." *Journal of Midwifery & Women's Health* 47 (2002): 2–15.

Rooks, J.P. *Midwifery and Childbirth in America.* Philadelphia: Temple University Press, 1997.
_____, N.L. Weatherby, E.K. Ernst, S. Stapelton, and A. Rosenfield. "Outcomes of Care in Birth Centers. The National Birth Center Study." *The New England Journal of Medicine* 26 (1989): 321.
Rothman, B.K. *Giving Birth: Alternatives in Childbirth.* Harmondsworth, England: Penguin, 1982.
Rosenberg, C.E. *The Care of Strangers.* New York: Basic Books, 1987.
Roush, R.E. "The Development of Midwifery—Male and Female, Yesterday and Today." *Journal of Nurse-Midwifery* 24 (1979): 27–37.
Schmidt, J.V. and P.R. McCartney. "History and Development of Fetal Heart Assessment: A Composit." *Journal of Obstetric, Gynecologic, and Neonatal Nursing* 29 (2000): 295–305.
Semmelweis, I.P. Excerpts taken from *The Etiology, the Concept, and the Prophylaxis of Childbed Fever* (1861). Translated by Frank P. Murphy in the series, *Medical Classics* 5 (January 1941). Reprinted in *Reviews of Infectious Diseases* 3 (1981): 808–811.
Shryock, R.H. *Medicine in America: Historical Essays.* Baltimore: Johns Hopkins Press, 1966.
_____. *Medical Licensing in America, 1650–1965.* Baltimore: Johns Hopkins Press, 1967.
Simpson, K.L. and J. Atterbury. "Trends and Issues in Labor Induction in the United States: Implications for Clinical Practice." *Journal of Obstetric, Gynecologic, and Neonatal Nursing* 32 (2003): 767–777.
Smith-Rosenberg, C. and C.C. Rosenberg. "The Female Animal: Medical and Biological Views of Woman and Her Role in Nineteenth Century America." *The Journal of American History* 60 (1973): 332–560.
Speert, H. *Obstetrics and Gynecology in America: A History.* Boston: Waverly Press, 1980.
Stampone, D. "The History of Obstetric Anesthesia." *Journal of Perinatal and Neonatal Nursing* 4 (1990): 1–13.
Stern, C.A. "Midwives, Male Midwives, and Nurse Midwives." *Obstetrics and Gynecology* 39 (1972): 308–311.
Stille, D.R. *Extraordinary Women of Medicine.* New York: Grolier, 1997.
Szasz, T.S. *The Manufacture of Madness: A Comparative Study of the Inquisition and the Mental Health Movement.* New York: Harper & Row, 1970.
Taylor, S.E., L.C. Klein, B.P. Lewis, T.L. Gruenewald, R.A.R. Gurung, and J.A. Updegraff. "Biobehavioral Responses to Stress in Females: Tend-and-Befriend, Not Fight-or-Flight." *Psychological Review* 107 (2000): 411–429.
Thacker, S.B, D. Stroup, and M. Chang. "Continuous Electronic Rate Monitoring for Fetal Assessment during Labor." A Cochrane Review. In *The Cochrane Library*, Issue 4. Chichester, UK: John Wiley, 2004.
Thoms, H. *Chapters in American History.* Springfield, IL: Charles C. Thomas, 1933. Reprint 1961.
Townsend, L. "Obstetrics through the ages." *The Medical Journal of Australia* 1 (1952): 557–565.
Undset, S. *Kristin Lavransdotter II: The Mistress of Husaby.* Translated by C. Archer. New York: Alfred A. Knopf, 1925. Bantam Edition, 1978 (Original title: *Husfriel.* Oslo: H. Aschebauy, 1921).
U.S. Congress, Office of Technology Assessment. *Nurse Practitioners, Physician Assistants, and Certified Nurse-Midwives: A Policy Analysis.* Health Technology Case Study 37, OTA-HCS-37. Washington, DC: U.S. Government Printing Office, 1986.
Vincent, P. *Baby Catcher.* New York: Scribner, 2000.
Webb, D.A. and J. Culhane. "Hospital Variation in Episiotomy Use and the Risk of Perineal Trauma during Childbirth." *Birth* 29 (2002): 132–136.
Wells, H.G. *The Outline of History.* New York: Macmillan, 1921.
Wertz, R. and D.C. Wertz. *Lying-In: A History of Childbirth in America.* New York: Schoekin Books, 1977.
White, D.G. *Aren't I a Woman? Female Slaves in the Plantation South.* New York and London: W.W. Norton, 1985.
Whitmont, E.C. *Return of the Goddess.* New York: Crossroad Publishing, 1984.
Williams, J.W. "Medical Education and the Midwife Problem in the United States." *The Journal of the American Medical Association* 58 (1912): 1–6.

Williams, S.R. *Demeter's Daughters.* New York: Atheneum, 1976.
Winkelman, C. *The Complete Guide to Pregnancy after 30.* Avon, MA: Adams Media Corporation, 2002.
York, R. "The History of Induction." *Midwife Health Visitor and Community Nurse* 20 (1984): 1–6.
Ziegler, C.E. "The Elimination of the Midwife." *American Association for the Study and Prevention of Infant Mortality. Transactions of the Annual Meeting* 3 (1912): 222–223, and 258.

Index

3